SPORT AND SOCIETY IN LATIN AMERICA

Diffusion, Dependency, and the Rise of Mass Culture

Edited by
Joseph L. Arbena

Contributions to the Study of Popular Culture, Number 20

Greenwood Press
New York • Westport, Connecticut • London

Library of Congress Cataloging-in-Publication Data

Sport and society in Latin America : diffusion, dependency, and the
    rise of mass culture / [edited by] Joseph L. Arbena.
        p.   cm. — (Contributions to the study of popular culture,
    ISSN 0198-9871 ; no. 20)
        Bibliography: p.
        Includes index.
        ISBN 0-313-24774-9 (lib. bdg. : alk. paper)
        1. Sports—Social aspects—Latin America.   I. Arbena, Joseph.
    II. Series.
    GV706.5.S696 1988
    306'.483'098—dc19   87-32271

British Library Cataloguing in Publication Data is available.

Library of Congress Catalog Card Number: 87-32271
ISBN: 0-313-24774-9
ISSN: 0198-9871

First published in 1988

Greenwood Press, Inc.
88 Post Road West, Westport, Connecticut 06881

Printed in the United States of America

The paper used in this book complies with the
Permanent Paper Standard issued by the National
Information Standards Organization (Z39.48-1984).

10 9 8 7 6 5 4 3 2 1

Copyright Acknowledgments

The editor and publisher gratefully acknowledge permission
to use portions of the following:

Joseph L. Arbena, "Sport and the Study of Latin American
History," in the *Journal of Sport History* 13:2, Summer 1986.

Janet Lever, *Soccer Madness,* University of Chicago Press, 1983.

With love to Scott and Robin and to all young people of the Americas! May they find in the worlds of sport and letters the enjoyment and satisfaction that I have been fortunate to experience.

Contents

Acknowledgments

My deepest personal gratitude to Alan Schaffer, Joe Turner, and Bill McLelland, whose imagination, determination, and generosity respectively, made possible the four annual Clemson University Conferences on Sport and Society (1981-1984), the last of which included the discussions around which this volume was constructed. Special thanks also to Mike Sutton for his assistance, in the face of great obstacles, in putting the manuscript on computer.

Sport and Society
in Latin America

1
Sport and the Study
of Latin American Society:
An Overview
Joseph L. Arbena

This introduction[1] starts from two basic assumptions: (1) that the academic study of sport no longer requires extended justifications or apologies; and (2) that modern sport, whose emergence accompanied the rise of industrialization from about the mid-nineteenth century, is qualitatively different from all sport in all societies that preceded it, though not necessarily thereby more or less important in its historical setting or more or less important as a subject of study.

Over the last several decades, pioneers in the study of modern sport have often felt compelled to justify their research or teaching focus, fearful--perhaps with good cause--that their colleagues would consider their work intellectually inferior and professionally frivolous.[2] While such concerns may linger, it seems obvious, in the Latin American context alone, that any activity that can repeatedly attract up to 200,000 spectators in many places at about the same time, support multimillion dollar betting pools, sustain profitable daily and weekly newspapers, fill hours of radio and television programming, justify significant governmental budgets, provide the theme for speeches by politicians from mayors to presidents, convince not-so-wealthy nations to bid for the right to host international competitions, and more--such an activity merits serious analysis.[3]

But to accept its legitimacy does not imply that the study of sport is without its problems. One such is that of definition. Attempts have been made to define sport, often in opposition to non-sportive games and play, but even the best leave imprecise areas.[4] For example, again in context, are bullfighting and rodeo (*charrería*) true sports? Is chess? Are young boys playing pick-up soccer in an open field engaged in sport? Turn-of-the-century cyclists touring the Mexican countryside? Ladies swatting tennis balls at the club? If not in each individual case, perhaps in a systemic structure. Or, perhaps in these gray areas, it doesn't matter very much.

Another problem concerns level of analysis. Children playing intramural basketball may validly constitute sport just as much as their country's olympic team, but qualitatively are they doing the same things? And the boys trading punches in the makeshift neighborhood ring may be doing sport as much as the millionaire middle-weight champ, but are we, in fact, witnessing the same process?

In a sense, these debates carry us into a third problem confronting the field of sports studies: the existence of conflicting theories or paradigms. To avoid making this too complex, we suggest that the broad philosophical or theoretical differences appear to revolve currently around a few basic issues: Is sport, as opposed to play and perhaps games, inherently enslaving or liberating or perhaps both simultaneously? Or is sport itself neutral, with the context determining its meaning? Is professional by definition more exploitive than non-professional sport, assuming one can define professionalism? Does sport always replicate the dominant or hegemonic culture or can it (should it) be a means of challenging that culture? Is sport in socialist societies meaningfully different from sport in capitalist nations?   The questions are exciting, the answers usually elusive.[5] Fortunately, there are a few areas of tentative agreement among sports scholars today.[6]

One appears to be that the foundations of nearly all modern sports (that is, all sports in their modern forms)--with their emphasis on rationalization, standardization, secularization, specialization, quantification, record-keeping and breaking--are located historically in England, or the North Atlantic region, and, less consistently, among the upper classes.[7] Often, though not always, then, the global history of modern sport is characterized by parallel processes of diffusion geographically outward from centers of innovation and hierarchically downward, spatially from more to less industrialized sectors and socially from upper to lower strata, processes that repeat and rerepeat themselves internationally and, on a smaller scale, intranationally.[8]

Even when sports evolve from the bottom up, there appears to be a tendency for the dominant classes either to suppress the popular activity or to concentrate control over production, distribution, and regulation of the previously more spontaneous, unstructured behavior. The result is often a severe loss of options and resources available to those players, spectators, and competing entrepreneurs with less power.

In that framework, Latin America is primarily a recipient region that, over the last century, has adopted sports mainly developed in other places and that has generally seen those adopted behavior patterns move from capital and/or major port city to the hinterlands and from elite to mass cultural phenomena.[9] In the process, older forms of popular sport and mass recreation were modified, reduced, or even eliminated.[10]

Put another way, the most popular sports in Latin America today have little connection with traditional society, not much with colonial society, and even less with pre-Columbian civilizations, though remnants or residual expressions of those pre-modern activities continue to express themselves, at times in surprising ways.[11] Rather, as in other parts of the world, including western Europe, the United States, the socialist bloc, and increasing portions of the Third World, modern sport seems intricately linked to the complex of cultural patterns and values associated with urban-industrial institutions and their spheres of influence.

What that suggests in turn is that the evolution of modern Latin American sport can be used to analyze various attributes of Latin America's increasing involvement in the capitalist world system. At the same time, given the infinite variety of creative outlets in the sporting experience as well as the diversity of historical and cultural mixes in the Latin American realm, sport also vividly expresses the unique ways in which different peoples have reacted to the penetration of so-called modern models and of transnational institutions with connections between metropolitan centers and weaker peripheries. In other words, the process of adoption/adaption, rather than true innovation, which marks modern Latin American sport, permits comparison among Latin American countries and perhaps between Latin America and other Third World areas.[12] In turn, the resultant international sports relationships may prove to be another graphic indicator, highly correlated with and partially determined by the economic, political, and military indices of Latin America's overall weakness and dependency in the world community.[13]

This is not to pretend that sport need be understood solely within this global "dependency" framework. Clearly sport, as a highly complex and pervasive social phenomenon with many interconnected dimensions and expressions, can offer insights into various related historical and contemporary processes on different levels. For, at one and the same time, sport has (at least) cultural, psychological, social, institutional, economic, and political content and ramifications, though, as suggested above, the nature and meaning of any of these is not always clear or predictable.

Nor is it to assert that sport is only a reflector of society, a mere indicator of these other dimensions. Rather, sport is a part of society, interacting with other parts often in a dialectical fashion. Sport, it appears, like other institutions, can be consciously or unconsciously manipulated by individuals or, more commonly, interest groups and classes in pursuit of ends which may be limited to the sports realm or which may have larger implications.[14]

Certainly in this volume we can't hope to examine the manifestations of all these themes over all of Latin America. But in this essay and those that follow we can offer some examples and suggest some tentative relationships.

In the cultural realm, sport may be both an expression of national or regional cultural characteristics, broadly defined, and a source of cultural creativity, in the narrower sense. In the first instance, for example, it has been argued that the style in which Brazilians play soccer is illustrative of other attributes of the Brazilian "character," and that the bullfight simultaneously reflects and reinforces the structure of the Mexican family.[15] In the second, sports themes have been used by various writers and artists as a metaphor, setting, or motif through which to communicate their intended message.[16] In one special case, that of the Chilean "university classic," the soccer match provided the physical and emotional ambience in which to practice artistic creativity, in the form of mass theater.[17]

The psychological implications of sport throughout Latin America are surely varied, difficult to determine, and subject to debate. In one circumstance, it may be suggested that the persistence of pre-modern games/sports is a source of self-respect and even a type of rebellion among people who have seen much of their traditional culture destroyed, especially under the wave of modernism imported over the last century in the name of progress.[18] A similar interpretation can be applied to the resiliency of indigenous forms of recreation throughout the centuries of European colonial rule.

In another situation, sport has been blamed for diverting popular attention away from more serious social and political problems,[19] though not all observers agree.[20] In fact, one Chilean maintains that, in an atmosphere of political repression, the soccer stadium may provide citizens a unique opportunity to choose (read vote) among two contenders and to act, through cheering, in a way that, they believe, will influence the outcome of events.[21] Brazilian anthropologist Roberto Da Matta proposes that another socio-psychological result of soccer may be to teach players and fans to live by standardized rules, operating in a structured environment, and to accept the outcome as being a result of merit, laying thereby the groundwork for constructing a "liberal" society.[22]

Two other interesting, and perhaps controversial, psychological interpretations of Latin American soccer include: (1) Luis Millones's proposal that weekend violence on the soccer fields and in associated rituals of Lima's neighborhood teams is a function of the pent-up hostilities deriving from the socio-economic frustrations suffered by the working-class players during the rest of the week;[23] and, (2) Marcelo Suárez Orozco's contention that the on-field style of play and the off-field nature of fan behavior and folklore suggest that Argentine males are excessively concerned with protecting their maleness and must symbolically avoid being penetrated from the rear--they are stuck in Freud's anal phase of development--hence players and the fans who identify with them are preoccupied with protecting their goal.[24] One result: more defense than offense.

No doubt, sport can also reflect, express, and even encourage class and/or racial cleavages. Despite the recent success of darker players such as Pelé, Brazilian soccer was marred in its early days by overt racism and discrimination; even today, critics contend, the black player earns less while playing and has little carry over into his retirement years.[25] In addition, it has been charged that one reason for Brazil's decline in international soccer in the late 1970s was a deliberate effort by the military regime to change the national team's style by "whitening" its complexion in pursuit of an allegedly superior European model.[26] In Yucatán, as Gil Joseph shows in this collection, baseball has long had specific class/race overtones; Deustua Carvallo, Stein, and Stokes illustrate how soccer in early twentieth-century Lima afforded both the exploiters and the exploited a mechanism for manipulation.[27]

As sports in Latin America have become more sophisticated and structured, they have elicited larger administrative/support institutions and bureaucracies. One frequent criticism heard among Latin Americans is that these institutions have not functioned to aid either athletes or athletics, a reflection of corruption or ineptness among the administrators and/or of inadequately developed institutions throughout the entire society and/or of insufficient funding.[28] Nevertheless, it has been argued that, in the best of cases, in organizing and managing teams, leagues, etc., people learn skills potentially applicable to other areas of life; in other words, sports administration, broadly defined, may be an aid to "development."[29]

Nearly all Latin American comments on sport arrive eventually at the question of money, either because too little is spent on sport or because what is spent is spent unwisely, an issue that ranges from the lowest scholastic programs to the highest professional ranks. In some cases, Latin Americans admit in frustration that their economies are poor and that they are lucky to do as well as they do.[30] Others condemn governments for incorrect priorities.[31] More recently, there has been an outcry against the so-called *espectáculo deportivo* (sporting spectacle) and concommitant administrative policies that, it is argued, have cheapened the product (usually professional soccer), reduced attendance and the gate, attracted too many unproductive hangers-on to the game, and reduced the clubs to selling players to keep from going bankrupt.[32] Some critics further link this to excessive commercialization, the "star system," and exploitation of athletes, all of which together undermine whatever positive educational or developmental value sport may theoretically offer.[33]

Though focusing on team sports in North America, Stephen Hardy has suggested that much could be learned about how sport becomes a commodity in terms of its activity or game form, its service role, and its marketing of related goods by studying those entrepreneurs, investors, and institutions whose decisions seem ultimately to limit the choices available to consumers.[34] Considering Latin America's general position as a dependent/recipient region and the fact that at least some of its sports are organized differently from those in the United States, Canada, and Commonwealth areas, there lies here a rich area for comparative analysis offering insights into such questions as the autonomy of local sports administrators, the penetration of transnational equipment and communications corporations, the existence of differing expectations for sports programs, and the degree to which modern sports are shaped by universal traits as opposed to regional or national cultural/social traditions. A good place to start would be the sports clubs which in Latin America often combine, among other roles, the functions performed in the United States by scholastic and professional sports.[35]

Whether intrinsically so or not, sport, like virtually everything else, has also become ultimately political.   Even if, contrary to John Hoberman's suggestion,[36] policies on sport and/or physical culture do not absolutely link governments to specific ideological traditions, certainly such policies can provide evidence of attitudes and objectives in such areas as health, education, social integration, mass mobilization, and foreign policy.   Sport law and sport legislation can also indicate power relationships among various interest groups and, especially on the professional level in capitalist societies, between owners and players.   And the funding and operation of sports federations, olympic committees, etc., may illustrate, as implied above, the workings of bureaucracies and the linkages among public, quasi-public, and private agencies.

There is no doubt, for example, that both Cuba and Nicaragua have developed "revolutionary" sports programs aimed at achieving specific domestic objectives and inculcating selected social values.[37] Cuba, in particular, has made sport a significant element in its foreign policy.[38] Mexico, in contrast, has until recently done little officially to raise the quality of its national teams, but it has been the conspicuous host of various international competitions with the aim, not only of earning tourist dollars, but of satisfying domestic constituents and favorably impressing the outside world.[39] On a smaller scale, the Guatemalans sought the same when hosting the Central American and Caribbean Games in 1950,[40] as did the leaders of Cali, Colombia, in organizing the Pan American Games in 1971.[41] It may be argued, returning to the dependency perspective alluded to above, that such an assertive, independent sports policy represents one way of symbolically, and perhaps even substantively, weakening those dependent relationships.

Of course, even when governments don't deliberately encourage it (the Brazilians in 1970 and the Argentines in 1978 can here join Fidel Castro), individual and team success against foreign foes can stimulate national consciousness, pride, and unity across broad spectrums of society.[42] It is interesting how many writers even from the smaller, poorer countries express pride in the achievements of their athletes or administrators when analyzed in the context of their own region, resource level, or athletic specialization.[43] One Argentine wrote, just two decades ago, that Luis Angel Firpo's boxing success, despite his second-round loss to Jack Dempsey in 1923, "affirmed to the world that we were more than a pasture populated by cows" and became part of the mythology by which Argentines have defined their national being.[44] Witness, also, the so-called Fernandomania within Mexico resulting from the athletic and financial triumphs of the screw-balling Valenzuela.[45] Moreover, the importation of foreign players has often aroused the nationalistic ire of numerous Latin Americans.[46]

In an example of politics from the bottom up rather than the top down, referring back to the question of the psycho-political implications of sport, there is evidence that one way the people of Chile expressed their quiet disgust, and perhaps lingering fear, growing out of the coup of September 1973, was to avoid attending events in Santiago's national stadium, where some of the military's most brutal actions had taken place.[47]

Despite the pervasiveness of sport in the Latin American experience and despite the rich archival, printed, and human sources available, Latin American sport remains a subject of limited systematic analysis. Pre-Columbian sport, above all in Mesoamerica, has earned notable attention,[48] but the colonial and early national periods have been almost completely ignored.[49] Modern sport is better covered, though in English only a mere handful of books and a few dozen articles reflect scholarly inspection.[50] Although more plentiful and often very good, work in Spanish and Portuguese tends to be impressionistic or anecdotal and thus far regionally and topically spotty.[51]

In the collection that follows we seek to achieve four ends:

1. To expose some of the sources that can be used to do sports studies in Latin America;

2. To expand the body of material available on modern sport in Latin America as a social institution and thus a subject of intellectual interest in its own right;

3. To suggest ways that sports themes can be used to illustrate and interpret other historical processes in Latin America; and,

4. To make available examples from the Latin American sport experience as contributions to understanding the universal sports realm and thus to building, if possible, more valid universal theory. (On this point, it is worth noting that, perhaps owing to the paucity of literature alluded to above, most major surveys and theories of modern sport contain fundamentally no references to Latin America, nor on much of the rest of the Third World.)[52]

To achieve these objectives we have prepared essays that focus on aspects of Latin America's evolving sport practices over this last century of diffusion, dependency, and the rise of mass culture. William Beezley illustrates how the Mexican fascination with cycling was part of a larger pattern of enthusiastic elite acceptance of foreign sports and other values and habits associated with modernization. Steve Stein discusses the ambivalent role of soccer in the lives of Lima's growing working classes, who sought dignity and security in a world that increasingly restricted their social space. Gil Joseph recounts the spread of baseball in the intriguing environment of Yucatán and the connection between that imported game and local political and social movements, as well as the peninsula's unstable economy.

Matthew Shirts and Janet Lever look at popular expressions of the soccer mania in Brazil, one in terms of community and club behavior, the other in relation to country-wide psychological and developmental patterns. Eric Wagner points out how two avowedly revolutionary societies, Cuba and Nicaragua, have implemented sports programs, at times in similar and at times in different ways. In his conclusion, Robert Levine appraises aspects of sport in the human experience and suggests some lines of future research in the Latin American area.

Our decision to focus on the modern era is not to deny the value of studying sports, games, and recreation in Latin America before 1850, either as meaningful areas of human behavior in their own right or as a way to approach other related themes, such as class and race, slavery, rural-urban dichotomies, the persistence of older traditions, resource allocation, space utilization, public ritual, and social values. In fact, we encourage scholars to attack these topics, if only to provide a fuller background against which to judge the impact of the later, modern sports.

What we are saying is that much, much more needs to be done before anyone can generalize about Latin American sport or claim to construct valid universal sport theory. For surely, whatever universal qualities may characterize modern sports--even of the "professional" variety--consideration must be given to the specific historical context that shaped the form, meaning, and values of those sports and to the evolving societies of which they remain an integrated element.[53]

Notes

[1] The original version of this chapter was presented at the Fourteenth Annual Convention of the North American Society for Sport History, Vancouver, B.C., May 23-26, 1986. A slightly different version was published in the *Journal of Sport History* 13:2 (Summer 1986): 87-96.

[2] Some basic arguments in favor of researching and teaching sport history are presented in Joan M. Chandler, "Towards the Teaching of Sport History," *Teaching History* 7:1 (Spring 1982): 34-40; Mary L. Remley, "Sport History: A Brief Overview," *OAH Newsletter* 11:3 (August 1983): 15-16.

[3] Angel V. Ruocco, "La trastienda del fútbol," in *El fútbol (antología)*, José Luis Buzzetti, et. al., (Montevideo: Centro Editor de América Latina, 1969), pp. 73-80.

[4] Allen Guttmann, *From Ritual to Record: The Nature of Modern Sports* (New York: Columbia University Press, 1978); John W. Loy, Jr., "The Nature of Sport: A Definitional Effort," in *Sport in the Sociolcultural Process*, eds. Marie Hart and Susan Birrell, 3rd ed. (Dubuque: Wm. C. Brown, 1981), pp. 21-37.

[5] On one level, for example, Eldon E. Snyder and Barbara A. Brown conclude that ". . . scholars have approached the study of social change in society and sport from diverse perspectives and hold differing views as to its outcomes for society in general and sport in par-

ticular." See their note, "Sport and Social Change," *Sociology of Sport Journal* 4:2 (June 1987): 140-43. The quote is from p. 142.

6   There is a growing body of good literature on sport theory. An introduction to some of the basic issues is found in: Jean-Marie Brohm, *Sport--A Prison of Measured Time*, trans. Ian Fraser (London: Ink Links, 1978); Hart Cantelon and Richard Gruneau, eds., *Sport, Culture and the Modern State* (Toronto: University of Toronto Press, 1982); Richard Gruneau, *Class, Sports, and Social Development* (Amherst: University of Massachusetts Press, 1983); Guttmann, *From Ritual to Record*; William J. Morgan, "'Radical' Social Theory of Sport: A Critique and a Conceptual Emendation," *Sociology of Sport Journal* 2:1 (March 1985): 56-71;   Alvaro Mutis, "La vergüenza del deporte," *Eco* 35:215 (September 1979): 557-59; Bero Rigauer, *Sport and Work*, trans. Allen Guttmann (New York: Columbia University Press, 1981);   David Whitson, "Sport and Hegemony: On the Construction of the Dominant Culture," *Sociology of Sport Journal* 1:1 (1984): 64-78.

7   Guttmann, *From Ritual to Record*.

8   John Bale, "International Sports History as Innovation Diffusion," *Canadian Journal of History of Sport* 15:1 (May 1984): 38-63; Loy, Jr., "A Paradigm of Technological Change in the Sports Situation," *International Review of Sport Sociology* 1 (1966): 177-93.

9   William H. Beezley, "The Porfirian Persuasion: Sport and Recreation in Mexico's Society of the 1890s," *Proceedings of the Rocky Mountain Council on Latin American Studies* (1983): 136-45; Gabriel Escobar M., "The Role of Sports in the Penetration of Urban Culture to the Rural Areas of Peru," *Kroeber Anthropological Society Papers* 40 (1969): 72-81;   Renato González, *El boxeo en Chile* (Santiago: Editora Nacional Quimantú, 1973); Ilan Rachum, "Futebol: The Growth of a Brazilian National Institution," *New Scholar* 7:1/2 (1978): 79-80.

10   Richard W. Slatta, "The Demise of the Gaucho and the Rise of Equestrian Sport in Argentina," *Journal of Sport History* 13:2 (Summer 1986): 97-110.

11   Isabel Kelly, "Notes on a West Coast Survival of the Ancient Mexican Ball Game," *Notes on Middle American Archaeology and Ethnology* no. 26 (1943): 163-75; Lilian Scheffler, et. al., *El juego de pelota prehispánico y sus supervivencias actuales* (Tlahuapan, Puebla, México: Premiá Editora, 1985).

12   João Lyra Filho, *Introdução a sociologia dos desportos* (Rio de Janeiro: Bloch Editores, 1973). For possible comparisons with the

African experience, consult William J. Baker and James A. Mangan, eds., *Sport in Africa: Essays in Social History* (New York: Africana Publishing Company, 1987).

13   Ignacio Martín Baró, "Munich 72: el ocaso de una mitología," *ECA; Estudios Centro Americanos* 27:288-289 (October - November 1972): 697-701; Fernando Reyes Matta, "The Olympic Games in the Latin American Press," in *Global Ritual: Olympic Media Coverage and International Understanding*, ed. Michael Real (San Diego: [p.p.], 1986), pp. 194-217; Alejandro Cadavel, *El deporte visto por los universitarios* (México, D.F.: Universidad Nacional Autónoma de México, [1979]).

14   André Corten and Marie-Blanche Tahon, "Sport et societé dans une cité pétroliére mexicaine: biographie d'une équipe de jeunes," *Canadian Journal of Latin American and Caribbean Studies/Revue canadienne des études latino-américaines et caraibes* 9:18 (1984): 57-73.

15   Alastair Reid, "The Sporting Scene: Shades of Tlachtli," *The New Yorker* 46:22 (18 July 1970): 60-71; Louis A. Zurcher and Arnold Meadow, "On Bullfights and Baseball: An Example of Interaction of Social Institutions," *The International Journal of Comparative Sociology* 8:1 (March 1967): 99-117.

16   Milton Pedroza, "Presencia del fútbol en la literatura brasileña," *Revista de Cultura Brasileña* 46 (June 1978): 53-88; Eduardo Galeano, ed., *Su majestad el fútbol* (Montevideo: Arca Editorial, 1968); Isaac Goldemberg, *Play by Play*, trans. Hardie St. Martin (New York: Persea Books, 1985). A survey of sport themes in various Latin American literary genre is offered in Joseph L. Arbena, "Sport and Sport Themes in Latin American Literature: A Sampler," forthcoming in *Arete: The Journal of Sport Literature* 5:1 (Fall 1987).

17   Osvaldo Obregón, "El 'clásico universitario' chileno: un caso singular de teatro de masas," *Revista Canadiense de Estudios Hispánicos* 7:1 (Fall 1982): 67-80.

18   René León Echaiz, *Diversiones y juegos típicos chilenos* (Santiago: Editora Nacional Gabriela Mistral, 1974).

19   Peter Flynn, "Sambas, Soccer and Nationalism," *New Society* 18:464 (19 August 1971): 327-30.; Robert M. Levine, "Sport and Society: The Case of Brazilian *Futebol*," *Luso-Brazilian Review* 17:2 (Winter 1980): 233-52.

[20] Philip Evanson, "Understanding the People: *Futebol*, Film, Theater and Politics in Present-Day Brazil," *The South Atlantic Quarterly* 81:4 (Autumn 1982): 399-412.

[21] Carlos A. Ossandón, "Las dos caras de fútbol," *Araucaria de Chile* 20 (1982): 192-94.

[22] Roberto Da Matta, "Esporte na sociedade: um ensaio sobre o futebol brasileiro," in *Universo do futebol: esporte e sociedade brasileira*, Roberto Da Matta, et. al. (Rio de Janeiro: Edições Pinakotheke, 1982), pp. 19-42.

[23] Luis Millones, "Deporte y alienación en el Perú: el fútbol en los barrios limeños," *Estudios Andinos* 1:2 (1970): 87-95.

[24] Marcelo Mario Suárez Orozco, "A Study of Argentine Soccer: The Dynamics of Its Fans and Their Folklore," *Journal of Psychoanalytic Anthropology* 5:1 (Winter 1982): 7-28. For a larger discussion of violence and aggression in relation to modern sport, see José María Cagigal, *Deporte y agresión* (Barcelona: Editorial Planeta, 1976).

[25] Janet Lever, "Soccer As a Brazilian Way of Life," in *Games, Sport and Power*, ed. George P. Stone (New Brunswick: Transaction Books, 1972), pp. 138-59; Robert M Levine, "The Burden of Success: *Futebol* and Brazilian Society Through the 1970s," *Journal of Popular Culture* 14:3 (Winter 1980): 453-64.

[26] Jacob Klintowitz, "A implantação de um modelo alienígena exótico e outras questões pertinentes: A seleção brasileira de futebol--1978," *Encontros com a Civilização Brasileira* 5 (November 1978): 113-18.

[27] José Deustua Carvallo, Steve Stein, and Susan C. Stokes, "Soccer and Social Change in Early Twentieth Century Peru," *Studies in Latin American Popular Culture* 3 (1984): 17-27.

[28] March L. Krotee, "The Rise and Demise of Sport: A Reflection of Uruguayan Society," *The Annals of the American Academy of Political and Social Science* 445 (September 1979): 141-54; Diego Morales Roca, *¿Existe el fútbol boliviano? (Problemas del fútbol nacional)* (La Paz: Ediciones Galaxia, 1977); Ernesto Vidales, *Nos dejó el tren . . .* (Bogotá: Editorial Kelly, 1961).

[29] Escobar M., "The Role of Sports." M. Stark and R. Clignet make a similar assessment of soccer's impact in Cameroon; see "Modernization and the Game of Soccer in Cameroon," *International Review of Sport Sociology* 9:3-4 (1974): 81-98.

30   Carlos Guerrero, *Grandes del deporte* (Santiago: Editora Nacional Gabriela Mistral, 1975).

31   Francisco Ponce, "Ocio y deporte," *Revista Mexicana de Ciencias Políticas y Sociales* 25:95-96 (January - June 1979): 79-90.

32   Hugo Angel Jaramillo, "El profesionalismo deportivo y la juventud," *Desarrollo Indoamericano* 6:20 (June 1973):   53-61;   Humberto Domínguez Dibb, *El fútbol paraguayo* (Asunción: Talleres Gráficos Cromos S.R.L., 1977);   Franklin Morales, *Fútbol: mito y realidad* (Montevideo: Editorial "Nuestra Tierra," 1969);   Juan José Sebreli, *Fútbol y masas* (Buenos Aires: Editorial Galerna, 1981);   Miguel A. Taboada, "Con el fútbol espectáculo comenzó la bancarrota que hoy ahoga a los clubes," *La Razón* (15 October 1984): 17.

33   "La corrupción del deporte," *Criterio*, 50:1773 (13 October 1977): 539-41;   Hugo Angel Jaramillo, "Los ídolos del deporte en la sociedad capitalista," *Desarrollo Indoamericano* 12:37 (April 1977): 27-31.

34   Stephen Hardy, "Entrepreneurs, Organizations, and the Sport Marketplace: Subjects in Search of Historians," *Journal of Sport History* 13:1 (Spring 1986): 14-33.

35   Edigar de Alencar, *Flamengo: Força e alegria do povo* (Rio de Janeiro: Conquista, 1970);   Club Colonia Rowing, *Libro de oro* (Colonia, Uruguay: El Ideal, 1973);   Daniel Samper Pizano, *Así ganamos . . . (Como fue campeón Santa Fe en 1975)* (Bogotá: Carlos Valencia Editores, 1975).

36   John M. Hoberman, *Sport and Political Ideology* (Austin: University of Texas Press, 1984).

37   R. J. Pickering, "Cuba," in *Sport Under Communism*, ed. James Riorden (Montreal: McGill-Queen's University Press, 1978), pp. 141-74;   David Russell, "Baseball, Hollywood, and Nicaragua," *Monthly Review* 34:10 (March 1983): 22-29; Brad Whorton and Eric A. Wagner, "Nicaraguan Sport Ideology," *Journal of Sport and Social Issues* 9:2 (Summer/Fall 1985): 26-33;   Eric A. Wagner, "Sport After Revolution: A Comparative Study of Cuba and Nicaragua," *Studies in Latin American Popular Culture* 1 (1982): 65-73.

38   Manfred Komorowski, "Cuba's Way to a Country with Strong Influence in Sport Politics: The Development of Sport in Cuba Since 1959," *International Journal of Physical Education* 14 (1977): 26-32.

39   See two books by Julio Mera Carrasco: *De Tokio a México: Los juegos olímpicos* (México, D.F.:   Ediciones Deportemas, 1968), and

Fútbol (La Copa del Mundo en sus manos) (México, D.F.: Editores Mexicanos Unidos, 1970).

40   [Benjamín Paniagua S., et. al.], *Guatemala* (Guatemala: Tipografía Nacional, 1950).

41   Alfonso Bonilla Aragón, et. al., *Cali Panamericana*, 2 vols. (Cali: Carvajal & Cía., 1971).

42   Manuel Velázquez Rojas, *Alex Olmedo: el cacique del deporte blanco* (Lima: Editora Contemporanea, 1959).

43   Miguel Angel Cospín, *Nuestro fútbol en su época de oro (anecdotario)* (Guatemala: El Imparcial, 1965); Alí Rafael Ramos Mirena, *Todos fueron héroes* ([Caracas]:   Ministerio de Información y Turismo, 1982).

44   José Speroni, "Firpo-Dempsey: el combate del siglo," *Todo Es Historia* 1:6 (October 1967): 26-32. For a contemporary expression of Argentine enthusiasm for Firpo's career, see Carlos Berdier Uriburu, *Hacia el campeonato mundial; las grandes peleas del "Toro Salvaje de las Pampas"* (Buenos Aires: Agencia General de Librería y Publicaciones, 1923).

45   David G. LaFrance, "A Mexican Popular Image of the United States Through the Baseball Hero, Fernando Valenzuela," *Studies in Latin American Popular Culture* 4 (1985): 14-23.

46   Angel Jaramillo, "El profesionalismo deportivo"; Morales Roca, *¿Existe el fútbol boliviano?*

47   D. Alonso Calabrano, "La cultura, el deporte y la juventud chilena," *Cuadernos Americanos* 200:3 (1975): 55-68.

48   Eric A. Wagner, "Sports," in *Handbook of Latin American Popular Culture*, eds., Harold E. Hinds, Jr., and Charles M. Tatum (Westport: Greenwood Press, 1985), pp. 135-150; this article contains a survey of the entire field of Latin American sports studies, as well as an un-annotated bibliography of over 100 entries.

49   Useful examples of such rare studies include Ricardo M. Llanes, *Canchas de pelotas y reñideros de antaño* (Buenos Aires: Municipalidad de la Ciudad de Buenos Aires, 1981); Eugenio Pereira Salas, *Juegos y alegrías coloniales en Chile* (Santiago: Editora Zig-Zag, 1947); Oscar Troncoso, *Juegos y diversiones en la Gran Aldea* (Buenos Aires: Centro Editor de América Latina, 1982); and, José Luis Buzzetti and Eduardo Gutiérrez Cortinas, *Historia del deporte*

en el Uruguay [1830-1900] (Montevideo: Talleres Gráficos Castro & Cía., 1965).

50   Janet Lever, *Soccer Madness* (Chicago: University of Chicago Press, 1983);   and C.L.R. James, *Beyond a Boundary* (New York: Pantheon Books, 1983) are the only significant books, and even the second of these is highly autobiographical and intuitive.

51   The author of this introduction is currently preparing an annotated bibliography of sport in Latin America from all periods and regions; projected publication date is 1989.   As of January 1988, the number of works actually consulted is over 1100.   Some further observations on current progress in the study of sport in Latin America are found in Arbena, "Winners Without Losers: Perspectives on Latin America Sport," forthcoming in *Studies in Latin American Popular Culture* 7 (1988).

52   Baker, *Sports in the Western World* (Totowa, NJ: Rowman and Littlefield, 1982);   Richard D. Mandell, *Sport: A Cultural History* (New York: Columbia University Press, 1984);   Guttmann, *Sports Spectators* (New York: Columbia University Press, 1986).

53   Conrad Phillip Kottack, "Swimming in Cross-Cultural Currents," *Natural History* 94:5 (May 1985): 2-11.

2
Bicycles, Modernization, and Mexico
William H. Beezley

Mexico experienced its most dramatic economic changes in the era of the dictator Porfirio Díaz, 1876-1911; along with political centralization and nationalization of the culture, Mexicans used foreign capital and indigenous labor to initiate the agricultural and manufacturing enterprises associated with modernism.   New attitudes resulted in continual discussions of change and, above all, progress. Technology meant change and change meant progress in the Mexico of Porfirio Díaz. Positivism's slogan Order and Progress offered collective nouns for political action in which bureaucratic administration predominated, and for economic growth in which foreign technology reigned supreme. The allure of modern fashion affected other aspects of Mexican life: clothing, cuisine, music, and amusements. These notions resulted in the rise of sport in Mexico. No recreation better expressed these sentiments than did bicycling.

Fascination with bicycling represented one sentiment that formed the temper of the times. Cycling became a fad, an obsession, much the way home computers have swept today's society. The locomotive expressed Porfirian society's access to technology; the bicycle represented the individual's acceptance of it. When a Mexican purchased a bicycle, he learned to ride it, repair it, race it, and replace it. He accepted technology, mass production, obsolescence, and other values that form the modern temper.

Bicycles were first shipped from Paris and Boston to Mexico City in 1869. The cycling rage, called the "Parisian mania," reached the capital when a French three-wheeled velocipede appeared on the streets. Soon a vehicle of Mexican invention, with four wheels, a seat at the back, and an umbrella that overspread rider and machine took to the Paseo. By midsummer, another Mexican velocipede appeared, this one a tricycle built for two. The unidentified Mexican inventor announced plans to build a machine in order for a family of five or six to ride together. This fad faded quickly as attention focused on the unsettled political situation that re-

mained several years after the execution of the Emperor Maximilian, and
because the common type of wheel, called the boneshaker, proved both
difficult and uncomfortable to ride. The only bicycle that Mexicans knew
much about before 1880 was the one ridden as part of a clown act at the
Chiarini circus.[1]

Another shipment of bicycles from the United States arrived in
Mexico in 1880. These were the so-called "ordinaries," high-wheeled bicycles famed for the headers taken by riders when they were hurled over
the handlebars. Cycling received encouragement from 1880 to 1884 when
a Michaux bicycle outlet was opened on the north side of the Alameda to
rent machines and to offer instructions to prospective riders. Converts to
the wheel soon organized the Club de Velocipedistas in the capital to
sponsor excursions led by President Wiener to the countryside. Dressed
in a uniform of hunter's green, the riders traveled to El Desierto and
neighboring suburbs.[2]

More competitive club members organized velocipede races, at first
down two streets bordering the Alameda, turning at the glorieta, and returning. Mario Garfias became the first champion racer. Despite his
popularity after winning several races in spring 1884, interest in cycling
soon waned. The Ayuntamiento contributed to the decline of cycling.
The council ruled that no wheels could be ridden in the Alamada because
of the number of accidents and upsets that had occurred there. The dor-
mant bicycle club roused itself to arrange races down Cinco de Mayo Avenue as part of the 1887 Independence Day celebration (although heavy
rains forced the races to be held at the French hippodrome at the La
Piedad, October 2). Nevertheless the fad attracted only a few partisans in
the early 1880s because of the high risk of accidents on these vehicles. At
the end of the decade, a prospective cyclist still had to order his machine
from Boston. The public did not rush to purchase boneshakers, or even
the more stable Brown Quadricycle, with two small front wheels, the usual
large wheels at the back, and steered by a joy stick. Few ordered them
from the Massachusetts dealer.[3] Mexicans waited for a better machine.

The machine that created a craze was the "safety" bicycle that arrived
in 1891 with the opening of the Columbia Bicycle Agency on Cinco de
Mayo Avenue. The safety was a machine with equally sized wheels and
soon came equipped with pneumatic tires. It was called the safety because
it greatly reduced the number of headers suffered by riders. Moreover, the
air-filled tires made it possible to ride on Mexico's nearly impossible
cobblestone streets and rutted roads. When the Germans Hilario Meenen
and Carlos Deeg imported their safety bicycles in 1891, enthusiasm leaped
forward, and by the following year safeties appeared throughout the capital, especially on San Francisco and Corpus Cristi streets and the Paseo
de la Reforma. Newspaper reporters predicted the cycle would soon become the major means of transportation in the nation.

Cycling clubs sprang up across Mexico--for example, the Veloce
Club founded by Meenen, Deeg, M. Biguard, and others, on July 25, 1891,
with riders usually adopting North American models, such as the Victor.
Prospective riders could buy American bicycles at Mexico City's Spaulding

outlet (a Columbia agency), or the W. G. Walz Music Store, or from company agents such as Eugene Roller, who represented the Pope Manufacturing Company, Columbia Bicycles, Meridian Britania Company, D. M. Osborne Company, and Mason Hanlon Company, or Holmes and Trachsel, sole agents for Victor bicycles.[4] One customer learned he could make the best purchase of a wheel from a protestant missionary who sold bicycles as a sideline to saving souls.[5]

The popularity of bicycling received a boost from touring racing teams. The Sterling bicycle team visited Mexico City and Puebla in 1894. A more elaborate tour occurred the following year, when an all-star racing team from the United States visited Mexico from January to March 1895. H. T. Roberts, of Roberts & Pomeroy Cycle importing company and owner of the Bicycle Riding School, had arranged the trip for Mexico's cycling clubs through promoter F. E. Spooner of Chicago. The five-man team included the nationally known professional riders L. D. Cabanne, the owner of the half-mile unpaved course record of 25 seconds; Dr. A. I. Brown, quarter-mile record holder; L. A. Callahan, road and track champion; E. F. Leonart, straight-away champion; and A. J. Nicolet, trick rider, who also served as photographer. The party comprised ten persons, including coaches and trainers.

The schedule called for races in Mexico City (opening January 23), with appearances in Guadalajara, Puebla, Monterrey, Durango, and San Luis Potosí. All these cities reportedly had active cycling clubs and racing tracks. The tour was to teach Mexicans how to attain higher speeds, especially with the use of pace-makers. The riders, in exchange, would receive fees, expenses, and become acquainted with Mexican society through balls and dances and the nation's sights through special excursions.[6]

The all-America team left Chicago for Mexico City on January 13, but did not have a chance to race until February 17, because the new La Piedad track experienced a three-week construction delay. This velodrome, located at Rancho Anzures, had a track that was a hard, smooth adobe oval three miles long, with a spacious grandstand a quarter-mile long, ten rows deep, and topped with boxes, and a concourse accommodating more than 2000 spectators.

On opening day, L. A. Callahan won the open mile and delighted the capacity crowd, who also enjoyed the one-mile novice race won by local favorite Felipe Flores, followed by Eduardo Trigueros. Another Mexican, G. Licea, captured the handicap contest and the following week won both races open to amateurs. The second day drew more than 2000 fans again, despite the fact that it was Carnival weekend. The audience gave its hardiest approval to the cycling tricks performed by Nicolet, who was persuaded to give a special benefit performance at Orrin's Circus before the tour left the capital.[7]

The delay in Mexico City severely abbreviated the tour. The team immediately headed for Guadalajara for its last stop in Mexico. The Biciclista de Occidente (the Western Bicyclist Club) sponsored the riders, and had prepared for their visit by financing a new $2000 track made of volcanic ash. Before leaving for El Paso, Texas, the North Americans gave two exhibitions that were both well attended by the Tapatíos (residents of Guadalajara), even though they occurred during the Lenten season.[8]

The exhibitions boosted cycling. The sport increased in popularity, but not with everyone. Members of what Silvestre Terrazas identified as "the lower part of the population" sneered at the vehicles and jeered at their riders. Their least offensive insults, reported Terrazas, included "locos" and "white devils." Many tossed rocks along with their catcalls. The Ayuntamiento cast a jaundiced eye at the wheel as well, and in 1891 prohibited both boneshakers and safety bicycles and any similar machines from the center of town, defined by a circle running through the city tollhouses (garitas) and passing through the statue of Carlos IV. The wheel was thus excluded from the Zócalo, the Alameda, and neighboring shopping districts. The statute allowed bicycles in only one fashionable district, the suburban residential area developing at the Hacienda de la Condesa in Chapultepec forest. Members of the Club Veloce immediately petitioned to have the law modified or reversed, but the Ayuntamiento stood firm against them. The riders then sent a delegation to President Díaz. Cycling enthusiast José O. Pastor headed the committee, and presented a request that the president intervene in behalf of the sportsmen. Díaz assented to the committee's proposal, and ordered the city ordinance revoked. The law remained in force for only a few months, but it indicated clearly that not everyone accepted the bicycle or the changes it represented in the Mexican traditional mentality.[9]

Opposition to the wheel and the opportunity to share excursions both encouraged riders to join clubs. Organizations similar to the Club Veloce quickly appeared around the country. Enthusiasts in Puebla organized Colón Club, October 12, 1892, and other communities followed. A second bicycle group appeared in the capital city when Mexican riders formed the Cyclists' Union Club, New Year's Day 1883. José Hilario Elguero, Federico Trigueros, Alejandro Rivas Fontecha and Francisco Rivas were the club's founders and they held the executive positions for the next several years. In 1895, for example, members elected the following officers: José H. Elguero, president; Alejandro Rivas, treasurer; and Federico Trigueros, secretary and trainer. The club's excursions to neighboring villages and tourist sites such as El Desierto, attracted many ardent cyclists, beginning with 70 riders on the first trip, 104 on the second, then 120 on the third, all in the first year of its existence.[10]

Club members and other wheelmen displayed all the attitudes, including the acceptance of technology, of modern society. These included secular expectations, equality of competition, specialization, rational rules, bureaucratic organization, record-keeping, and production (in sport, the drive to set records especially for speed).[11] The Cyclists' Union Club financed the $25,000 La Piedad bicycle track, built by developer Salvador Malo. Club members clocked laps and races, recorded elapsed time to suburban towns and further to Amecameca and Cuernavaca, had their own bureaucracy, and kept records of the first woman to ride from one place to another, and of the fastest Mexican in the mile and at other distances. Such events sprang from exhibitions during Lent, demonstrating a new secular attitude.[12]

Speed lured many from biped to bicycle. Mexican cyclists developed an interest in the capabilities, especially the speed, of their metal steeds. This concern resulted in an awareness of mechanics, new models, different brands, demonstrations. Above all, Tlalpam hosted the grand races of May 1893, dominated by René Sarre, who earned accolades as the first champion of Mexico. Shortly afterward, Puebla's cyclists inaugurated their new track with a series of races. The capital city riders sponsored races on Plateros and San Francisco streets (in the area the city council had once closed to riders) in September. Once again Sarre dominated by winning four of the events. The following year a new champion emerged when Luis Brauer won the championship of Mexico at both long and short distances. These Mexican cyclists, along with Lecca, Flores, Trigueros, and Jiménez, became popular figures. Society was stunned when the most celebrated rider, Carlos Buenabad, died of typhus, November 7, 1895. His funeral cortege was escorted through town by all the city's bicycle clubs.[13]

The drive for speed, equality of the conditions for competition, and specialization served as motives for the construction of new cycling tracks. The offical inauguration of the La Piedad track with a full season of racing in December 1895 saw the new '96 Rambler bicycles win three of five races. Customers quickly bought the entire shipment of new Ramblers.[14] These purchasers had adjusted to the planned obsolescence that apparently originated with bicycle manufacturers and became a part of their marketing strategy in the United States and elsewhere in 1895.[15] Demonstrations of different brands occurred with the arrival of company agents and riders in Mexico. Colonel Albert Pope, whose company manufactured the Columbia, traveled to Mexico in the winter of 1895-95, and there was great disappointment when he announced that he would have to cancel his 1895 return.[16] The E. C. Stearns Company sent Howard F. Tuttle, who stayed with Federico Trigueros while displaying his machine for admiring wheelmen. California's outstanding rider, M. Stewart, arrived to exhibit his new racer.[17]

Mexico's wheelmen were a cosmopolitan crowd. In the capital, the editor of the *Mexican Herald* commented on the widespread interest in bicycling, saying he had observed ". . . . Mexicans, Americans, English, French, Spaniards, and an African or two" riding through town.[18] Young Frenchmen formed the Velo Club Touriste with M. Clement as chairman. Most of the riders chose French bicycles, but a few imported their mounts from the United States.[19] Englishmen belonged to the older and more sedate Bicycle Society Limited, but the largest and most active club remained the Mexican-dominated Cyclists' Union Club.

The cycling clubs corresponded with counterparts in Puebla, Monterrey, and other towns around the country and obtained information on cycling matters in the United States, England, and on the continent.[20] Newspapers included a wheelmen's department, with international news, such as the report that Colombian President Miguel Antonio Caro's son had imported and begun riding the first wheel in Bogotá.[21]

As in other nations, cyclists in Mexico worked for better roads and traffic management and claimed that the bicycle itself would reform society; these efforts were credited with the decision to pave one hundred blocks of street in Mexico City with asphalt.[22] Another proposal called on the city council to purchase the Hacienda de la Condesa, near Chapultepec Castle, to convert to a park with paths for horsemen and wheelmen. This proposal explained that Mexico City had no genuine park; the Alameda, although beautiful, was too small; the Zócalo, the central garden of the Plaza Mayor, was the breathing spot for the lower classes; Chapultepec forest offered possibilities, according to the plan, if the commissioners acted wisely in their efforts to preserve the giant Cyprus trees.[23] The *Mexican Financier* argued that the city council could provide a park, if it would buy the Hacienda de la Condesa from the Escandón family, and it could reclaim the cost by developing a residential district in one section of the property for those who wanted to be near an ideal location for cycling.[24]

Thefts, accidents, collisions with pedestrians and carriages, and conflicts over the right-of-way on streets raised questions of traffic management. Reports of stolen bicycles pointed to the need for a licensing policy; the city council began selling license plates, good for a two-month period for $1.25 pesos.[25] The licenses may have helped the police identify the missing wheels, but thieves continued to sneak off with Ramblers, Sterns, and Columbias.[26] Charles Van der Velde rode his Victor, license 238, to the YMCA reading room one evening. As his bicycle could not read, he explained, he left it outside and a daring thief rode off on it.[27] Bicycle clubs soon considered a fund to provide rewards to witnesses who helped bring bike thieves and hit-and-run coachmen to justice.[28]

Collisions and injuries resulting from questions of right-of-way represented more serious problems for the community than did the individual loss of bicycles. As early as January 1891, a bicycle rider collided with a goat cart in the Alameda. Both the rider and the goat escaped injury, but the animal displayed its displeasure by chewing up one of the vehicle's rubber tires.[29] A number of accidents occurred in 1895. Pedestrians received a warning that at intersections, anyone walking the streets would be held responsible for damages in the event of a collision with a wheelman.[30] More serious than pedestrians for cyclists were the crashes with coaches and hacks. Jean Girald, a young Frenchman, was run down on Juárez Avenue by a Red Hack in December 1895. Girald suffered no permanent injury, but John C. Hill from the U.S. was struck and killed by a hit-and-run coach. Hill might well be the first traffic death involving a bicycle in Mexico. Officials reacted quickly. The United States Consul-General Thomas Crittenden demanded all efforts be made to capture the unknown coach driver and that new laws be drafted for the protection of riders.[31] The governor of the Federal District, Pedro Rincón Gallardo, pressured the police to complete the investigation (which proved unsuccessful) and reissued a set of rules that supported this technological innovation.

Rincón Gallardo had first opened all streets of the city, the towns of the federal district, and adjacent roads to two-, three-, and four-wheeled vehicles during Holy Week, 1892. His restrictions prohibited use of the sidewalks, immoderate speeds, and traveling more than three abreast. He also warned that beginners attempting to master the wheel would not be tolerated on the streets. His safety measures required a bell, a lamp at night, riding on the right side of the road, and passing on the left; the decree prohibited riders from lifting either foot from the pedal, since this might result in the loss of control. His proclamation concluded with an order for the police to protect wheelmen, arresting anyone who assaulted, whistled at, swore at, or annoyed the riders in any way. With official protection, the bicycle remained popular in Mexico until the advent of the automobile. This decree was reissued in September 1895.[32]

Wheelmen believed their metal mounts offered a way to speed the progress of society. Healthful, wholesome exercise was the most apparent benefit. One Mexican father outfitted his three teenage sons with bicycles costing 750 pesos in the hope that cycling would keep them away from barrooms. A Boston journalist, reporting the popularity of the wheel in Mexico, said, "The sport is in high favor among progressive people, who see in it a means of giving vent to the surplus energy of youth." The same anonymous reporter claimed that the bicycle worked against Mexico's national preoccupation with pills, potions, and patent medicines, which soon ". . . give way to a passion for exercise, and we shall see here a wonderful change." The greatest opposition to the wheel, he asserted, came from the apothecaries who saw an end to their lucrative business in patent medicines.[33]

Silvestre Terrazas, a Chihuahua journalist, wrote Mexico's first book on bicycling, in 1896. In his volume, he stressed speed, health, and self-reliance through the mastery of basic mechanics to do maintenance repairs. The book demonstrates clearly the author's acceptance of modern notions and his effort to promote them among other Mexicans. For prospective racers, Terrazas translated Thomas W. Eck's primer, *Points of Training*, because the methods were the ones known and used by all the top Mexican racers. He recommended that the ideal age to take up Eck's training program for racing was between eighteen and thirty, recalling that Carlos Buenabad, one of the outstanding Mexican racers, had been fifteen at his untimely death; had he lived he would have become one of the world's greatest cyclists. Terrazas's own counsel contains much good sense, for example, reminding corpulent riders that their bodies create too much wind resistance for them to expect much success on the racing circuit. Moreover, he insisted that the successful racer needed what he described as two moral conditions: intelligence and energy. The first would develop sound strategy and the ability to recognize the slightest advantage that could be used to claim victory; energy, he explained, enabled the rider to overcome difficulties during the race and to struggle until the opportunity came that would enable the rider to win. Riders fell into three cate-

gories as racers: the formidable, the less formidable, and duffers.   The
Cyclists' Union Club divided racers according to the International Cyclists'
Association classification that recognized amateurs and professional riders.

Eck's advice began with a trumpet call for hygiene and aristocracy:
the unkempt rider, he declared, was "repulsive"; he counseled that a man
should dress in clean clothing for racing just as he would to walk out in
the streets, because one never knew ". . . when he will be seen by ladies
or gentlemen." In his section called the "Development of Speed," Eck
suggested a reasonable twice daily program of endurance training and
sprint intervals, with the caution that the prospective racer should begin
"the work" of repeating these exercises as much before the race as possible,
preferably in the early spring. Following each workout, he directed that
the rider go immediately to the locker room to towel off and rub in
liniment to prevent catching cold. For supple muscles and soothing relief,
he encouraged the use of a mixture of bay rum and alcohol.[34]

Besides his own and Eck's advice to prospective racers, Terrazas also
provided encouragement for those duffers who wanted to ride for their
health. He included a chapter of medical advice for riders, warning away
critics of the sport with the assertion that eminent doctors of all
nationalities had praised cycling for its contributions to physical fitness.
Most of his information he drew from two doctors from Chihuahua City,
Angel J. Nieto and D. J. Enríquez y Terrazas, both of whom had published articles in local newspapers. They reported that the bicycle contributed to wholesome skin, because the rider was exposed to the sunlight,
and his muscles gained from the exercise, but they argued that the nervous
system received the greatest benefit from the good circulation of blood;
moreover, cycling encouraged the secretion of gastric juices, aiding di-
gestion that contributed to good health and robust individuals. Finally,
Terrazas concluded that cyclists should learn to breathe correctly to garner
the greatest benefits form the exercise; the cyclists' breathing method called
for the rider to inhale through the nose and exhale through the mouth.
Altogether cycling created a happy, robust individual.[35]

Terrazas offered information for the beginner.   His concluding
chapter reprinted instructions, from several newspapers, on learning to
ride. This basic information was supplemented with a glossary of cycling
terms, including the parts of the vehicle and the racing vocabulary (including many words borrowed from English, such as handicap, mile, and
time-keeper), illustrations showing how to change and repair a tire, and a
discussion of the parts and accessaries to reduce vibration, to alter gear
ratios, and to increase the enjoyment the bicycle could offer.[36]

Knowledge of the machine, its parts and repair, modifications for
speed, preparation for racers understood and described as work, a training
regime comprised of the repetition of the necessary functions (e.g.
sprinting) for the production of speed--Terrazas offered Mexicans the experience of modern life through bicycling.

The bicycle also represented modernization as it challenged traditional behavior, demeanor, and fashions of Mexican women. Señoritas looked on the sport as an opportunity for a broader, freer life. They could escape the humdrum of a shut-in existence by mounting a wheel, often riding off in the company of a young gentleman, leaving behind the *dueña* who could not or would not learn to ride a bicycle.[37] These señoritas could not ride in the traditional dress, so they had to modify their wardrobe. Some of them adopted the daring "bloomer" costume. "To be or not to be" in bloomers, described as "a pair of trousers very baggy at the knees, abnormally full at the pistol pockets and considerably full where you strike a match," was the question agitating the feminine mind in Mexico City. Opponents argued that women should be held responsible for accidents caused by their provocative garments; others averred women would tarnish their reputations by appearing nearly disrobed in public. Reports soon circulated that shoplifters were renting the cycling costumes because the roominess of the garment made it easy to hide stolen goods. Despite critics, the wheelmen and women believed progress was the result of exercise, mobility, new fashions, and companionship offered by the bicycle.[38]

Progressive society returned from their suburban homes along the Viga Canal on two pneumatic tires to Mexico City during the Lenten season. Traditionally high society had escaped the onerous rules of Lent, but the wheel brought them back beginning with the tour by the North American riders in 1895. The following year, the capital's city council arranged a bicycle parade to celebrate the Carnival season, offering over $500 in awards to winners. The display was regarded as a stunning success. Trigueros, dressed in a cerise, blue, orange, and black-and-white costume with his wheel decorated with "rare tropical flowers, shaded by a canopy of gardenias," tied for first honors; but Zozoya claimed the prize with a coin flip. Only the presence of large numbers of the rabble, who could not be controlled by the police, marred the event, according to reporters. After this 1896 parade, riders began to spend the entire season, with reduced regulations, in the city. These events soon led to pushing the traditional celebration of such Holy Week events as the Burning of Judas out of the Zócalo into the plazas and streets of the working-class neighborhoods.[39]

With all the interest in the bicycle, eventually commercial efforts to repair them and the manufacture of Mexican wheels had to come. R. R. Shepard opened a repair shop in the Calle de Dolores in 1896, offering spare parts and making adjustments. Charles Leo Browne obtained contracts on November 15, 1905, and March 12, 1908, to establish a factory to manufacture both bicycles and automobiles. For reasons that remain unclear, Browne's efforts never went beyond the planning stage, and on February 10, 1909, the government rescinded his contracts. Nevertheless, the modern Mexican mounting his wheel and weaving in and out of the crowds during the afternoon's *paseo* on the Reforma demonstrated his wealth, position, and above all his progressive character.[40]

Those who became bicycle riders expressed an ambivalence toward modernization. Their machine seemed to be the miracle of technology; it also offered them the means to escape the crowded, dirty, congested, and dangerous modern city. The bicycle became a vehicle to flee progress and its consequences.[41] The Cyclists' Union Club and other bicycle groups sponsored excursions into the country. Individuals often pedaled into the countryside, either consciously or subconsciously escaping to bucolic surroundings. A few riders found more adventure than they wanted outside of town. T. Philip Terry and a companion, in 1897, took a bicycle trip from Mexico City to Acapulco. As they neared Guerrero, a bandit gang galloped after them and attempted to lasso the cyclists. Both riders crouched low over the handlebars so the lasso would not fit over them. Still Terry felt one lariat "as hot as any live electric-light wire" hit his forehead, burn its way down his back taking his cap with it, and ring his camera that was hooked behind his seat. The bandit got away with the camera.[42] Most Mexicans found the calm, restful country that they sought rather than highwaymen on their excursions. These escapes from the city may represent the first stirrings of a critique by the elite of modern life and what it was doing to Mexico.

The bicycle as a metaphor for the dictator's policy of modernism remained a safe target of criticism. The Liberals believed in the power of the press, so that much of their critique appeared in newspapers, such as *El Hijo de Ahuizote*. Cartoons correctly identified Porfirian modernization as a policy leading to new roles for women in society. These sketches tried to make oblique hints of an effeminate regime because it fostered female activities. Many of the parodies correctly connected the bicycle with the changing dress, behavior, and outlook of women, while attacking women's continued dependence on the church and the man of the house. "Did you know, Juan," asked one jest, "that the Pope has permitted Priests to use bicycles?" "Don't tell me, man!" "Exactly." "Well, I'm not going to allow my wife to make confession."[43] The association between the bicycle and the modern woman clearly accounted for the snap decision to keep the wife from confessing. Other jeering comments reflected the same association. In cartoons, women riders in the 1890s are almost always drawn with short, knee-length skirts and long socks, revealing the exact form of their legs and ankles that modesty would not allow even if covered when not riding. One such cyclist said, "This bicycle cost me 250 *pesos*. Do you think, neighbor, that there might be a cheaper one?" "Yes, neighbor, the one that your boyfriend buys you, because it will be free."[44] Still another, entitled "What will Probably Happen in the Twentieth Century--The Emancipation of the Woman Will Probably be a Reality" revealed this dreaded prospect: the cartoonist drew a woman dressed in an army officer's uniform and carrying a cigarette.[45]

The Porfirian modernism represented by its bicycles, that offered only one of several new opportunities for women, called forth criticism from the Liberals, who parodied the dictator's regime by mocking its symbols. "An End of the Century Duel" showed two dandies fencing from the seats of their bicycles. One finally claimed victory after a series of thrusts and parries by the quick stab that punctured the other's front tire.[46] In the same sarcastic manner, another caricature listed the benefits offered by the bicycle to Mexican citizens. One should ride a bicycle, according to the artist, for enjoyment, for the amusement of the people in the streets, to become thinner, in order to pay the wages of a quack pillpusher, to pay a debt at the end of the month (by giving the debtor a ride), for love, and for the enjoyment of children.[47] Not one of these reasons seemed worthy to the Liberals.

The leisure interests of Mexicans in the 1890s revealed attitudes, notions, and proclivities that constituted the Porfirian persuasion. This temper showed a rush to accept European, and especially American, activities that included sport. Baseball particularly reflected the growing influence of the United States, the most important group of foreigners in the country, whether measured in number of residents, importance of occupations, or value of investments. Boxing not only expressed this mimicry, but also revealed the new security and routine established by the Díaz regime that resulted in a quest for excitement in what had abruptly become an "unexciting" society. Above all Mexicans recognized the importance of progress, speed, and modernization through technology as they turned to bicycles. Cycling became the sport of the times.

Perhaps these attitudes do not seem surprising to those familiar with the Porfirian economic and political system. But no political pressure from the *rurales*, military, or administration, nor economic necessity from the need for work, ownership of the means of production, or relationship to the land compelled the adoption of these diversions. Mexicans freely chose the sport that expressed the Porfirian persuasion.

Notes

1   "Velocipede Notes," *Scientific American* 20 (29 May 1869): 343; Norman L. Dunham, "The Bicycle Era in American History" (Ph.D. diss., Harvard University, 1956), p. 159; *Two Republics* (21 April, 3 July 1869).

2   Silvestre Terrazas, *El ciclismo: manual de velocipedia* (Chihuahua: Tip. de Silvestre Terrazas, 1896), p. 22.

3   Ibid., p. 24; *New York Times*, 25 January and 29 February 1880.

4   Terrazas, *El ciclismo*, p. 24; *New York Times*, 25 January and 29 February 1880; *Two Republics*, 18 March 1884, 1 May, 5 August, 22 September, 4 October, 1888; *Mexican Herald*, 29 September 1895; *El Financiero*, 21 March 1885.

5   *Mexican Herald*, 23, 29 September, 13, 21 November, 1 December 1895;

6   *Mexican Herald*, 18 October 1895.

7   *Mexican Herald*, 16 April 1896; *New York Times*, 9 January 1895. "Dute" Cabanne endured a two-year suspension (reduced from a lifetime ban) when he was discovered conspiring with Fred Titus and Charles Murphy to fix the three premier races on the U. S. professional circuit in summer 1895. E. F. Leonart rode a mile in one minute thirty-five seconds, beating the time of the champion race horse Salvator, settling the question of speed in favor of the machine. See Robert A. Smith, *A Social History of the Bicycle: Its Early Life and Times in America* (New York: American Heritage Press, 1972), pp. 143, 157-58.

8   *New York Times*, 6 March 1895.

9   *New York Times*, 9 and 11 March 1895.

10   "Cyclist to Editor," *Mexican Herald*, 26 October 1895.

11   Terrazas, *El ciclismo*, p. 29.

12   Allen Guttmann, *From Ritual to Record: The Nature of Modern Sports* (New York: Columbia University Press, 1978), pp. 15-55, discusses these attributes of modern society and sport. A discussion of some of these characteristics in Mexico is the substance of Hugo Hiriart, *El universo de Posada: Estética de la obsolescencia, Memoria y Olvido: Imágenes de México* 8 (Mexico: Secretaría de Educación Pública, 1982).

13   *Mexican Herald*, 15 October, 5, 13 November, 2, 9, 18 December 1895. On U.S. bicycle exports to Mexico, see *U.S. Census Report, 10, 12th Census 1900: Manufactures, Part IV: Special Reports on Selected Industries* (Washington, D.C.: Government Printing Office, 1900), p. 335. For a comparison of the impact of the bicycle in the United States, see: Dunham, "The Bicycle Era in American History"; Smith, *Social History of the Bicycle; Mexican Herald*, 8 and 10 December 1895.

14   *Mexican Herald*, 23 December 1895; Terrazas, *El ciclismo*, pp. 29, 31.

15   Smith, *Social History of the Bicycle*, p. 19.

16   Pope was one of the fathers of the American bicycle industry; see
     Smith, *Social History of the Bicycle,* pp. 8-12, 18-19, 36-40, 207-09;
     Mexican Herald, 24 November 1895.

17   *Mexican Herald,* 10 October and 20 November 1895.

18   Ibid., editorial, 9 December 1895.

19   Ibid., 8 December 1895.

20   Ibid., 20 September 1895.

21   Ibid., 7 November 1895.   There was also an international curiosity
     about bicycling in Mexico that was satisfied in part with articles such
     as T. Philip Terry, "In Aztec Land Awheel," *Outing* 23 (6 March
     1894): 461-63, and Terry's "My Ride to Acapulco: A Cycling Ad-
     venture in Mexico," *Outing* 29:6 (March 1897): 593-96.

22   *Mexican Herald*, 29 September 1895.

23   Ibid., 16 November 1895.

24   Ibid., 15 October 1895; *Mexican Financier*, 15 October 1895.

25   *Mexican Herald*, 20 October 1895.

26   Ibid., 18 September 1895.

27   Ibid., "Editorial," 9 December 1895.

28   Ibid., 15 October 1895.

29   *Two Republics*, 21 January 1891.

30   *Mexican Herald*, 7 and 8 December 1895.

31   Ibid., 19 December 1895.

32   *Siglo XIX*, 14 April 1892.   These rules were reissued; see *Mexican
     Herald*, 28 September 1895.

33   *Mexican Herald*, 28 September 1895.

34   Terrazas, *El ciclismo*, pp. 39-40, 49, 51.

35   Ibid., pp. 32-38, and especially p. 39.

36   Ibid., p. 44.

[37]   Ibid., 22 September and 5 October 1895.

[38]   Ibid., 19 January and 19 February 1896.

[39]   *Mexican Herald*, 5 February 1896.

[40]   Fernando Rosenzweig, "La industria," in *La Vida económica,* I, p. 467, of Cosío Villegas, *Historia moderna.*

[41]   For this explanation of the bicycle, I have drawn on Richard Harmond, "Progress and Flight: An Interpretation of the American Cycle Craze of the 1890s," *Journal of Social History* 5 (Winter 1971): 235-57, especially p. 236.

[42]   T. Philip Terry, "My Ride to Acapulco," pp. 593-96.

[43]   *El Hijo del Ahuizote*, 12 August 1894.

[44]   Ibid., 31 October 1897.

[45]   Ibid., 14 November 1897.

[46]   Ibid., 30 January 1898.

[47]   Ibid., 23 January 1898.

3
Forging the Regional Pastime: Baseball and Class in Yucatán
Gilbert M. Joseph

Introduction

The Mexican people's love of sport is world renowned. In 1968, Mexico City was the site of the Summer Olympics, and 1986 marked the second time in two decades that Mexico has hosted the finals of the World Cup (Mundial)--remarkable achievements for a Latin American or developing nation. The hosting of soccer's most prestigious event testifies to that sport's tremendous vitality at the nation's grassroots. While Mexicans have embraced a variety of sports as participants and spectators--boxing, bullfighting, baseball, basketball, and distance track come most readily to mind--unquestionably, *fútbol* has traditionally been Mexico's most "popular" sport.

There is, however, one notable regional exception. In the remote southeastern Yucatán peninsula, baseball has been and seems certain to remain the chief pastime, or, as *yucatecos* proudly refer to it, *"el rey de los deportes"* ("the king of sports"). In this regard, the Yucatán (and certain other parts of the Mexican Gulf) would seem to conform to a larger circum-Caribbean pattern, having more in common sportswise with such Antillean baseball bastions as Cuba, Puerto Rico, and the Dominican Republic, and with isthmian Nicaragua and coastal Venezuela, than with the rest of Mexico.[1]

There is no disputing baseball's popularity in the peninsula. Professionals and party functionaries, middle class merchants and housewives, cabbies and street vendors, factory workers and henequen laborers, even backcountry *milperos* (maize-growing peasants)--all typically are *béisbolistas*. As such, they regularly play or follow the game through a well-organized, multitiered regional network of leagues, and fanatically support Yucatán's Double A-level franchise in the Mexican League, the Mérida-based Leones (Lions). Year after year, the club's attendance figures top the league, easily outdistancing the gate receipts of teams in Mexico City, not to mention those of franchises in larger regional centers. Invariably, the Leones's twenty thousand-seat Kukulcán Park is filled to capacity for important games, and local fans have justly earned a reputation for being at once the most sophisticated and verbally intimidating in the Mexican League. In 1984, they were rewarded with the club's first league championship in twenty-seven years, an event that triggered around-the-clock celebrations in Mérida and the surrounding towns that lasted for two days, brought business to a standstill, and dwarfed more traditional Independence Day, New Year's, and Carnival Week revels. Minor League baseball may never again see the like of it, unless, of course, the Leones repeat as champions.[2]

This chapter attempts to account for this colorful regional phenomenon. Specifically, what historical factors explain baseball's surprising popularity in Yucatán, particularly among the working classes, and most dramatically among Maya *campesinos*? Why has *béisbol* been preferred by Yucatán's humble country folk, whereas *fútbol*, traditionally Mexico's most popular sport, has been relatively neglected?[3] The essay will focus on baseball's formative period in Yucatán, from the sport's introduction by Cuban immigrants in the 1890s until the Great Depression. An effort will be made to relate pivotal trends in the region's political economy to important developments in the game. Initially, we will see that the sport was appropriated by an exclusive urban-based regional oligarchy that prided itself on imitating the latest *fin d'siécle* trends in foreign recreation and leisure. Later, during the first two decades of this century, *béisbol* shifted its base to the emerging middle sectors, particularly the small urban working and artisan class, and first penetrated the Yucatán countryside. Yet it is the pivotal juncture of the Mexican Revolution that follows that merits special attention. During the 1920s, Marxist Governor Felipe Carrillo Puerto and subsequent administrations of his Partido Socialista del Sureste (PSS) systematically promoted baseball among the numerous inhabitants of the interior Maya *pueblos* and hacienda communities and, in the process, launched the institutionalization of the sport at the grassroots level.

Foundations: Oligarchs and Immigrants (c. 1890-1894)

Like so much Porfirian Mexico, Yucatán was thoroughly transformed by the requirements of North American industrial capitalism and governed by its fluctuating rhythms.[4] The invention of a mechanical knotting device for the McCormick reaper-binder (1878) revolutionized the grain industry and expanded demand for fiber and twine geometrically. The production of Yucatán's monocrop, henequen (sisal hemp), increased furiously during the Porfiriato (1876-1911), when annual exports rose from 40,000 bales of raw fiber to more than 600,000 bales. By the end of the nineteenth century, the green cornfields and idly grazing cows of the peninsula's colonial-style haciendas had been replaced by endless rectilinear rows of bluish-gray spines and the brisk factory-like pace of the modern henequen plantation. The final destination of this raw hemp would be New Orleans or New York, where stateside cordage manufacturers would convert the fiber into binder twine for the wheat farmers of North America.

Mérida was no longer the dingy, muddy overgrown village it had been in 1850. By the turn of the century, it was the republic's "White City," immaculate and modern, a fitting seat for Yucatán's newly minted henequen millionaires. Universally recognized as the world's most active fiber market, Mérida boasted a population of almost 70,000--roughly double the figure of 1875--as well as urban services and amenities that Mexico City was hard pressed to match.

If Mérida was blossoming, its streets scientifically numbered and well lit, the port of Progreso was flourishing comparably. Founded upon a mangrove swamp in 1870 to replace the insalubrious, more distant and shallower port of Sisal, Progreso had survived a mosquito-infested infancy to become modernized and redecorated by a newer, more affluent generation. By century's end, the best *meridanos* were building luxurious resort homes along the port's beach wall, and the U.S. Consulate had transferred its offices from Mérida to Progreso (twenty-two miles away) to be closer to the increased pulse of daily commercial transactions. New wharves and fiber wharehouses were under construction, and a variety of trading houses had moved to the port or opened branch offices there. By 1900, Progreso had about 5,500 inhabitants and, among Mexico's ports, only Veracruz shipped and received a greater volume of goods.

All of these material transformations, and the regional elite that carried them out, owed their existence to henequen. Yet if Yucatán's three to four hundred planter families collectively constituted one of the wealthiest classes in Porfirian Mexico, their economic condition was among the least secure. In most cases, these henequen *hacendados* were not only big spenders but speculators, constantly seeking new ways to maximize profits amid the problematical turns of the export economy and often overextending themselves in the process. The world fiber market subjected planters and Yucatecan society as a whole to an extended rollercoaster ride, with alternating boom and bust surges the norm rather than the exception throughout the Porfiriato.[5]

Sudden price turns and periodic cycles worked to concentrate henequen production in fewer and larger hands. Around the turn of the century, a small cohesive group of about thirty families came to form a dominant oligarchical faction, or *camarilla*. This "Divine Caste," based upon the Olegario Molina-Avelino Montes *parentesco* (clan), had homogeneous interests, a relatively closed membership, and owing in part to its collaboration with the principal buyer, manufacturer, and financier of raw fiber, the International Harvester Company, such control over the economic and political levers of power in the region that it was able to thwart the opportunities of rival elite factions. With increasing frequency after the turn of the century, members of Yucatán's henequen elite became indebted to Molina and Montes's *camarilla* and were forced to advance their future product at slightly less than the current market price to cover present obligation.   Access to larger amounts of Harvester's capital at critical junctures enabled the Molina-Montes faction to acquire mortgages, purchase estates outright, and progressively consolidate a hold on regional communications, infrastructure, and banking--all of which guaranteed control of local fiber production and generally worked to depress the price in Harvester's interest prior to the arrival of the Mexican Revolution in the region in 1915.[6]

Although the vast majority of Yucatán's large producers and merchants remained outside the exclusive faction that collaborated with International Harvester, and bitterly railed against it, Yucatán's preponderant share of the world's hard fiber supply, coupled with minimal production costs, generally ensured profits attractive enough to soothe most irate members of the agrocommercial elite.   In effect, the Maya *peon* underwrote the planter's profits even under difficult market conditions, laboring on estates under miserable, deteriorating conditions, often for fewer than fifty *centavos* per day.

The rise of henequen monoculture dramatically transformed the lives of the tens of thousands of *campesinos* who comprised the labor force. The plantation devoured what independent peasant villages remained in the northwestern quadrant of the peninsula--the so-called "henequen zone"--then began to encroach upon peasant communities beyond the zone. By the turn of the century, the great majority of free Maya *pueblos* had lost their land base. Unable to hold off the expanding henequen plantations, Yucatán's *campesinos* were first pulled onto the estates and then isolated on them. *Hacendados* made sure that their work forces were heterogeneous groups, combining Maya *campesinos* with small contingents of ethnic and linguistic strangers: Yaqui deportees, indentured Asians, and central Mexican *enganchados* (contract workers).   Not only did *peones* have no contact with their fellows on other estates, but they were also isolated from potential allies in the urban areas. Yucatecan planters hoped that these precautions, coupled with a demanding labor regimen and a multilayered system of surveillance and repression, which included private bounty hunters and secret police, would preclude another "*guerra de castas.*" In the apocalyptic Caste War of 1847, rebel Maya had come close to driving their white masters from the peninsula and destroying sugar production in the southeastern portion of the peninsula.[7] A half century later, the white masters still lived in constant fear of large scale rural uprisings.

Indeed, in many respects, Yucatán's social formation during the late Porfiriato had much in common with the colonial plantation and slave societies of an earlier period of Latin American history.   An enormous chasm separated the two extremes on the social scale: the tiny minority of planters and the great majority of "slaves" (*peones*).   Nor was there

much of a social infrastructure between these extremes. The urban working class was limited in its growth by the insignificant level of industrialization in the region, owing to the persistence of monocrop agriculture and
the failure of an internal market. With minor exceptions, the little capital
that had gone for industrial development had been put primarily into unsuccessful attempts to produce binder twine or manufactured goods locally, or into service industries directly related to the production and
transport of henequen (e.g., railroads, tramways, fiber processing plants,
and repair shops).

Late Porfirian Yucatán also possessed a "middle class" that was small
even by the Latin American standards of the time: three to five percent
of the population. These middle sectors consisted mostly of intellectuals,
journalists, professionals, small merchants, and small rural producers, most
of whom served the agrocommercial elite and appropriated its social outlook.   Nevertheless, there was an increasingly vocal minority that felt
pinched by a lack of opportunity in the society. For in the stifling atmosphere of large-scale plantation agriculture, there was little room for any
other major activity.

Such were the parameters of Yucatán's Ancien Regime when it first
encountered baseball. It was perhaps inevitable that the local oligarchs
would embrace the North American pastime. They eagerly appropriated
every other major trend in foreign fashion and leisure around the turn of
the century, and a good many of these were far less appropriate to the regional environment. No sooner had heavy corsets made their appearance
in the solons and boutiques of Paris and New York than they were being
worn, despite the sweltering heat, by the society matrons of Mérida, determined to appear wasp-waisted at any cost. No matter that Yucatán had
no lakes, rivers, or even a protected harbor, and no paved roads outside
of Mérida, motor cars, sailboats, and luxury yachts were all the rage.
Baseball, in turn, not only appealed to the *Casta Divina's* heightened tastes
for imported, "modern" leisure pursuits; it was eminently suited to the
tropics. Moreover, their sons were already playing ball on the diamonds
of North American prep schools and universities.

Chauvinistic *yucatecos* would have us believe that *béisbol* was played
earlier in the peninsula than elsewhere in the republic. Baseball's origins
in both Yucatán and the rest of Mexico will, no doubt, remain shrouded
in myth and continue to spur debate among provincial *cronistas*. Certainly, Yucatán was one of several regions where the game was first played
in the early 1890s. What is interesting is that, whereas baseball was introduced into the national capital and other (mostly northern) centers by
U.S. miners, engineers, and railroad employees, the North American pastime came to Yucatán indirectly, via Cuba. U.S. merchant seamen had
first introduced baseball to Cuban cargo handlers in the 1860s, and the
sport quickly flourished among the popular classes. Indeed it had taken
root in the camps of the *mambises,* the predominantly black and mulatto
guerrilla fighters who spearheaded the island's struggle for independence
from Spain during the last third of the nineteenth century. Fleeing the
turbulence of their homeland, many Cubans sought a haven in neighbor-

ing Yucatán or the Gulf port of Veracruz, bringing their passion for the game with them.[8]

According to local tradition, the origins of regional baseball might well be traced back to a June day in 1890 when three homesick Cuban teenagers--Juan Francisco, Fernando, and Eduardo Urzáiz Rodríguez-- fresh off a boat from Havana, unpacked their suitcases in Mérida and made some friends on their new block:

> The other kids their age were gathered to play *toro* . . . . The Urzáiz boys began to "play ball" with a bat and an old ragged Spaulding, astonishing their new friends with the strange game. Within a short time, the neighborhood kids joined in and street baseball began in Mérida at the corner of 61st and 68th.[9]

"Street baseball" began to catch on in Mérida and Progreso's working and middle class barrios in the early 1890s. Boys in their early teens spilled into the *plazuelas* of Santiago and San Juan near the center of Mérida and played ball well into the evening. Old timers still recall their fathers' embellished account of adventures in the "days of the Xtoles," Mérida's first corps of urban police. Responding to neighbors' complaints of truancy and excessive noise, or those of irate pedestrians who had been "beaned" by stray balls (*pelotazos*), the constables mounted a concerted campaign against these first *béisbolistas*. Somehow the street urchins continually managed to elude the grasp of "El Chivo" ("Billy Goat") Escamilla, the exasperated police chief, and reclaimed their terrain after each sweep of the neighborhoods.[10]

These first young players were much less concerned with rules and rigorous competition than with the spontaneous fun their games and antics produced. Most often, they played barehanded--many barefooted as well--with makeshift bats and balls stuffed with rags or raw henequen fiber. Frequently they played ten or more to a side, inventing a new position they called "Rey Xiol" ("Right Short"), between first and second, with the second baseman standing on the bag itself. In the early 1890s, their efforts were aided by touring performers of the U.S. "Circo Orrin," who enjoyed playing pick-up games with the boys and imparted to them some of the finer points of the game.[11]

Although "street ball" would continue in the years ahead, in 1892 the peninsula's first organized teams were formed in Mérida and Progreso. The influence of the regional oligarchy in the early promotion of baseball as an organized sport was pervasive. Although the majority of the early teams were neighborhood-based and were formed by barrio youths, many of them recently arrived Cuban workers, invariably it was members of the Divine Caste who sponsored these amateur clubs, bore the cost of uniforms and equipment, arranged for the rental or purchase of playing fields, and ultimately, constructed the first ball parks.[12] The greatest of these early patrons of the game, Don Pablo González Anzar, who built the first ball field in suburban Chuminópolis and served as a benefactor for several neighborhood teams, took great pride in his reputation as a *"distinguido* sportman." He believed that "baseball could be a great element in the health, vitality, and morality of Yucatecan youth, as well as a restraining factor on their unhealthy passions."[13]

But the Divine Caste's promotion of the sport went beyond *noblesse oblige*. If baseball fit nicely into the oligarchs' roseate turn-of-the-century vision of a grander, more modern Yucatán founded upon the virtues of physical vigor and competition, they would lead by example. In 1892, the "Champion Club" of Mérida was created by young gentlemen to pursue both cricket and baseball. An early team photograph suggests their seriousness of purpose, not merely to become champions, but to look the part in the best Anglo-Saxon manner, complete with striped polo shirts, knickers, hair slicked and parted down the middle, and waxed handlebar mustaches.[14]

Other elite-based clubs would form that same year, but none of them, nor the migrant-dominated neighborhood teams, proved a match for "El Sporting Club," founded in Mérida by Don Pablo González and Enrique Cámara Zavala, and stocked with members of the powerful Molina-Montes *camarilla*. Unlike the young, hastily improvised barrio clubs, "El Sporting" was composed of players twenty and over, who had learned the game at U.S. boarding schools and colleges. Its roster read like a *Who's Who* of the incipient oligarchy: Cásares, Hubbe, Regil, Peón, Ancona, even Avelino Montes himself! "El Sporting's" star hurler, Miguel Peón Cásares, was over six feet tall, had blazing speed and a drop curve that had won him trophies and lured major league scouts in the States.[15]

"El Sporting Club" remains the only team in the region's history to go undefeated. Through 1892 and 1893, its games ranked among Mérida's important social events. Special trams brought elegant ladies with parasols and picnic lunches to Chuminópolis to watch their heroes; stirring music accompanied the action.[16] By 1894, however, the fad had peaked. The sudden death of Don Pablo, the game's most enthusiastic promoter, coupled with the demoralizing supremacy of "El Sporting," highlighted the fragility of organized baseball in Yucatán. More important, the financial panic of 1893-1894 and the worldwide economic recession that followed, knocking the bottom out of the fiber market, demonstrated how closely the fortunes of baseball and patterns of leisure were tied to fluctuations in the region's monocrop economy. Spontaneous street ball among the popular classes would continue, but the organizational impulse was temporarily checked.[17]

Resurrections: Broadening the Base (c. 1901-1915)

The new century arrived with new possibilities; the Spanish- American War breathed new life into the depressed fiber market of the mid-1890s. The outbreak of the conflict in 1898 had curtailed supplies of Filipino manila, henequen's chief competitor, and quotations for Yucatecan sisal hemp skyrocketed, quadrupling by 1902. Although prices began to fall thereafter--no doubt affected by the post-war restoration of competition between manila and henequen, as well as by a secret 1902 agreement between International Harvester and the Molina faction to depress the price of fiber--quotations would remain at a reasonably high level until the worldwide financial panic of 1907-1908.[18]

Signs of renewal abounded and Olegario Molina's Divine Caste presided over the new *auge* (boom). No sooner had President Díaz confirmed Molina as governor in 1902 than Don Olegario embarked on a massive public works program to further beautify Mérida and improve the port facilities at Progreso. By 1906 the capital's streets had been paved and drained--at substantial cost and by the governor's personal firm!--and *meridanos* could now admire their own version of the Champs Elysees, the elegant Paseo de Montejo. Such urban growth and renewal often had the effect of displacing barrio youths from the vacant lots and *plazuelas* they had hastily improvised into diamonds. Street players were now pushed to Mérida's urban periphery; indeed more organized groups of *béisbolistas* frequently traveled by train to neighboring villages such as Umán and Caucel to play[19]

The ever-increasing torrent of henequen income stimulated new businesses and industrial ventures and a dramatic increase in the region's communications and transportation network, although it was still almost exclusively tied to the export sector. As the pace of the export boom quickened during the final years of the Old Regime, Yucatán's modest urban-based middle sectors grew in number and performed more diverse and essential roles in the development process. Increasingly they began to demand a louder political voice and greater socio-economic opportunity. Railroad and dock workers spearheaded a fledgling urban labor movement that included *sindicatos* of mechanics, construction workers, carters, carriage drivers, barbers, and food caterers. These artisans and workers fought first to establish job security, then to maintain their real wages amid the fluctuations of the monocrop economy. Meanwhile, in the regional press, disgruntled middle class intellectuals issued their first challenges to the dominance of the Divine Caste. Yet none of these middle strata concerned themselves with the countryside or the sad plight of the enslaved Maya *peon*. Thus, despite the fabulous wealth generated by the fiber boom, the century's first decade evolved into a "summer of discontent" for the vast majority of regional producers, merchants, white collar functionaries, urban workers, and *campesinos*, all of whom found themselves subordinated, in one way or another, to the *Molinista* oligarchy.[20]

The deepening economic, political, and social contradictions that beset the last years of the old Porfirian order conditioned the manner in which *béisbol* was revived and began to develop following the turn of the century. With the return of good times, the oligarchy was again well disposed to act as catalyst and patron; indeed, now the game might well serve an important social control function, co-opting or diffusing dissent in Yucatán's factories, railroad yards, and hacienda communities. But at the same time, the broadening of society's base, coupled with the prosperity of the boom, gave greater initiative to the popular classes. With increasing regularity, first in Mérida and Progreso, and then in some of the smaller centers of the interior, students, artisans, mechanics, and even groups of village-based *campesinos* spontaneously formed their own baseball clubs. In some instances, they sought and received the traditional support of elite benefactors. However, more commonly they now opted for an independent existence, forming their own *juntas directivas* and establishing monthly dues to pay for their own equipment and upkeep.

Baseball's new epoch formally began in May of 1901, with the founding of "El Trovador," an elite-based team.[21] But it was not until 1904 that the sport began to set down roots and competition began in earnest among teams representing a variety of points on the social spectrum. The public would be receptive, since popular diversions at the turn of the century were few: annual religious festivals in the barrios and *pueblos*, bullfights in season, occasional *bailes populares*, and visits by touring circus and drama troupes. The *cine* (movies) would not delight the masses for several more decades.[22]

For their part, the scions of the Divine Caste, fresh from their schooling in the United States, formed the "Pablo González Baseball Club." By adopting the name of the founder of "El Sporting," the Pablistas sought to claim their predecessor's mantle of success. Money was no object: Spaulding balls and gloves and "Louisville Sluggers" were imported from the States, and in 1904 the Pablistas converted an amusement park in the fashionable suburb of Itzimná into Yucatán's first real baseball stadium, modeled after Ebbets Field.[23]

The oligarchy also invested heavily in the best working-class teams of the day, "El Fénix," "Railway," and "Club Colón."[24] "El Fénix" was the baseball club of "La Industrial," a short-lived factory that specialized in the manufacture of binder twine. La Industrial had been created by the Molina *parentesco* following the panic of 1893, when prices had dropped to the point where raw fiber export was ceasing to be profitable and the Casta sought to try its hand at fiber manufacturing in a well-capitalized effort to reap the value traditionally added by the North American cordage factories. Interest in the venture had already waned by 1902, with raw fiber prices soaring again and the Molinas now working closely with International Harvester, the acknowledged giant in the binder twine field. After a fire swept the plant's premises around the turn of the century, Molina and Montes moved to divert La Industrial from twine production into other non-competitive applications, and ultimately let the venture quietly slip into oblivion on the eve of the Mexican Revolution.[25] High wages and job security may have been lacking for the factory's mechanics and artisans--a great many of whom were recent Cuban immigrants--but management attempted to bolster their morale on the baseball diamond.

Don Olegario's Cuban-born son-in-law, Luis Carranza, La Industrial's manager, encouraged factory personnel to play for "El Fénix," granting time off for team practices and rewarding on-the-field heroics with special bonuses. Olegario Molina's son, Luis Augusto Molina Figueroa, was appointed the club's manager, and backed by his cousin, Luis Demetrio Molina, contracted for 10,000 square meters of prime urban real estate, which in 1905 became "Fénix Park," the best facility of the period. The name of the ball park and the team were intended dramatically to suggest La Industrial's rise from the ashes of the fire and the brighter days ahead for the plant and its workers.[26]

These, of course, would never arrive. Nevertheless, the ball club played a great part in the resurrection of the regional pastime, drawing mass crowds numbering in the thousands and undisputedly establishing itself as the peninsula's premier nine, "the people's team."[27] Ironically, the Casta Divina had armed the very opponents who would deny their Pablistas the supremacy that "El Sporting" had previously enjoyed. During one stretch in 1904-1905, "El Fénix" defeated "Pablo González" thirteen straight times![28]

The Pablistas never beat "El Fénix" and their record against the urban working class's two other strongest contenders, "Railway" (made up of the workers from "La Plancha," the machine shops of Ferrocarriles Unidos de Yucatán) and "Club Colón" (comprised of the port workers employed by Progreso's Agencia Comercial) was only mediocre.[29] The game was passing the oligarchy by.

Increasingly, baseball in the regional capital and port seemed to revolve around the major enterprises and workers' groups: La Industrial and the railroad yards in Mérida; the Agencia Comercial and the docks in Progreso. The workers played the game after a hard day's work, mostly for the pleasure of it, but also to earn a few extra pesos. In addition to the modest bonuses that management might extend to its best players, there were always special gimmicks arranged by promoters and advertisers. At Itzimná Park, for example, batters won 100 pesos every time they hit the large box of "La Paz" cigarettes painted on the left-field fence. Decades after his playing days were over, Dr. Saturnino Borges would claim that these bonuses and incentives financed the medical studies that freed him from a childhood of poverty. For Agustín Osorio Polanco, there was little upward mobility.[30] "El Chato" ("Flat Face") combined an amateur career as a ballplayer with work on the Progreso docks, at 6 pesos per day, and moonlighted as a *picador* during bullfighting season. Baseball occasionally provided a little pocket money, but more important were the memories that Chato continued to nurture of afternoons spent with teammates such as "El Zorro" ("The Fox") Amaro, "Joloch" ("Cornhusk") Patron, and a rifle-armed catcher from Veracruz known simply as "Escopeta" ("Shotgun").[31]

For Federico ("Chivi") Cardeña, who had worked his entire adult life riveting boilers at "La Plancha," and earned a salary that hadn't held up in the years of his retirement, baseball had afforded a special kind of release:

> Locomotives, smoke, steam, and grease . . . all kinds of noise: pounding hammers, hissing engines, blaring horns . . . A racket everywhere, a mass of humanity, workers coming and going in every direction . . . . Then, suddenly, it was 4 o'clock--time to play ball.

During the weekends, baseball was equally a part of Cardeña's routine. He recalled the crazy afternoon he pitched "hungover" ("*crudo*"). Game time had arrived but he had forgotten he was the starting pitcher for "Railway." His brother "Mike" organized a search party and found "Chivi" at his favorite watering hole, the Gran Hotel. He was bundled off to Fénix Park and installed on the mound. "My catcher had to put a *granizadero* [crushed flavored ice] under my cap to sober me up. Somehow I managed to pitch a shutout."[32]

Meanwhile, baseball clubs proliferated among the *meridano* and *progreseño* middle class. Students and white collar employees were particularly effective in organizing new, often ephemeral, teams with imaginative names.[33] Scores formed in Mérida in 1904 alone, among them: "New York," "Iron Baseball Club," "Walk Over," "Pickup Nine," "Kickers," and "Mauser."[34] By the end of the same year, Progreso itself boasted sixteen clubs, and baseball had spread to the interior county seats and to the capital and principal centers of the neighboring state of Campeche. The first encounters in Yucatán's rural hinterland pitted clubs from places such as Temax, Motul, and Hunucmá, which, in somewhat surreal fashion, had randomly chosen their names from the headlines of the Mérida papers: "El Cometa Halley," "Japón," and "Rusia."[35]

Nevertheless, baseball's revival following the turn of the century did not spread widely in the *campo*. In addition to the *cabeceras*, the game found its way to a number of the Maya villages that had managed to survive in the henequen zone or on its fringes.[36] Moreover, some planters--avid aficionados such as Delfín Salazar--appreciated the recreational benefits of the game and organized Sunday afternoon games among their laborers.[37] But even here paternalism had its limits. Peons were never permitted to travel to neighboring haciendas for games. Planters were loathe to tamper with the isolation and mechanisms of social control that maximized fiber production and minimized the chances of rural revolt. They carefully regulated the flow of ideas and people between city and countryside and between the estates themselves. Thus, for most of the peninsula's country people, and certainly for tens of thousands of hacienda peons, baseball was an idea whose time had not yet come.

In Mérida and Progreso, however, people were playing and talking about baseball again. The trams, cantinas, and cafes percolated with discussions of stellar plays and upcoming contests.[38] In 1904, *El Eco del Comercio,* a Mérida daily, helped fan the baseball fever by publishing a low-cost brochure of the official rules of the game.[39] The Mérida town council, recognizing the sport's burgeoning popularity, passed an ordinance classifying baseball as an *espectáculo*--a major public event--and making provisions for police presence at all major games. Apparently, mass crowds had brought vulgar language and rude behavior offensive to the ladies present, and complaints had been registered. The council also responded to the transportation tangle that was developing on game days by increasing tram and carriage service to Fénix and Itzimná parks.[40]

As baseball emerged as a true pastime in the capital and port, entrepreneurial members of the regional elite began to seek ways to tap its

economic potential.   A sports weekly--*El Coacher*--dedicated almost entirely to *béisbol*, was founded by a member of the Divine Caste.[41] In the
fall of 1904, a committee was convened to form a new "Liga Yucateca de
Béisbol," which would develop the best local talent, import foreign stars
("*refuerzos*"), and strive to provide a quality product for the new mass
market.   The planning committee was dominated by members of the
Molina *camarilla,* led by Avelino Montes, but also included representatives   of   their   principal   factional   rivals,   the   Eusebio   Escalante
parentesco.[42] The Escalantes's import-export firm was the oldest house in
Yucatán and O. Molina y Cía's bitterest rival in the local fiber market.
Besides the commercial house in Mérida, the extended family had mam-
moth investments in haciendas, urban real estate, banks, and utilities, including substantial shares in Ferrocarriles Unidos de Yucatán. Finally, the
Escalantes owned the Progeso based Agencia Comercial, S.A., whose
warehouses, docks, lighters, and other means of transport enabled them to
move fiber from hacienda to steamship.[43]

Like the Molina *camarilla,* the Escalante faction had taken a keen
interest in baseball. Both provided assistance to Mérida's "Railway" club,
since both had substantial interests in Ferrocarriles Unidos de Yucatán.[44]
The Escalantes, however, were primarily concerned with the development
of baseball in Progreso, where many of their chief investments lay.   The
manager of Agencia Comercial, Menalio Marín Cordoví, was a Cuban-
born businessman, who had been educated in the United States.   Apart
from his own deep love of the game, he appreciated the positive social
impact that a well-financed company team might have on the hundreds
of families the Escalantes's firm employed. In 1904, Marín Cordoví reor-
ganized "Club Colón" (originally founded in the early 1890s) and created
"Progreso," recruiting for these teams the stevedores and port workers who
were becoming the focus of appeals by anarchosyndicalist labor organizers.
A year later, Marín Cordoví inaugurated a spanking new ball park for
"Club Colón," which he personally managed.[45]

The new Yucatecan Baseball League never survived its maiden season.   It fell victim to the same intraelite rivalry and bitterness (*disgusto*)
that plagued late Porfirian regional society as a whole.   Things began
smoothly enough.   The league's directors agreed to a thirty-game season
that would run from mid-January to May 1905 and pit four of the
strongest teams--"El Fénix," "Pablo González," "Club Colón," and "El
Aguila," a Veracruz-based club[46] --for the regional championship. All
teams were permitted to charge admission to their games and to recruit
professional *refuerzos* abroad. While these North American and Cuban
stars would be paid well, local players would compete for the regional
"pennant," a very modest cash bonus, and a new pair of imported baseball
spikes.[47]

It quickly became apparent, however, that the rival elite factions involved in the league were bringing the same no-holds-barred approach to
their baseball operations that had generated such animosity in their competition over the spoils of the monocrop economy. First, the clubs failed
to reach an understanding on the selection of umpires and the division of

gate receipts. Then, a recruiting war began for foreign *refuerzos*. Neither the Molina nor the Escalante faction would agree to limit the number of foreign players on their teams' rosters. Early on, the season degenerated into a series of mercenary spectacles in which "El Fénix's" (read the Molinas's) *"cubanitos de color"* battled "Club Colón's" (the Escalantes's "gringos"), with local ballplayers increasingly relegated to the bench. The proud Pablistas, no longer enamoured of a sport that was seemingly turning professional and in which they were now unable to compete successfully, withdrew from the league. "El Aguila" remained, but lacking the financial backing of its rivals, offered only token resistance on the diamond.[48]

For a brief period, local crowds reveled in the imported spectacle. On one afternoon, "Club Colón's" promoters, featuring five Triple A players from Shreveport, made close to $18,000 pesos from the sale of tickets variously priced at two, five, and six pesos.[49] Not to be outdone, the Molinas sent their agent, José Millet Heredia, to Havana to offer Cuba's best talent "whatever they want to earn" to come play for "El Fénix." Millet sailed back to Yucatán with nine of the island's best ballplayers, including José María García ("El Inglés"), who old timers regard to have been "the Cuban Ty Cobb." As a consequence of the Molinas's raiding, the Cuban League was forced to suspend its own Championship Series in 1905.[50]

Ultimately, however, the feuding oligarchs behind the Liga Yucateca could not sustain their expensive artificial creation. "Club Colón's" North American *refuerzos* had other engagements in the United States and refused to extend their short-term contracts with Menalio Marín Cordoví. Nor could "El Fénix" control its all-star Cuban players, who raised their prices to a point where even the Molinas balked, then embarked on a barnstorming tour of the North American Negro Leagues. Midway through its initial season, with each elite faction accusing its rival of greed and sabotage, the Liga Yucateca suspended its operations.[51]

The 1905 collapse of Yucatán's first baseball league was a minor setback compared to the economic crisis that shook the export economy two years later. Bonanza fiber prices from 1898 to 1904 had pushed property values up, giving planters a false sense of security. Many borrowed heavily during the boom, securing additional mortgages on their haciendas. Loose credit practices fueled a spiral of speculation in real estate, new industrial ventures, and regional infrastructure. But as the price of henequen began to decline from 1904 to 1907, the artificially high prices of peninsular stocks could not be maintained. The bubble burst in 1907, as Yucatán began to feel the prolonged impact of an international economic crisis that would ruin business and financial institutions throughout the United States, Europe, and Mexico. One of the first local casualties was the Escalante house, and its *quiebra* (failure) in 1907 served to destabilize a number of other prominent local firms and individuals. The dominant Molina *camarilla* had a hand in bringing it about. The Escalante failure removed the Divine Caste's principal rivals in the fiber trade and permitted it to strengthen its hold on banks, railroads, and henequen production.[52]

Although fiber prices did not fully recover until World War I and the aftershocks of the panic of 1907-1908 continued to be registered in foreclosures throughout the final years of Yucatán's Ancien Regime, baseball was not among the permanent casualties. La Industrial and the Agencia Comercial shut their door, but "El Fénix's" and "Club Colón's" best local players found new teams to play for in both the capital and port. In the countryside, some of the earliest municipal and *pueblo* nines disbanded in the wake of the panic, but as the economy began to perk up in the early 1910s, most of these revived and baseball continued its gradual penetration of the interior.[53] By the end of the Porfiriato, the game had expanded its social base and was too deeply rooted in the regional imagination to be dislodged by periodic swings in the political economy. In fact, as things turned out, even the Mexican Revolution worked to institutionalize *béisbol* as the regional pastime.

Mobilizations: "Hasta los Pueblitos" (1915-1924)

If in the rest of Mexico baseball never went beyond elite mimicry of a foreign pastime during the Porfiriato, the apocalyptic Revolution of 1910 only postponed its arrival as a popular sport.[54] Hundreds of thousands of Mexicans perished in the fighting alone, a sizable loss for a nation of only fifteen million in 1910. Related causes--hunger, malnutrition, illness-- killed many times that number. Free-ranging violence wrought havoc with the Mexican society and economy throughout much of the north, west, and central parts of the republic. It was not until well after the "epic Revolution" (1910-1917), during President Alvaro Obregón's regime of reconstruction (1920-1924), that baseball began to gain a foothold among Mexico's popular classes. As prosperity gradually returned to the country and the new centralizing Revolutionary state sought to legitimize itself in the eyes of the people, private promoters and government teachers and officials alike brought baseball into Mexico's urban neighborhoods and rural villages. Foreign ballplayers, particularly individual *refuerzos* and barnstorming teams from the U.S. Negro Leagues, also were instrumental in enhancing the game's popularity after the fighting ended.[55]

In southeastern Yucatán, however, *béisbol's* popular development continued virtually without interruption. The middle and working classes had already embraced the game prior to 1910, and the Mexican Revolution followed a rather different course in the peninsula. It took almost five years to reach Yucatán and, although the region quickly became a celebrated laboratory for radical social reforms, the Revolution proceeded with little loss of life or property. Indeed, the peninsula's population actually increased by about 25,000 during the national decade of violence, and

Yucatán's henequen industry enjoyed a golden age in terms of production and earnings.[56] In 1915-1916, at the height of the bitter war between competing revolutionary factions, when writer Martín Luis Guzmán described the Mexican Revolution as a "fiesta of bullets," the U.S. consul in Yucatán observed rather matter-of-factly that "peace is raging down here as usual."[57]

It was no accident that the Revolution was delayed five years in reaching Yucatán. The peninsula's geographical isolation made it difficult for would-be revolutionaries to obtain news of the progress in the rest of the republic of the movement that began with Francisco Madero's revolt against Díaz in November 1910. More compelling, however, was the regional elite's deep-seated reluctance to join the revolutionary tide. The old Porfirian order gained an extended lease on life in Yucatán because the peninsula's rulers had, through skillful adaptation to the changing configuration of national events, maintained a hold on the levers of local economic and political power. Isolated disturbances erupted and subsided in the countryside, and discontented intellectuals continued to conjure visions of the impending deluge in the cafes and solons of Mérida, but the objective conditions for a local revolutionary movement plainly did not exist. Only a military stroke administered from the outside could curb the political and repressive power of the great planters and topple the oligarchical order.[58]

Revolution came from without in March 1915. Venustiano Carranza, the first Chief of the powerful Constitutionalist faction, who was increasingly desperate for money to wage his struggle against the rival Villistas and Zapatistas, coveted Yucatán's rich henequen receipts and ordered an invasion of the peninsula to gain access to them. Backed by an 8000-man army of occupation, Constitutionalist General Salvador Alvarado made short work of a Yucatecan elite force barely one-tenth the federals' size in what amounted to skirmishes with limited casualties. Then, over the course of the next three years, the enlightened, if egocentric, caudillo devoted himself to dismantling the monopolistic structures and repressive mechanisms of the Ancien Regime, and to introducing a nucleus of political, social, and economic reforms upon which later revolutionary regimes could build. That Alvarado was able to accomplish so much in so short a time is attributable to his monopoly of armed force within the region, his organizational ability and singleminded commitment to social change, the relatively large measure of autonomy from Carranza and Mexico City that he enjoyed during the Revolution's chaotic pre-constitutional phase, and the record prices that henequen commanded on an inflated World War I market.

Alvarado's revolutionary program was characterized by an effective blend of idealistic, bourgeois reform in the social areas and pragmatism in the political sphere. Perhaps most important, the general put an end to "slavery" in Yucatán. He changed the relations of production on haciendas, substituting the wage relationship for existing forms of peonage and forced labor, and, in a modest way, began the process of mobilizing the region's *campesinos*. At the same time, he realized that to be lasting, his incipient revolution would have to be institutionalized. To that end, he created pilot institutions like a state party and a centralized network of local revolutionary organizations (*ligas de resistencia*), which would, in time, become the party's constituent units. Alvarado also patronized the incipient urban labor movement, based in Mérida and Progreso, then successfully incorporated it into his regional revolutionary coalition.

In the economic sphere, the general expanded the state's control over the henequen industry, creating an exclusive producers' cooperative that bought fiber directly from local *hacendados* and sold it directly to the North American twine manufacturers. In the process, the Molina-Montes *camarilla's* all-powerful intermediary role as agent for International Harvester was nullified. Yet never a Marxist, Alvarado was not inclined to expropriate the henequen plantations on behalf of Yucatán's *campesinos*. Moreover, although he created resistance leagues in the countryside as a means of co-opting the rural masses and giving them a stake in the political process, Alvarado was reluctant to encourage a systematic political mobilization of the rural sector. He feared that excessive politicking in the *campo* might interrupt the steady flow of henequen revenues that appeased his boss in Mexico City and lent harmony to his populist regional coalition.   Ever the liberal, Alvarado offered the *campesino* increased wages and education in lieu of mass mobilization. He established a thousand new schools, the majority of these in remote, previously untouched hamlets and hacienda communities.

With the rest of Mexico burning, but with the peninsular economy booming, and General Alvarado forcefully opening up regional society to the popular classes, baseball in Yucatán prospered. Oldtime *béisbolistas* recall that it was during the early years of the Revolution that an *época de oro* began, one which would last until the Great Depression.[59] Cash was seemingly everywhere. Industry and commerce extended fat bonuses to local players while simultaneously stepping up the recruitment of black Cuban professionals. Julio Molina, the hard-living "poorer" (middle class) relation of Don Olegario's Divine Caste, symbolized the exuberance of the period. Blessed with an imposing physique and a blazing fastball, Molina, "El Diamante Blanco," was worshiped by the *meridano* and *progreseño* fans almost as much for his off-the-field exploits as for his heroics on the mound.   Although he nominally held a job at the Casa Montes in Progreso, "the White Diamond" was perhaps the first *yucateco* to earn his living as a ballplayer, starring for clubs like "Comercial," the "Yucatán Stars," and the "Amateurs" in the 1910s and 1920s.[60]

Julio Molina and other local stars were periodically called upon to respond to challenges by visiting foreign teams, occasionally made up of the crews of commercial U.S. ships that put in at Progreso. Fans placed extravagant bets on the outcomes and players shared the fine points of the game.   Saturnino Borges, one of "El Diamante's" teammates on the Mérida "Amateurs," recalls the historic day they played the crew of the freighter *Olympia* and the regional pastime was introduced to the "spitter":

They had this pitcher who had a wet pitch. The ball came up to the plate dripping with saliva. In those days these pitches were permitted. The American pitcher chewed his tobacco and administered a "salavazo" ("glob of spit") to each pitch . . . It was disgusting (Un asco)! Luckily their club was pretty bad and we had Julio pitching.[61]

Molina and another local hurler, Eliseo Gómez, "El Pan de Umán," were also a match for the better Cuban *refuerzos,* one of whom, Luis Tiant, is today as well remembered in Yucatán as his son and namesake, who for many years was a charismatic big league star. Tiant, Sr., would later return with the great "Bacardí" and "Cuban Stars," teams that toured the peninsula in the 1920s and featured Eusebio Cruz, the legendary "Quince y Medio." Renowned for his extraordinary combination of power and speed, Cruz earned his nickname when a Yucatecan sportswriter timed him around the bases on an inside-the-park homerun in 15 1/2 seconds.[62]

The Cubans were not only great crowd pleasers but also generous teachers and friends. Several of the best local players of this *época de oro,* including the brothers Cardeña, later admitted that they had learned many of their skills and imbibed a real love of the game from the Cuban stars who came to Yucatán.[63] The Cubans, in turn, were impressed with the progress of their pupils. Moisés Quintero, a well-paid veteran Cuban *refuerzo* of the day, predicted that it wouldn't be long before the *yucatecos* would be able to dispense with foreign imports. He observed that whereas baseball once was played only by those who had been to fancy schools in the United States, now anyone could play.[64]

In fact, thanks to general Alvarado's historic 1916 decree abolishing debt peonage and forced labor, increasingly everyone *was* playing, even Yucatán's hacienda laborers. Planters no longer had the power to restrain the mobility of their workers; violations of the 1916 law were sternly punished by Alvarado's military regime. Significant numbers of the approximately 80,000 freed *peones* exercised their newly won right of movement and left the estates, most only temporarily; the great majority stayed on, but traveled to market and visited family and friends on Sundays. The hermetic isolation of Yucatán's interior was broken, rural-urban exchanges increased and, despite the poor road network linking the various *pueblos* and haciendas, *béisbol* now spread quickly throughout the countryside.

The ballclubs that had earlier established only a precarious existence in the interior municipal and county seats--teams such as the "Motul Stars," "13 de Motul," Temax "Mireya," and Conkal "Plus Ultra"--now constructed proper ball fields in their town plazas and traveled weekly to play each other. Boom conditions enabled them to increase membership dues, buy new uniforms and equipment, and host visiting teams.[65] Meantime, increased prosperity and mobility enabled much smaller, more remote *pueblos* and hacienda communities to create their first ballclubs. Competition among them often took place later on Sunday afternoons, following lengthy journeys on foot or horseback by the *campesinos* of the visiting teams.[66] Spearheaded by dedicated *béisbolistas* and would-be country impresarios like Juan Uso Muñoz, a modest builder and sporting goods manufacturer, the first tournaments were held in the interior during the revolutionary period.[67] Championships were contested at the town and district levels, and, increasingly, the better rural clubs sought the kind of stiffer competition that could only be found in Mérida and Progreso. Motuleno Emilio Manzanilla recalls the excitement surrounding one of these first rural-urban duels in the early 1920s. In order to raise the first-class train passage and lodging expenses necessary to lure "Escuela Modelo," one of Mérida's better middle class teams into the *campo*, he and his teamates of "13 de Motul" whitewashed walls the week before the game.

> Our eyes were red from the lime, and after three days of hard work painting 100 meters of wall we were bushed, but we played like never before . . . The entire plaza was filled; people poured in from the surrounding villages--Telchac, Dzemul, Sinanché, Baca--and from the neighboring *fincas* as well. There must have been over 2,000 people there.[68]

Manzanilla's Motul club lost that day; as a rule the early country nines rarely upset the city teams. But their time was coming.

Once again, larger social forces figured prominently in the development of the regional pastime. Baseball in the interior received unexpected support from a powerful benefactor in the early 1920s, socialist revolutionary Felipe Carrillo Puerto. Carrillo Puerto had assumed the leadership of Yucatán's revolutionary party from the more moderate Alvarado when the general was suddenly reassigned by President Carranza in 1918. Almost immediately, Carrillo Puerto attempted to move the revolution to the left.

The opposition of Carranza's conservative central government was prompt and formidable. Federal troops launched a reign of terror against Carrillo's radicalized Partido Socialista del Sureste (PSS), sacking the offices of its more active resistance leagues and driving Carrillo Puerto and the party's chief cadres into exile. The PSS went underground, then, following Carranza's ouster in 1920 by the forces of Carrillo's national allies, Alvaro Obregón and Plutarco Calles, began to reconsolidate its power. Political mobilization and social reform had also been impeded by the collapse of the lucrative wartime fiber market, but by 1922, the year Carrillo Puerto was elected governor in a political landslide, the monocrop economy was experiencing a modest recovery. At last, Don Felipe, as the *campesinos* came to call him with both affection and respect, had the regional mandate, the national patronage, and the economic means to attempt a social transformation of Yucatán.

The PSS's program represented both an extension and a radical redefinition of the theoretical precedents and reforms brought about by Alvarado. The general had recognized the validity of grievances by workers and peasants, but had sought to redress them within the limits of the capitalist system. He had used the power of a strong revolutionary state to eliminate what he identified to be the main obstacles to industrial growth and progress: coerced labor, nonproductive uses of the land, and foreign control of the export economy. Carrillo Puerto, however, was no bourgeois revolutionary, but a socialist, committed to the ultimate abolition of capitalist relations in Yucatán; whereas Alvarado was reluctant to let the masses actively participate, let alone rule, once they were brought into the political process, Carrillo began his career as an agrarian agitator, politicizing the *campesinos* and encouraging them to accept responsibility for their own political destiny. Alvarado had cultivated the urban middle sectors, particularly the small proletariat, as his chief civilian allies. Carrillo dispayed little interest (and some hostility) toward the longshoremen and railroad workers, who comprised what he viewed as a "labor aristocracy." Yucatán was overwhelmingly an agricultural region and he reasoned that the *campesinos* and local bosses and middlemen (*caciques*) in the agrarian sector would provide his party with the bases of power it needed during the social transition. Alvarado had been prepared to initiate only a moderate agrarian reform, and even that had been thwarted by Carranza. Carrillo Puerto, however, had demonstrated from his earliest days as an agrarian leader that land was the focal point of his social vision. During his leadership of the Revolution in the peninsula, the pace of agrarian reform accelerated to the point that Yucatán had distributed more land than any other state, save perhaps Zapata's Morelos. By the time of his death in 1924, Carrillo Puerto had made sure that virtually every one of the state's major *pueblos* had received at least a basic ejidal grant.[69] His regime and life were snuffed out--hardly a coincidence--just at the moment he seemed ready to initiate a more sweeping agrarian reform that would have expropriated the region's henequen estates and turned them into collective farms owned and operated by their former *peones*.

Under Carrillo Puerto, the Mexican Revolution in Yucatán became a Yucatecan movement. His use of locally trained cadres of agrarian agitators and activist schoolteachers and his network of alliances with local *caciques* stands in contrast to Alvarado's greater reliance on outside intellectuals and his own military commandants. Moreover, Don Felipe reinforced the regional character of his revolution in a variety of symbolic ways, most of which sought to wean the *campesino* away from the traditional attitudes and institutions of the Ancien Regime and inculcate within them a sense of ethnic pride in addition to class consciousness. The speaking of Maya and the teaching of Mayan culture and art forms were encouraged, for example, and every effort was made to recall the great tradition to which the *campesinos* were heir. Weekly cultural programs known as *lunes rojos* (Red Mondays) were scheduled at the headquarters of the local resistance leagues. The leagues organized work details to construct serviceable roads to the breathtaking but largely inaccessible ruins of Chichén Itzá and Uxmal, both of which Carrillo was restoring in collaboration with a team of archaeologists from the pestigious Carnegie Institution of Washington.

Carrillo Puerto's repeated use of Mayan myth and symbol was calculated with great care. More than cultural edification was at stake. Don Felipe hoped to reclaim for the Indian masses the revolutionary tradition they had established in conquest times, which developed through a series of rebellions during the colonial period and culminated in the mid-nineteenth-century Caste War. Carrillo shrewdly realized that, given the Maya *campesino's* economically impoverished and culturally despised position, the development of ethnic pride would also work simultaneously to promote class consciousness.

Thus, like other twentieth-century socialist revolutionaries, Carrillo Puerto had made a synthesis, bringing modern political theories and mobilization strategies to bear upon the backwardness and social injustice of his own land. Through his own rudimentary understanding of Marxism-Leninism, Carrillo hoped to provide *yucatecos* with a new way to perceive their society and the means to integrate it fully into the modern world. His party's idiosyncratic and eclectic socialism sought simultaneously to allow Yucatán's *campesinos* to preserve their immediate folk traditions, recover a sense of their past, and gain a belief in change through faith in the power of the working class. For Carriilo, the revolutionary state was the mechanism that could articulate past glories and present possibilities. "We will have a Yucatán," he wrote, "that will preserve all that is rich, beautiful and useful in the traditions of the Mayas and at the same time one that will have absorbed all that can be used of the new and the modern in science."[70]

Although few writers or old timers appreciate it today, *béisbol* became a strategic component of the PSS's campaign to mobilize its rural-based socialist regime. Promotion of the larger Western athletic tradition of competitive sports and physical culture (*cultura física*), and of the regional pastime in particular, squared nicely with both the party's ideological amalgam and its tactical objectives. Here, Socialist officials emphasized, was a revival of old-time athletic prowess, a chance to reverse the physical and spiritual degeneration into which the Maya race had fallen. Did not the ancients have their ball courts, their own Olympic Games immortalized on the walls of the great temples at Chichén and Uxmal? Now, a carefully programmed "scientific" regimen of *cultura física* in the schools, as well as the state's commitment to broad-based participation in recreational amateur sports such as baseball, basketball, boxing, soccer, swimming, wrestling, and tennis, would play an important role in the party's renovation of Yucatecan society and the creation of the new revolutionary man.[71] In Don Felipe's words:

> It will make them better men physically, but, far more important, they will grow up with the understanding that every man has a right to recreation. It will be good for their bodies, but it will be even better for their souls . . . . They have been slaves so long that they have forgotten how to play--slaves do not play; and people who play are not slaves.[72]

Shortly following Carrillo Puerto's inauguration, the state budget was amended to hire physical education instructors at all levels of the educational system.[73] The PSS's Liga Central de Resistencia created a special Sports Section and chose Compañero Ignacio Moreno, Profesor de

Cultura Física, to head it. The Sports Section's first order of business was the promotion of *béisbol,* which even then was acknowledged as "the king of sports." The Liga Central made a commitment to organize baseball clubs and lay out diamonds in the most out-of-the-way hamlets and haciendas--*"hasta los pueblitos,"* as Carrillo Puerto put it. Moreover, it would provide travel subsidies for rural-urban competitions, with a view to shortly sponsoring a statewide championship. Finally, the Liga Central would begin drawing up plans for a new 10,000-seat stadium, which the Socialists envisioned as the future mecca of Yucatecan baseball.[74] The party's decision to make *béisbol* the centerpiece of its *política deportiva* was a masterful stroke. Baseball was already rooted in the regional environment and, as the Revolution had opened up the countryside, the *campesinos* had demonstrated a particular fascination with the game. The regional pastime had always counted upon powerful and interested benefactors in the private sector, a role Carrillo Puerto's party might now preempt from rural *patrones* and urban businessmen alike.

At the First and Second Workers' congresses in Motul (1918) and Izamal (1921), party leaders had discussed the tactical value of team sports, particularly baseball, within a larger strategy of grassroots mobilization.[75] Popular pursuits that helped to build socialism and break with old social attitudes were to be encouraged. Baseball seemed singularly appropriate to the social transition that the party would carry out in Yucatán. It was a game that in itself marked the transition from individual to corporate values. *Béisbol* preserved elements of personal accountability and enabled the individual to achieve recognition, but inevitably it was a team game that subsumed the individual into the collective. Effective team play often depended upon the individual's willingness to sacrifice his personal glory for the common cause. However distinguished, the individual was only a part of a larger entity, whose success depended upon the transformation of individualism into collective conscience.[76] Waxing eloquent about baseball's virtues, Carrillo Puerto optimistically (though unrealistically) predicted that the game's popularity would soon sound the death knell for bullfighting, the "cruel and degrading . . . Spanish-inherited pastime" that he regarded as an emblem of the selfish and exploitative Ancien Regime.[77]

Moreover, the proliferation of baseball clubs throughout the peninsula and the intensification of competition within the interior and between urban and rural clubs would strike at the traditional isolation that impeded the socialist transition. Baseball would make an immediate contribution to the party's goal of social integration, even in advance of projected improvements in regional communication and transportation, which would take the government years to bring about. Baseball games would bring people together, not only to engage in friendly competition, but also to share fellowship and perhaps to reaffirm the hopes and dreams of the new revolutionary society under construction.[78] The Liga Central made sure, for example, to schedule the most popular games--occasionally featuring its own powerful club "Yucatán Rojo" ("Red Yucatán")--to coincide with holidays or important public occasions, such as government land distributions, public works inaugurations, or the weekly cultural events of local resistance leagues.[79]

Thus, although *béisbol* had undeniable value as a tool for enhancing the popularity of Carrillo Puerto's party, it was at the same time a component of the more global approach that the PSS brought to social organization. The party not only addressed the *pueblo's* most pressing social problems; it also attended to its daily concerns and simple pleasures. The local *ligas de resistencia,* which Don Felipe entrusted with the implementation of his baseball program, collectively numbered about 70,000 members in 1923 and had become the basic units of communal organization in Yucatán. The local league was part ward club, part night school, part producer and consumer co-operative, and part sports center. It was the embodiment of Carrillo's "new Yucatán" and he boasted that it "was more vitally a spiritual institution than the church ever was."[80] In reality, however, Don Felipe's network of resistance leagues was still a rather new and transitional phenomenon. Rather than a massive grassroots mobilization in response to his charismatic leadership or the party's ideological message, the league structure in great part represented a reaccommodation by the Socialist Party of existing *cacique* power bases.[81] Liberally financed by party headquarters in Mérida and patronized locally by Socialist deputies and bosses, the *ligas* organized or rejuvenated teams in the *campo*, luring new converts in the process.[82]

During his brief Socialist regime in 1922-1923, Governor Carrillo Puerto implanted *béisbol* in the farthest reaches of the state. He distributed over 20,000 U.S. dollars worth of gloves, bats, and balls and organized ballclubs in over 70 percent of the state's *pueblos* and hacienda communities.[83] During one two-week period alone in 1923, forty-seven new teams were created in the interior.[84] Former peons on henequen haciendas like "Cuca," "Ticopo," and "San Juan Koop" wrote their governor warm letters in Maya, which Don Felipe spoke fluently, expressing their gratitude.[85] *Milperos* in even more remote places, with unpronounceable Maya names like Tixcacaltuyu and Tacchubchen, took the field for *liga* clubs named "Soviet" and "Agrarista."[86] Meanwhile, in Mérida and Progreso, the "Carlos Marx" League battled rivals like "Emiliano Zapata," "Máximo Gorki," and "Los Mártires de Chicago."[87] Carrillo Puerto instructed the state's railroads, now government controlled, to provide petitioning groups of *béisbolistas* with free passes, so that they might travel to distant points throughout the state on game days.[88] The governor also made the state's official military band available to play at tournaments in the interior.[89] Baseball had indeed arrived *"hasta los pueblitos"*--out to even the smallest towns.

Epilogue

Don Felipe's socialist experiment ended suddenly and tragically in January 1924, when Yucatán's federal garrison pronounced in favor of the national de la Huerta rebellion and toppled the PSS government, which had remained loyal to President Alvaro Obregón. Carrillo Puerto and many of his closest supporters were rounded up and executed by the insurgent federals, who had the financial backing and encouragement of Yucatán's large planters. By April 1924, the de la Huerta revolt had been quelled and the PSS returned to power in Mérida, but now with a social program more in tune with the moderate policies of Obregón and Calles in Mexico City. The regional party cut back its expenditures for social programs and never again allocated large sums to the popularization of sport. Yucatecans would wait until the 1950s for their 10,000-seat baseball stadium.[90]

The party continued to promote baseball on a more modest scale during the late 1920s. In 1925, championship series were inaugurated for boys in the public primary and secondary schools in Mérida and Progreso.[91] In the *campo*, local PSS *caciques* sponsored new hacienda teams and delivered on their promises to obtain the necessary equipment from their superiors in Mérida. In turn, their rural clients named the new nines in their honor.[92] Increasingly rare were the colorful, combative names of international Marxism. Carrillo's militant party had been domesticated, brought into the fold of Mexico's Institutionalized Revolution.

By then, the regional pastime had also been institutionalized. Fans throughout Yucatán, in both town and country, petitioned Carrillo Puerto's Socialist successors for annual visits from Cuba's best professional teams and turned out by the thousands when they arrived.[93] In 1928, Governor Alvaro Torre Díaz, aided by Mérida's Socialist mayor, Pablo Garza Leal and his chief of police, Alfredo Pierce, all rabid *béisbolistas*, promoted a Yucatecan amateur league with fifteen clubs spread out across the state in centers as diverse as Mérida and Cansahcab, Progreso and Temozón, Motul and Umán. Before the Great Depression scuttled the league, it became amply clear that country baseball had finally arrived. Stars like Eliseo Gómez--"El Pan de Umán"--or Temax's Luciano Ku, another exceptional Maya pitcher, frequently led their teams to victory over the Mérida and Progreso clubs and became the objects of intense bidding among promoters in the capital and port.[94]

Gómez and Ku, and scores of other players who would star in the regional games in the 1930s and 1940s, were the first products of baseball's penetration of the peninsula's interior. They grew up speaking Maya, working in the henequen fields, and playing ball in the plaza of their *pueblos* and hacienda communities on makeshift diamonds painted out in lime and ashes. Fans remember "El Pan de Umán," a force to be reckoned with on the mound but still wearing the traditional white cotton pants, field apron, and straw hat of the henequen *peón*.[95]

The backcountry pick-up games of the teens and twenties that launched Gómez and Ku on their careers, as heralded if modestly paid semi-pro ballplayers, likely echoed with the same patois of Maya and Spanish that one hears on the hacienda diamonds today: *"Conex, conex, jugar béisbol . . . ten quécher, tech pícher y tech centerfil"* ("Come on, let's play ball . . . I'll pitch, you catch, and you play centerfield").[96] Today the leagues are still named after politicians of the official party and also after

Fernando Valenzuela, whose screwball first drew the attention of Dodger scouts in Mérida, where he was pitching for the Leones. And now there are more and more women's teams, particularly in the *campo*, where, even in age of disco music, foreign movies, and video arcades, *"el rey de los deportes"* still reigns supreme.[97]

Abbreviations Used in Notes

AGE	Archivo General del Estado de Yucatán
DdS	*Diario del Sureste* (Mérida)
DdY	*Diario de Yucatán* (Mérida)
DO	*Diario Oficial* (Mérida)
EdC	*El Eco del Comercio* (Mérida)
HAHR	*Hispanic American Historical Review*
LARR	*Latin American Research Review*
NdY	*Novedades de Yucatán* (Mérida)
P	*El Peninsular* (Mérida)
PO	*El Popular* (Mérida)
RdM	*Revista de Mérida*
T	*Tierra* (Mérida)

Notes

1   The Yucatán peninsula, which encompasses the modern states of Yucatán, Campeche, and Quintana Roo, offers numerous exceptions to generalizations about Mexican history and culture. There are indeed "many Mexicos," but distant and separatist Yucatán has traditionally been viewed as more marked in its regional identity than any other entity within the republic. It was not until the end of World War II that the peninsula was even connected by land with central Mexico. Before that, communication by sea with the port of Veracruz occasionally took longer to reach Yucatán than it did from some points in the United States. In a real sense, for much of its modern history, Yucatán has been an "island," oriented toward the Gulf and the Atlantic, and away from the Mexican "mainland." Not surprisingly, the region's pronounced geographical affinity for the United States and Cuba translated over time into close commercial and cultural links--as this essay will demonstrate. Since events and actors in the densely populated state of Yucatán have traditionally shaped the history of the rest of the peninsula, and since the combined historical writing on Campeche and Quintana Roo is scant, this essay

will focus primarily on Yucatán. For an examination of both Yucatecan "exceptionalism" and the relevance of the region's past to larger Mexican problems, see Gilbert M. Joseph, *Rediscovering the Past at Mexico's Periphery: Essays on the History of Modern Yucatán* (Tuscaloosa: University of Alabama Press, 1986), and "From Caste War to Class War: The Historiography of Modern Yucatán (c.1750-1940)," *HAHR* 65:1 (1985): 111-34.

2   These judgments are based on over a decade of informal "participant observation," including residence in Yucatán throughout the course of the championship season. During 1984-1985, the author conducted a series of unstructured interviews with *yucatecos* representing all walks of life, including amateur and professional players, and attended (and occasionally played in) baseball games in Mérida and several outlying *pueblos*. Regarding the Leones's impressive attendance figures, the quality of local fan support, and the gala celebrations that followed the Mexican World Series, see *DdS*, 18 July, 20 Aug. 1984; *DdY*, 22 July, 10-11, 20-21 August 1984; *NdY*, 18-20 August 1984, 10 January 1986.

3   Soccer has found its deepest niche in the state capital, Mérida, particularly in private schools for more well-to-do suburban youth. Even so, at present the state can only support Division Three-level *fútbol*. For a discussion of soccer's failures to gain a mass following throughout the peninsula, see "Tres clubes de segunda?" *NdY*, 9 January 1986.

4   The following discussion of the social, economic, and cultural transformations that occurred in the region during the Porfirian henequen boom draws heavily on Allen Wells, *Yucatán's Gilded Age: Haciendas, Henequen and International Harvester, 1860-1915* (Alburquerque: University of New Mexico Press, 1985); G. M. Joseph, *Revolution from Without: Yucatán, Mexico, and the United States, 1880-1924* (Cambridge: Cambridge University Press, 1982), chapters 1-3; and Joseph and Wells, "Corporate Control of a Monocrop Economy: International Harvester and Yucatán's Henequen Industry During the Porfiriato," *LARR* 17: 1 (Spring 1982): 69-99.

5   Attempted corners by local exporters and North American buyers, a rise or fall in manufacturers' demand, international wars and crop failures, stateside binder twine competition, and the saturation of the market by overzealous producers--all these combined to play havoc with the planters' ability to predict prices and punished the foolish investor. See Joseph and Wells, "Corporate Control," p. 87.

6   Some North American neoclassical economists and economic historians have recently minimized the impact that Harvester's collab-

oration with Molina's Divine Caste had on local market trends. See
particularly the freewheeling exchange of views in *LARR* 18:3 (1983):
193-218.

7   The most thorough and readable account of the great rebellion remains Nelson Reed, *The Caste War of Yucatán* (Stanford: Stanford
University Press, 1964).

8   For baseball's origins in the republic, see William Beezley's article in
this volume, and his "Judas, Rabelais and Abner Doubleday: Carnival
Laughter and Modernization in Porfirian Mexico" (Paper presented
at the Annual Meeting of the Rocky Mountain Council on Latin
American Studies, Tucson, 1984).   For the "Yucatecan interpretation," see Joaquín Lara C., *Historia del béisbol en Yucatán
(1890-1906)* (Mérida: Editorial "Zamma," 1953), pp. 7-8.   The
game's origins in Cuba are discussed in Eric Wagner's essay in this
volume, and in Lara C., "El Aguila de Veracruz: Las primeras raíces
del equipo," *DdY* (1 September 1986), which also discusses the Cuban
transmission of baseball to Veracruz and Yucatán.

9   Lara C., *Historia del béisbol*, p. 8; cf. the almost identical version
found in Luis Ramírez Aznar, "El béisbol en Yucatán: Carta del Dr.
Eduardo Urzáiz Rodríguez," *NdY* (6 January 1986).

10   *EdC* (28 March 1893);   *RdM* (29 April 1894); Lara C. *Historia del
béisbol*, p.9. The popular reference to the constables as "Xtoles" deserves some explanation. *Xtol* was intended as an unflattering Maya
corruption of the Spanish word *tolete*, the club or nightstick the po-
licemen carried.   Yet in the Maya-speaking countryside *Xtol* also referred to the long, thin member of a bull, which the *tolete* resembled.

11   Lara C., *Historia del béisbol*, pp. 8-9; Ramírez Aznar, "Béisbol en
Yucatán: Carta del . . . "; "Historia del béisbol yucateco: El 'Dzol'
Peraza y el juego de 21 entradas," *NdY* (31 December 1985).

12   Lara C., *Historia del béisbol*, pp. 9, 15; Ramírez Aznar, "Béisbol en
Yucatán: Carta del . . . "; *RdM* (20 December 1892).

13   Quoted in Lara C., *Historia del béisbol*, pp. 11-12.

14   *EdC* (5 November 1892). The photo of the "Champion Club," as
well as team and action photos of a number of the early nines, can
be found in the Fototeca "Guerra" at the Universidad Autónoma de
Yucatán's Escuela de Ciencias Antropológicas.

15   Young Miguel Peón Cásares's family, wealthy planters, were not impressed by the big league scouts' attention. *Béisbol* was fine as an
amateur pastime, but only "vagabonds and people with no future"

would think of playing it for a living. For "El Sporting's" founding and make-up, see *RdM* (7, 23 June 1892; 11 August 1892); 20 October 1892); Lara C., "De nuestro béisbol: La novena invencible," *DdY* (26 July 1970); Ramírez Aznar "Béisbol en Yucatán: Carta del . . . ."

[16] *RdM* (18, 27 October 1892); *EdC.* (18 October 1892, 2 February 1893); Lara C. *Historia del béisbol*, pp. 10-12, and "De nuestro béisbol."

[17] On Don Pablo's death: *EdC* (21 November 1893), *RdM* (1 March 1894); for the economic downturn's effect on fiber prices, see Joseph and Wells, "Corporate Control," p. 81.

[18] Joseph and Wells, "Corporate Control," especially pp. 21, 87-88.

[19] Lara C., *Historia del béisbol*, p. 14, and "Arturo Millet Heredia: Primer pelotero estrella local," *DdY* (25 May 1969). For Governor Molina's urban renewal, see Joseph, *Revolution from Without*, pp. 34-38.

[20] Joseph, *Revolution from Without*, pp. 82-89; Joseph and Wells, "Summer of Discontent: Economic Rivalry among Elite Factions During the Late Porfiriato in Yucatán" (Paper presented at the Seventh Conference of U.S. and Mexican Historians, Oaxaca, 1985).

[21] *RdM* (May 1901).

[22] Lara C., *Historia del béisbol*, pp. 25, 48.

[23] Ibid., pp. 18-19, and "De nuestro béisbol: Parques, umpires y peloteros," *DdY* (1 March 1970).

[24] The theme of paternalism and co-optation is also examined in Steve Stein's essay in this volume.

[25] On the sad history of La Industrial, see Joseph, *Revolution from Without*, pp. 50-51, 63-64, and Joseph and Wells, "Corporate Control," pp. 83, 96-97 nn. 48-49.

[26] Lara C., "Arturo Millet Heredia," "Del béisbol nuestro: Detalles y minucias que se olvidan," *DdY* (23 January 1970) and *Historia del béisbol*, pp. 15, 16.

[27] Lara C., "De nuestro béisbol: Parques . . . ," and "Arturo Millet Heredia". Millet Heredia, an eighteen-year-old spray-hitting outfielder during the team's heyday in 1904-1905, was the son of a prominent Casta family on an otherwise working class team.

28   *RdM* (22 Jan. 1904, 10 April 1904); *P* (23 March 1904, 17 September
      1904, 3-4 October 1904); *EdC* (20 January 1904, 23 March 1904, 9,
      12 April 1904, 23 May 1904, 4 October 1904); Ramírez Aznar,
      "Béisbol en Yucatán: 'Chato' Juanes, primer cátcher técnico," *NdY*
      (18 January 1986); Lara C., "Del béisbol nuestro: Detalles . . . ." The
      "Fénixistas'" margins of victory over their chief rivals were often
      lopsided, with final scores more appropriate to the gridiron. In gen-
      eral, contests during these early years were offensive displays, with the
      hitting well ahead of the pitching.

29   Menalio Marín C., "La precoz infancia del béisbol en Yucatán," *DdY*
      (1 January 1934); Lara C. *Historia del Béisbol*, chapters 2 and 3.

30   Lara C., "Peloteros de otros tiempos: Saturnino Borges," *DdY* (2 July
      1967).

31   Lara C., "Pelotero y picador: Agustín 'Chato' Osorio Polanco," *DdY*
      (8 December 1968); cf. Lara C., "48 años detrás del jom: Pedro
      Gutiérrez García," *DdY* (15 September 1968).

32   Lara C., "Béisbol local de antaño: Federico Cardeña, 'Chivirico',"
      DdY (14 April 1968). Ramírez Aznar, "El béisbol en Yucatán:
      Federico 'Chivirico' Cardeña," *NdY* (20 January 1986).

33   *P* (3 May 1904, 14 July 1904, 15, 29 September 1904, 3, 8 October
      1904, 14 November 1904); Lara C., *Historia del béisbol*, pp. 18-19,
      and "Arturo Millet Heredia."

34   *EdC* (10 May 1904); *RdM* (11, 15, 17, 21 May 1904, 4, 16 October
      1904); Lara C., *Historia del béisbol*, pp. 19, 29-31.

35   For the spread of baseball to the larger towns in the interior, see, e.g.,
      RdM (28 July, 16, 20 August 1904) (Tizimín); *RdM* (14 August, 20
      September, 27 October 1904) (Tekax); *RdM* (25 August 1904)
      (Hunucmá); (11, 29 October 1904) (Tixkokob); and Lara C.,
      Historia del béisbol, pp. 19, 22, for the naming of some of these early
      nines and *béisbol's* arrival in Campeche.

36   E.g., see Lara C., "Peloteros de antaño: Emilio Manzanilla Gómez,"
      DdY (7 July 1968); and "Béisbol de antaño: El deporte de
      Cansahcab," *DdY* (29 March 1970).

37   E.g., see Lara C., "Peloteros yucatecos: Leonardo 'Zurdo' Pérez,"
      DdY (15 December 1968); Ramírez Aznar, "Béisbol en Yucatán:
      Federico 'Chivirico' Cardeña."

38   Lara C., *Historia del béisbol*, p. 20.

39   Ibid., p. 21.

40   *RdM* (14 June, 14 September 1904);   Lara C. *Historia*, p. 27.

41   Lara C., "Béisbol y cine: Joaquín Espinosa Cásares," *DdY* (8 November 1970).

42   *RdM* (27 September 1904);   Lara C., *Historia del béisbol*, pp. 25-27.

43   Joseph and Wells, "Summer of Discontent."

44   *RdM* (15 June 1904); *P* (13 June 1904).

45   Martín C., "La precoz infancia";   Ramírez Aznar, "Béisbol en Yucatán: Primera gran recaudación: $18,000," *NdY* (21 December 1985);   Lara C., *Historia del béisbol*, pp. 19, 29-31, and "De nuestro béisbol: Parques . . . ."

46   Originally formed solely by recent Cuban immigrants and based in Veracruz, "El Aguila" had come to include a number of *progreseños*, underscoring the close commercial links between the two Gulf ports. Around 1906, Progreso dock workers formed a new club with the same name.   See Lara C., "Novenas del recuerdo: El 'Aguila' de Progreso," *DdY* (20 September 1970), and "El Aguila"; Marín C., "La precoz infancia";   Ramírez Aznar, "Béisbol en Yucatán: Primera gran recaudación," and "Béisbol en Yucatán: El 'Chivo' de Halacho," *NdY* (4 January 1986).

47   Lara C., *Historia del béisbol*, pp. 25-27, 48;   Marín C.   "La precoz infancia."

48   *EdC* (21 March 1905);   Ramírez Aznar, "Béisbol en Yucatán: Primera gran recaudación";   Marín C., "La precoz infancia"; Lara C., "Del béisbol nuestro: Detalles . . . ," and *Historia del béisbol*, chapter 3.

49   Ramírez Aznar, "Béisbol en Yucatán: Primera gran recaudación"; Marin C., "La precoz infancia";   Lara C., "Del béisbol nuestro: Detalles . . . ."

50   Lara C., "El año dorado de 1905:   Yucatán paralizó el béisbol cubano," *DdY* (28 December 1969).

51   Ibid., and *Historia del béisbol*, pp. 96-98;   Ramírez Aznar, "El béisbol en Yucatán: Fernando Escamilla Rejón," *NdY* (8 January 1986).

52   Joseph and Wells, "Summer of Discontent," and "Corporate Control," especially pp. 81-82.

53   Lara C., "Peloteros de antaño: Emilio Manzanilla," and "Béisbol de antaño: El deporte de Cansahcab."

54   See William Beezley's essay in this volume.

55   William Beezley, personal communication, 20 June 1984.

56   For analyses of the revolutionary period of the region's history, which emphasize the unique characteristics of the Yucatecan case, see Joseph, *Revolution from Without*; Ramón D. Chacón, "Yucatán and the Mexican Revolution: The Pre-Constitutional Years, 1910-1918" (Ph.D diss., Stanford University, 1982); and Francisco J. Paoli and Enrique Montalvo, *El socialismo olvidado de Yucatán: Elementos para una reinterpretación de la Revolución Mexicana* (Mexico City, 1977).

57   Martín Luis Guzmán, *The Eagle and the Serpent*, trans. Harriet de Onis (Garden City, New York, 1965), p. 163; U.S., Department of State, *Records of the Department of State Relating to the Internal Affairs of Mexico, 1910-1929*, Record Group 59, Washington, D.C., Microfilm Copy 274, 1959, *Correspondence*, 1916, I, 125.3, Claude E. Guyant to William P. Young, 10 June.

58   See, especially, Joseph, *Revolution from Without*, chapter 3. The discussions of the Alvarado and Carrillo Puerto regimes that follow draw mostly upon Joseph, *Revolution from Without*, chapters 4-5 and 7-8, respectively.

59   See, e.g., Lara C., "Peloteros yucatecos: Leonardo 'Zurdo' Pérez," and "Peloteros de antaño: Emilio Manzanilla."

60   Lara C., "Pelotero y picador," and "Peloteros de otros tiempos: Saturnino Borges"; Ramírez Aznar, "Béisbol en Yucatán: 'Chato Juanes'." Local fans still embellish tales of Molina's ability to pitch with either hand and take the mound under the influence of cocaine.

61   Lara C., "El primer doble juego en Yucatán: Bragaña lanzó 19 actos," *DdY* (19 May 1986), and "Peloteros de otros tiempos: Saturnino Borges." Borges also relates another episode in which his local team was shut out by the crew of the USS *Desmoines*, a gunboat sent into Yucatecan waters to ensure that henequen shipments to the United States were not delayed following Alvarado's invasion of Yucatán.

62   Ramírez Aznar, "Historia del béisbol yucateco: El 'Dzol' Peraza," "Béisbol en Yucatán: La Serie con el 'Bacardí'," *NdY* (14 January 1986), and "El béisbol en Yucatán: El debut de Ramón Bragaña," *NdY* (10 January 1986); Lara C., "La emoción del recuerdo: Feria

de jonrones," *DdY* (17 April 1966), "Peloteros de otros tiempos: Eliseo Gómez ('Pan de Umán')," *DdY* (14 April 1966) and "48 años detrás del jom." According to local tradition, several of the Cuban stars developed a fascination for ladies in the best circles of *meridano* society (and their affections were returned).

63   Lara C., "Béisbol local de antaño: Federico Cardeña."

64   Lara C., *Historia del béisbol*, p. 156.

65   Ramírez Aznar, "Béisbol en Yucatán: El campeonato de 1928," *NdY* (15 January 1986), and "Béisbol en Yucatán: El debut de Ramón Bragaña"; Lara C., "Peloteros de antaño: Emilio Manzanilla," and "Peloteros yucatecos: Leonardo 'Zurdo' Pérez."

66   See, e.g. Lara C., "Peloteros de antaño: Juan Burgos," *DdY* (15 February 1970).

67   Ramírez Aznar, "Béisbol en Yucatán: El 'Chivo' de Halacho," and "Historia del béisbol yucateco: El 'Dzol' Peraza"; Lara C., "Peloteros de antaño: Emilio Manzanilla."

68   Lara C., "Peloteros de antaño: Emilio Manzanilla."

69   Ejidal grants were part of the land reform/redistribution program initiated as a result of the Revolution of 1910 and the Constitution of 1917.

70   Felipe Carrillo Puerto, "The New Yucatán" *Survey* 52:3 (1 May 1924): 138-142 (quotation, p. 142); cf. José Castillo Torre, *A la luz del relámpago: Ensayo de biografía subjetiva de Felipe Carrillo Puerto* (Mexico City, 1934), p. 104.

71   *T* (1 July 1923, 14, 21 October 1923, 4, 18 November 1923); *DO* (6 November 1923); *PO* (5 August 1922). Also see Ernest Guerning, "A Maya Idyl: A Study of Felipe Carrillo, Late Governor of Yucatán," *The Century Magazine* 107 (April 1924): 832-36.

72   Quoted in Ernest H. Gruening "The Assassination of Mexico's Ablest Statesman," *Current History* 19:5 (February 1924): 736-40 (quotation, p. 739); Carrillo Puerto, "The New Yucatán," p. 141; cf. *T* (15 July and 19 August 1923).

73   *DO* (17 January and 6 July 1923).

74   *PO* (10, 21 July 1922); *T* (6 May 1923, 4, 18 November 1923).

75 E.g., see Alvaro Gamboa Ricalde, *Yucatán desde 1910*, 3 vols. (Mexico City: 1955), vol. 3, pp. 106-7; Paoli and Montalvo, *El socialismo olvidado*, pp. 168, 172; David A. Franz, "Bullets and Bolshevists: A History of the Mexican Revolution and Reform in Yucatán, 1910-1924" (Ph.D. diss., University of New Mexico, 1973), pp. 180-81.

76 For a provocative discussion of the relevance of baseball to societies in transition, which argues the game's "congruence" with capitalist values, see Stephen Gelber, "Working at Playing: The Culture of the Workplace and the Rise of Baseball," *Journal of Social History* 16:4 (Summer 1983): 3-22. Wagner's essay in this volume explores *béisbol's* fit with emerging socialist values in Cuba and Nicaragua.

77 Carrillo Puerto, "The New Yucatán," p. 141; Gruening, "The Assassination of Mexico's Ablest Statesman," p. 739. Yucatecans (Carrillo Puerto included!) would continue to attend *corridas*, although the PSS issued a decree in 1922 tempering some of the crueler aspects of the spectacle. See *DO* (24 August 1922).

78 See the Lever essay in this volume for a discussion of sport's (soccer's) integrative function in modern Brazil.

79 E.g., see *T* (1 May, 1 July, 5 August 1923); *PO* (22 November 1922).

80 Carrillo Puerto, "The New Yucatán," p. 141; also see Gruening, "A Maya Idyl," p. 834, and "The Assassination of Mexico's Ablest Statesman," p. 739; and, Paoli and Montalvo, *El socialismo olvidado*, pp. 168-73.

81 Joseph, *Revolution from Without*, chapter 7 , and "The Fragile Revolution: Cacique Politics and Revolutionary Process in Yucatán," *LARR* 15:1 (1980): 39-64.

82 E.g. see *PO* (1 December 1921, 24 February 1922, 3, 9 March 1922, 5, 6, 17 July 1922, 8, 28 August 1922, 16 October 1922, 13 December 1922, 8 January 1923).

83 Robert L. Brunhouse, *Sylvanus G. Morley and the World of the Ancient Mayas* (Norman: University of Oklahoma Press, 1971), p. 176. And see *PO*, particularly for the final months of 1922 and the first months of 1923, when scores of *poblaciones* petitioned for and received baseball equipment from the Liga Central.

84 *T* (18 November 1923).

85 These letters of gratitude may be found in AGE, Ramo del Poder Ejecutivo, 1922-1923; also see the expressions of thanks appearing in

the "Ecos de la Península" section of *PO*, particularly during January and February 1923.

[86] E.g., see *PO* (9 February 1922, 19 September 1922, 7 March 1923).

[87] E.g., see *PO* (10 June 1922, 19 September 1922, 27 March 1923).

[88] *PO* (15 November 1922, 27 February 1923).

[89] *PO* (27 October 1922).

[90] For a discussion of the fall of Carrillo Puerto and the restoration of a more moderate PSS, see Joseph, *Revolution from Without*, chapter 9 and Epilogue.

[91] See AGE, Ramo del Poder Ejecutivo, 1925; and *Boletín de Educación Primaria* 2 (1 May 1925): 11-12, 16-17.

[92] See *DdY*'s regular column, "Notas de Sport," during the late 1920s for illustrations of this patron-client arrangement.

[93] Ramírez Aznar, "Béisbol en Yucatán: La serie con el 'Bacardí'" and "Béisbol en Yucatán: El debut de Ramón Bragaña."

[94] Ramírez Aznar, "Béisbol en Yucatán: El campeonato de 1928"; "Béisbol en Yucatán: El debut de Ramón Bragaña"; "Béisbol en Yucatán: Federico 'Chivirico' Cardeña"; Lara C., "Peloteros de otros tiempos: Eliseo Gómez."

[95] Ramírez Aznar, "Historia del béisbol yucateco: El 'Dzol' Peraza"; interview with Nicolás Cruz, Sacapuc, 10 June 1985.

[96] See traveler Thomas Gann's observations on rural baseball during the early 1920s in his *In an Unknown Land* (New York, 1924), pp. 177-78. Baseball's linguistic influence in the Maya countryside is also discussed in Alfredo Barrera Vásquez, "El idioma español en Yucatán" in *Enciclopedia Yucatanense*, 8 vols. (Mérida, 1944-1947), vol. 6, p. 346.

[97] Interview with Lina Cruz, Sacapuc, 10 June 1985; interviews with team members of the "Naranjeros de Oxkutzcab," 29 July 1984; interview with Dom Fucci, "Leones de Yucatán," 6 August 1984. The majority of women's teams play softball, but there is a growing interest in competitive hardball among rural women.

4

The Case of Soccer in Early Twentieth-Century Lima

Steve Stein

It might seem redundant and not particularly profound to state that the principal characteristic of the life of Latin America's poor has always been misery. Nevertheless, this simplistic redundancy carries with it a series of questions that students of Latin American society have long been trying to answer with varying success. If misery has acted in different situations and at different times as a kind of sieve through which the life of the poor has passed, how has it shaped popular values and institutions? On another level, how have the essentially oppressive societies of Latin America--oppressive at least from the standpoint of the poor--survived during years, decades, centuries? What have been the major forces of cohesion, both external and internal to the Latin American popular sectors, that have helped hold these societies together?

An essay on soccer in early twentieth-century Peru could hardly purport to answer such complex questions.[1] Yet this case study of the development of the sport among the growing popular sectors in Lima from 1900 to 1930 reveals a variety of significant forms of social control, from the production and dissemination among the urban poor of conservative ideological norms to the preemption of potential popular self-consciousness and unrest through the institutionalization of one of this group's primary forms of diversion and autonomous expression. At the same time, we may see through the emergence of soccer how the popular sectors in an expanding metropolis created new forms of space--living space--in a world highly stratified in social and economic terms, which offered them precious little of such space. In short, the growth and progressive institutionalization of popular soccer exercised a dual impact on the urban poor. First, the consolidation of greater "living space" through participation in and attendance at soccer games made the life of some members of the popular sectors more bearable, at least in psychological terms.   Second, the increasing institutionalization of popular sport made for greater identification between lower class players and fans on the one hand, and the dominant elite and the state on the other.

Popular soccer began as the most informal of diversions at the turn of the century in Lima; thirty years later, when Peru fielded its first national team in World Cup competition, the sport seemed to have come full circle, from being a major form of autonomous lower class expression to being a major form of elite supportive social control. This study traces the drama of soccer as popular expression versus soccer as social control and attempts to explain its resolution.

Throughout Latin America the emergence of popular soccer was directly related to the birth of mass cities. The close intertwining of these two processes was evident in Lima during the first three decades of this century. In these years the Peruvian capital began to undergo an almost revolutionary transformation. For the first time the urban area began to extend geographically beyond its colonial limits. New paved streets and avenues, new houses for the rich and to a lesser extent for the poor, new public plazas, and new multistoried edifices all combined to give the city the image of a rapidly expanding modern metropolis. But even more than the physical evidence of change, the most dramatic feature of a growing Lima was expressed in the human dimension. Between 1900 and 1931 the total number of inhabitants rose over 125 percent, from approximately 165,000 to 376,000. The popular masses grew even more spectacularly, by more than 200 percent in the same period. The largest scale rural-urban migration in Peruvian history to that date was the major cause of this overall growth.

Simultaneously, the urban masses became plainly visible on the urban landscape: they labored on the numerous construction projects that exemplified the city's growth; they sold everything from vegetables in the city's expanding markets to lottery tickets in the new public squares; they worked in the textile, shoe, and beer factories; they inhabited the growing number of *callejones, casas de vecindad*, and *casas subdivididas* that had sprung up to meet the need for lower class housing. The emergence of the popular masses as a political force was also undeniable. This was clear in the initial organization of bakers and textile workers, in the general strikes of 1913 and 1919, and in growing support for political candidates, first in street demonstrations and later as members of Peru's earliest organized populist parties.

In terms of popular culture, soccer quickly became the most significant expression of the massification process. The fact that by the 1920s more than 25,000 people would have gathered in a stadium in Lima to watch a soccer match, as they often did, is testimony to both the emergence of Lima as a mass city and the importance of soccer as a mass sport.

Lima's first recorded soccer match took place in 1892, and in its initial form popular participation and appeal were totally absent. As in the case of all the sports practiced in Peru around the turn of the century-- riflery, bullfights, bicycle and boat racing--soccer was restricted to Lima's elite groups and was a foreign import. Peru's elite, increasingly integrated into the international economic system, was quick to imitate the cultural patterns of the core's elites. As with other European imports, soccer arrived in Peru in the 1880s aboard an English ship. The sport's English origins were immediately apparent, for example, when the first press account of the sport (1892) referred to it as "Football," a term which is retained today:

> On Sunday, August 7, a *Football* challenge will occur, between Limeños and Chalacos [residents of the port city of Callao] in Santa Sofía, Lima, organized by señores Larranaga and Fonkes, beginning at three in the afternoon.[2]

Still today in Peruvian soccer one speaks of the "offside," "corner," "forward," and "wing." These terms were also used in the early twentieth century and represented a clear expression of elite cultural dependency on Europe, specifically Great Britain.

In 1893 two exclusive soccer clubs were formed: Lima Cricket and Football Club, composed almost exclusively of foreigners resident in Peru; and Unión Cricket, composed both of foreigners and of Lima's young "gentlemen," or sons of the elite. These clubs combined soccer with other sorts of games such as cricket, polo, boat racing, and fencing. This was also true of the Club Cyclist Lima at the turn of the century, where members participated in both bicycle races and soccer matches. The kind of young men who were active in these clubs conformed to a specific social type: the "eminent *sport-man*" ("*conocido sport-man*"). The typical "*sport-man*" was energetic, athletic, carefree, and the member of a wealthy and prominent family.[3]

In the final years of the nineteenth century, soccer matches were often organized among groups--not always through such formal institutions as Lima Cricket or Unión Cricket--from areas that included central Lima, Callao, and the wealthy suburbs or summer retreats of Barranco and Chorrillos. There was a gradual increase in the number of spectators at these games, played on open fields, although no seating was available and no admission charged. Spectators, who were still almost exclusively members of the elite, began to have "favorite" teams with which they identified and whose progress they followed. In 1897 admission was charged for the first time at a soccer game; soccer began to have a more public character, although its participants were still drawn from the elite. By the turn of the century people began regularly to attend soccer games (*ir al fútbol*).

In sum, when soccer first became absorbed into the Peruvian cultural panoply, it conformed to the mold of various other elite, exclusivist sports and institutions of the era. Later, against the backdrop of a changing social context, soccer would come to play a very different role.

Among the effects of early urbanization and industrialization in Lima was that ever larger numbers of people were thrown into ever more densely concentrated social spaces: neighborhoods, factories, etc. Possibly this generalized process of collectivization favored the popularization of

collective sports.   It was in the port city of Callao where soccer as a
working-class sport first took root.   Sailors from English vessels demonstrated the sport to the inhabitants of this poor city.   Later, spontaneous
matches would occasionally be played between the young aristocrats of
Lima Cricket and workers who had observed their play with curiosity.

Soon these informal matches between dock workers or fishermen
and English sailors in Callao, or between players of Lima Cricket and
workers in the capital, led to growing popular participation in soccer.   In
some instances, the patronage of the aristocratic clubs allowed working-
class clubs to be established, which in turn would provide competition for
the patron clubs.   The aristocratic clubs encouraged workers' teams, pay-
ing them small "tips" or quotas for matches in which the two teams met.
More frequently, workers began to form their own teams without upper
class patronage.   In February 1901, the first such "spontaneous workers"
club was formed, "Club Sport Alianza," later to become well known as
Alianza Lima.   A year later, Alianza's early rival, Club Atlético Chalaco,
was established in Callao.   By 1910 a whole series of working-class teams
had appeared;   these included: Sport José Gálvez, Sport Tarapacá,
Miraflores Sporting Club, Club Atlético Grau, Sport Inca, Sport Jorge
Chávez, Club Atlético de Lima, Sport Vitarte, Sport Progreso, and
Sporting Tabaco (later Sporting Cristal).[4]

These clubs, composed of players from the lowest social strata, were
formed in a variety of ways.   Some began with the enthusiastic backing
of the working-class neighborhoods or districts of the city where the players lived.   Such was the case of Unión Buenos Aires Callao, located in the
Buenos Aires district of the port city, and of Sport Alianza, which had its
home and original allegiance with the new factory district La Victoria.
These   types   of   clubs   were   usually   formed   spontaneously   and
autonomously by workers who played together regularly.   Alianza, for
example, was originally established by men who were employed to care for
the race horses of Augusto B. Leguía, future president of Peru.   They
would play soccer near the stables every afternoon after work.   According
to one account: "One fine day the idea came up to found a soccer club just
like the *gringos* of Lima Cricket and the 'whites' of Unión Cricket."[5]   One
worker who recalls the early days of working-class soccer in Peru, reflected
on the growing importance of these neighborhood teams during this period:

> Each neighborhood had its club, but these clubs were informal, and their
> interest was in playing.   You would see soccer from eight o'clock in the
> morning until eight in the evening.   All those teams!   All different kinds
> of teams with their uniforms.   Boys who played for the sport of it, no?
> There were no other motives;   they played for sport.   When Alianza
> [Lima] won, La Victoria won.[6]

In the first decade of the twentieth century, when these initial neighborhood or district teams were formed, Lima was more a series of semi-autonomous neighborhoods than an integrated city. One's identification was first with one's *barrio* or district--El Rímac, La Victoria--and only second with Lima as a whole. And these soccer teams were often the most visible symbol or representative of the *barrio*. The victory of one club over another in a soccer match symbolized the victory of one area over another.

But in the early years of the century, most workers experienced soccer through less formalized channels than established clubs. On the way home from school, or just walking around the neighborhood, one would inevitably stumble upon spontaneous soccer games played in the streets or in vacant fields. The early experience of Antonio Maquilón, who was to become the first captain of a Peruvian team to participate in a World Cup match (Montevideo, 1930), was probably typical of most: "I began to play in school. I would even play hooky in order to play soccer. We used to play in pastures where we had to clear out rocks to make a playing field."[7] Miguel "Quemado" Rostaing, a working-class black who would become a reknowned player in the 1910s and 1920s, tells of a similar initiation into the sport: "We used to play in the neighborhood, sometimes five against five. In the kind of field that you found all over then. In those days Lima was still all farms. Groups of us boys used to play."[8]

Neighborhood soccer, then, was played with few material objects. The playing fields were simply open spaces with goals delineated by stones. The teams played with "rag balls" (*pelotas de trapo*), which were made of women's stockings filled with rags, wool, and sometimes a stone for weight. The more established teams played with rubber balls and began wearing uniforms "thrown together any which-way," according to one player.[9] These uniforms, usually nothing more than T-shirts of a given color and style, were paid for with the players' own small monthly contributions or, in some cases, with a donation from a better off neighbor who would then be named president of the club.[10]

For young men of the poorest social sectors, who lacked resources and support institutions, soccer came to have an importance in daily life beyond casual recreation. Through the sport, they began to expand their "living space" in a variety of ways. For example, the small soccer team grew into a close-knit network of friends who were involved in each others' lives, on and off the soccer field. According to Maquilón: "We on the team were very close. We used to go to the movies. We would fool around together, play with tops, make mischief. My best friends were the ones who played [soccer] with me."[11]

On a more basic level soccer came to represent a significant form of autonomous popular expression. From the dawn of the sport to the present day, the distinctive characteristic of Peruvian popular soccer has been what is called *picardía*. Miguel Rostaing explains clearly what *picardía* meant on the soccer field and how, in his experience at least, a dominant style of play was simply a reflection of a dominant style of living:

The *pícaro* player is the guy who doesn't let himself get kicked all the time. They weren't going to be kicking us. So you had to find [a way], jumping here, jumping there. And sometimes you had to give back a little so that they would be afraid of you. You're born with it, you're born with *picardía*. A quick witted person is called a *pícaro*. To be quick witted when you play is not to let yourself get kicked. To face life, because life is like a soccer game, you have to be quick so that you don't get hit that way in life.[12]

Rostaing's concern with maneuvering more than with winning is not unusual in a world where, as Peruvian sociologist Abelardo Sánchez León has stated, political, social, and economic power was "so immense, vast, and unfathomable that you could not directly confront it. Rather you had to deal with it by dribbling around it, making feints, dodging so that with a strange psychological reasoning, the lower class person opposed a power superior to him by trying to weaken it or wear it out."[13]

Soccer as self-expression and intangible personal reward was most clear in the experiences of the early players, even from the most prestigious clubs like Alianza Lima or Atlético Chalaco, who through the beginning of the 1920s played largely for love of the sport, since participation in soccer at that point represented a material sacrifice rather than material rewards. Nevertheless, certain special benefits did exist. Some players were attracted by the admiration and enthusiasm of the spectators: "The crowd began to buzz," according to Miguel Rostaing, "when one player faked out another, dribbling around him. And the crowd would join in and shout for you."[14] Another player of the era recounts that "when you made a good play and they cheered you, you felt like God. You really felt you could do anything."[15] Or on an even more basic level, Rostaing states: "You feel pride, pride that you're worth something."[16] For the Lima poor who suffered the humiliation and "defeats" of daily life, these feelings had enormous significance. In a society that continually denigrated their basic human worth, soccer was one of the few areas in which players who were poor could feel valuable, whole, accepted, and even revered.

More concrete than this relatively amorphous sense of personal fulfillment was that, for many working-class players, success in soccer led to the attraction of friends, male and female. "In those days that was the satisfaction of the soccer player, to attract women to dance. Then came respect, special consideration, the esteem of friends."[17] Often this esteem was expressed in the rounds of beer the fans bought the players and in the neighborhood parties that fans and family members sponsored after games. Israel Bravo Ríos, who played on Sporting Tabaco, remembered that

. . . games never ended without dances following them. The most important thing for us, the players, was getting together after the game at the club's locale. Girls would come, and there would be music, a party. And you were like a hero, you got a lot of attention from the girls. Of course, you didn't have only low intentions, it wasn't all a question of excesses. Respect and esteem were foremost. Of course we knew what we wanted; that's part of human nature.[18]

In addition, as the 1910s became the 1920s, there were increasingly more tangible rewards for soccer players and clubs. The clubs organized tournaments in which certificates, medals, and sometimes trophies were given out. The players themselves, together with other members of the clubs and their presidents, contributed toward the purchase of these prizes. For many players, winning a certificate or a "gold medal"--usually made of copper--was an event of great importance. Even players of the stature of Miguel Rostaing, who went on to play in international competition, placed a high personal value on those early prizes. Asked in 1982 what had been the most important part of his career, Rostaing insisted that "For me, the gold medals, the certificates, those are the most gratifying memories. But it costs a lot to frame them. In hard times I've had to pawn the medals."[19]

This world of soccer, created by the working-class players themselves, had become a genuine manifestation of popular culture. Allowed to evolve autonomously, the solidarity that emerged between players and fans might have later translated into forms of class solidarity and perhaps class consciousness among the popular sectors as a whole. Nevertheless, just as the seeds of soccer as popular expression were visible in this early period, so were the seeds of soccer as social control. The first evidence of attempts on the part of other social sectors to utilize the sport to fortify their own positions vis-a-vis the urban poor was the establishment and financing of soccer clubs for lower class players by members of the dominant elites. A clear example of this--and also a first step toward the professionalization of soccer--was the creation of clubs by the owners of the principal textile factories of Lima and in the nearby factory town of Vitarte. Apparently the idea for such clubs emerged when managers saw workers playing soccer after work in empty fields near the factories. First the managers established teams from different sections of the same factory and gave one *sol* to the winning team in intrafactory matches. Slightly later, teams were formed to represent entire textile factories: Sport Inca, of the Inca Cotton Mill; Sport Progreso, of the Fábrica del Progreso; Sport Vitarte, of the Fábrica de Tejidos Vitarte; and José Gálvez, of the Fábrica de Tejidos de La Victoria. The founding of José Gálvez was described in the following manner:

> The José Gálvez Club was formed on May 2, 1907. It was made up of the workers of the factory. The man in charge of it all was Sr. Ricardo Tizón y Bueno [president of the factory]. The factory donated uniforms, shoes, everything. They gave the team a free locale. They didn't charge them rent. And everyone who played for the team was given work in the factory.[20]

In recruiting players with offers of relatively privileged and well-paying jobs (compared with non-industrial occupations), the textile factories pushed soccer one step further toward professionalization. Frequently it was the player who approached the company's management, either directly or through a friend already there. According to a man who came to play for Sporting Tabaco in just such a manner,

> The manager would say, "we'll give him a chance. Let's see him play."
> Then they would watch him. If they liked what they saw, they gave him
> a job, even though it might just be cleaning up, or sweeping. The impor-
> tant thing is that you were working in the factory. You had a good
> salary.[21]

And there were some additional benefits as well. The soccer players left work early for practice, without losing any income. Some occasionally received from management loans that were not available to other workers.

These practices occurred mainly, but not solely, in the textile factories. In addition to the Club Sporting Tabaco, created by the cigarette factory, the owners of various haciendas around Lima created "company teams."

For their part, the hacienda and factory owners' motives probably went beyond pure sportsmanship. In the case of the factory teams, their creation clearly corresponded with the desire of owners and managers to forge bonds of loyalty between themselves and their workers. By sponsoring the teams, buying their equipment, providing the clubs with locales, and   sometimes   subsidizing   the   post-match   celebrations,   the presidents/owners/managers created strong clienteles among their workers. This description, provided by a player of Sporting Tabaco, illustrates the strong element of paternalism inherent in these initiatives:

> The president, who at that time was don Juan Carbone, would arrive [at
> the post-game party]. Carbone was very lively. Whether we had won,
> lost, or tied the game, he always came with a contribution and to see if
> we were getting along with each other. He would come, stay for a little
> while, then get in his car and say "Have fun. Here's a donation for your
> beer." And then all of us, grateful, would continue the party. And we
> were in such good physical condition in those days that we'd get up at six
> a.m., and by seven we were in the factory. The president didn't participate
> in the party. He looked in to make sure there were no bad feelings among
> us, difficulties, problems. He was like a father. Really. And we all came
> through with our obligations, because we admired him, like he admired
> us.[22]

A player from another club interpreted the gestures of his "patron" differently: "The thing is that those people are smart. You take care of him, the Señor. If you have workers, you have to reward them. So that the workers will watch out for you, instead of robbing you."[23]

For the owners of factories and haciendas, the sponsoring of popular soccer produced another even more tangible benefit. Matches between factory or hacienda teams distracted some workers from political or union-related concerns, and created divisions among members of the working class. According to some union leaders of the era, these actions had a negative impact on their ability to forge worker solidarity:

It was in the interest of the factory to use sports to break the labor movement. It pulled people away. They had tournaments between factories, and the union struggle suffered somewhat. Because everybody in the factory liked sports, pushed sports. It was a tactical move on the part of the owners to create disunity in the organization. That's where rivalries began; there were actual fights between the clubs. In Vitarte, when the soccer team played against La Victoria, there were fights.[24]

Workers who had fought among themselves on the soccer field found it more difficult afterward to unite in seeking social revindication.

Working-class soccer also created rivalries in contests between neighborhood or *barrio* teams. Independent of the influence of upper class patrons, these matches sometimes ended in brawls between players and fans, who identified with different districts of the city. These forms of internal conflict surfaced in both the "spontaneous" and "institutionalized" forms of the sport.

This picture of the emergence of popular soccer in early twentieth-century Lima is one filled with contradictions. The same sport that seemed to have the potential for stimulating class unity also produced conflicts between members of the popular classes. The game that constituted a highly significant form of popular self-expression and self-affirmation seemed to be easily turned to the purposes of elite social domination and ideological hegemony. Yet even within these uses of the sport for social control, there appeared important popular responses. As we have seen, at least some workers were well aware of factory owners' manipulative motives. And popular sector players were equally willing to manipulate the game for their own purposes. As one player from an hacienda recalls:

When I worked on the hacienda, I played soccer also, with the other peons. We made don Enrique Pardo, the hacienda owner's son, president of the team. He gave us a set of shirts, so we made him president. He gave us a trophy and paid for meals. We used to go on Sundays to other haciendas to play. We played because we loved the game. We made the hacienda owners captains, not so they would play, but so they would give us something. They were the owners. They gave us shirts, shoes, balls. We took advantage of it.[25]

This player astutely observed that the peons encouraged the owners' patronage, not only because it facilitated their play, but because in doing so they saw themselves as "taking advantage" of the hacienda owners. Hence, within these attempts of upper class sponsors to use the sport to consolidate their own positions, workers played at a similar game. At the same time that soccer became an effective means of social control, a way of reproducing the existing class structure through new mechanisms and clientage, workers did not seek to escape these mechanisms, but rather to exploit them for their own benefit. The very efforts on the part of the upper classes to use the sport to promote their self-interest led to the creation of opportunities for increased living space, in material and psychological terms, for lower class players at least. While some of these players might have been induced to sincere expressions of clientelistic loyalty to their patrons--"He was like a father . . . we admired him"--others found in the relationship that emerged elements of class opposition as well as elements of vertical social cohesion--"They were the owners . . . We took advantage of it."

With the coming of the 1920s, soccer would begin to take on a much greater importance in the life of the city's popular sectors. That decade marked soccer's transformation into a major spectator sport. It would be in the burgeoning soccer stadiums that seated the growing numbers of spectators where the battle between soccer as popular expression versus soccer as social control would be decided.

One immediately evident feature of the new decade was the virtual disappearance of elite soccer clubs composed entirely of the rich, the white, the *gente decente de buena familia* [decent people of high lineage]. Unión Cricket and Lima Cricket were the only representatives extant in the early 1920s of the old guard, and soon they too were inundated by the new popular clubs. Various factors led to the retreat of oligarchic teams from the top ranks. They found themselves continually defeated on the soccer field by lower class teams that could recruit their players from a much larger pool. Furthermore, for the exclusive members of Lima Cricket, it would have been absolutely unacceptable to play on the same team with a black or a mestizo; this would mean not only close contact with their "inferiors" in training and in games, but also--what was much worse--contact in the locker rooms.

What was happening with soccer teams reflected a larger social trend: public life in general, and specifically the sphere of organized sports, was becoming dominated by the popular sectors. In the case of soccer another cause and an important effect of this domination was the growth of sports consumers, the spectators who in ever larger numbers attended soccer matches. The overwhelming majority of these spectators belonged to the urban lower classes. Soccer crowds were made up of working men and women: taxi drivers, textile workers, construction workers, fishermen, stevedores, maids, and peons from the haciendas surrounding the capital. They came together in their scarce moments of leisure, on Sundays and holidays, to watch this magical game played by their peers. Soccer matches were a form of amusement, a way of escaping, at least momentarily, from the heavy burdens of working-class life. Soccer was a spectacle, a social occasion, a kind of collective release, for fans as well as players, a new kind of "living space."

Before the 1910s, soccer "stadiums" had no walls or seats. They were simply open fields surrounded on a Saturday or Sunday by a hundred or so spectators, who, in the early years, were mostly relatives or friends of the players. Of course, admission was rarely charged for those early games. During the decade 1910-1920, however, these arrangements gave way to more formal settings, as benches began to be placed around the fields, and people now had to pay to see most games. Even in these makeshift stadiums a division between first- and second-class seats was established; in

1914, for example, typical ticket prices were 50 *centavos* for the "Preferential" section and 20 for the "Popular" seats.[26] With the sale of food and beer, matches turned into true fiestas. To give some idea of the size of these events, contemporary reports estimated that some 7000 people attended a game in 1918 between Atlético Chalaco and José Gálvez, a record for the period.[27]

By the end of the 1920s not only had the number and size of soccer stadiums increased, but also the price and variety of tickets. The following types of seats were available for a 1930 game between the two top teams, Alianza Lima and Universitario de Deportes: first class, child's seat in first class, first class unreserved, railing unreserved, and second class.[28]

Although it is very difficult to confirm exact numbers of spectators for these games, the report on the above match gives a good idea of the massive nature of these events:

> Days before the date fixed for the playing of the game . . . the demand for tickets was truly extraordinary . . . . The demand for tickets greatly exceeded the capacity of the National Stadium to seat the spectators in a normal fashion. As a consequence, violence broke out . . . thousands of people were unable to enter the stadium in spite of having in their hands their legitimate tickets.[29]

One important facet of the growing number of soccer spectators was the appearance of the *barras*, or rooting sections, for specific teams. The affection of the *barra* and of the individual fan for the club was a function of the growth of the city and of changing urban life styles. There existed a long tradition of identity with one's neighborhood, and many soccer teams had become informal institutional expressions of that identity. On a broader level, the teams responded to a need for identification on the part of a growing, heterogeneous urban mass population. Like the regional associations that integrated new migrants, religious brotherhoods that integrated the faithful, and labor unions and political parties that integrated those with common concerns for their own welfare and that of the larger body politic, soccer clubs provided a sense of belonging, a sense of place in the ever-changing, at times uncertain, metropolis.

The *barras* emerged with particular energy in the 1920s, above all on the occasions of the first *clásicos*, the games between the archrival teams Alianza Lima and Atlético Chalaco, that informally represented Lima against the neighboring port city of Callao. As Callao did not yet have a soccer stadium, the games generally took place in Lima. The *barra* of Atlético Chalaco, made up largely of fisherman and stevedores, was greatly feared by the Lima populace, as well as by the Alianza Lima players. The *barra* from Callao would arrive by train and, according to the account of Antonio Maquilón, "They went on foot to the stadium. The mobs that came! And through all the streets [screaming] *chimpún* Callao, *chimpún* Callao!"[30] (The term *chimpún* comes from the small sticks of dynamite carried by the fishermen.) Pedro Frías further describes the behavior of the *barras* during the games:

People started fighting each other. It was a terrible thing when the Callao team played the Lima team. It was like a war. It was like the Chileans and the Peruvians, natural enemies. There was tremendous passion. If a Callao team lost, if Alianza won, uf!³¹

The enthusiasm of the *barras* affected the players as much as the spectators. Miguel Rostaing, who played for a period with Alianza Lima, relates his experiences with the inflamed fans from the perspective of those on the field:

We had to play with a knife in our hand to stick any of those fans who got mean, to scare them. They were tough, those guys from Càllao. Lots of bad people. The fishermen came with dynamite. They had their dynamite ready. So the Lima *barra* couldn't take it. How could they defend themselves? They had to leave on the run. Those fishermen almost blew up a back who we had when they threw a stick of dynamite next to where he was going to kick the ball. And another time they beat us when some fans, who were in back of the goal, stuck a knife through the net and cut Segalá [the Alianza goalie] in the behind. Segalá turned around, and the ball went in the net. They had to take Segalá out and give him five stiches. Their *barra* was terrible. You had to run off the field at the end of the game with your pants in your hands.³²

Among other things, these experiences demonstrate that soccer had taken root in the consciousness of the Lima popular masses. It had, in fact, become almost the sole sport of the urban popular sectors and, for many, a central concern in their daily lives. In the words of one who felt the attraction of soccer:

When I was young [in the 1920s], I liked soccer more than anything else. There was no other sport except soccer. And besides Independence Day and Carnival, there was nothing, nothing else. But soccer really stirred me up because it had everything, even better than girls.³³

Related to the general popularization of soccer and the emergence of the *barras* was the appearance of the so-called idols, of players of clearly lower class origins, who filled the sports pages and the conversations of all groups attracted to soccer. These were men with whom the young and even the old of working-class Lima could identify, one of the few positive role models that came from the same social and racial strata as themselves. The idols were men to imitate; they represented forms of behavior to which to aspire. And they were essentially spontaneous creations in an age prior to broadcast media, one in which even the print media was just beginning to devote substantial coverage to sports.³⁴

The impressive growth in soccer's popularity did not escape the attention of Peru's dominant elites. The large crowds, unbridled enthusiasm, and frequent outbreaks of violence at the games provoked a degree of fear in the upper classes. To many, "savage soccer mobs" and "violent soccer emotions" must have seemed to be particularly dangerous manifestations of the growing mass presence in Lima. The excesses of soccer would need to be curbed just like the more obvious dangers of popular sector emergence, such as strikes and political demonstrations. The creation of a series of formal institutions to regulate sports activities constituted a major response to these concerns.   The first signs of this enthusiasm for institutionalization were the tournaments organized by those factories that had teams: trophies and pennants were awarded to the winners, and the events were invariably followed by parties paid for by the firms. In 1912 the first step was taken to organize soccer on a wider plane with the foundation of the Peruvian Soccer League (Liga Peruana de Fútbol). It is interesting to note the social origins of the two presidents of the league: Eduardo Fry, a member of Lima's social elite, and H. G. Redsaaw, a prominent representative of the local British community. The English sportsman Sir Thomas Dewar donated a silver plaque to be awarded to the winning club each season. It was with the foundation of the league that admission was normally charged for soccer games.

Despite its yearly championships between 1912 and 1921, the league was plagued with difficulties from the outset. It did not have an office and suffered from a perpetual shortage of funds. Ultimately the league was unable to impose its authority over its member clubs, and in 1922 an internal schism developed that led to its demise. One faction of the league thereupon founded the Peruvian Soccer Federation (Federación Peruana de Fútbol) in August 1922, and in 1924 the latter affiliated itself with the international soccer organization, FIFA.[35] The emergence of the federation coincided with the opening of Lima's National Stadium, a gift of the British community in Lima on the occasion of Peru's centennial celebrations. Decisive steps had been taken in the institutionalization of soccer and its recognition as an "official sport." This marked the initiation of a process through which sport as an expression of popular culture would be distorted by the state acting as a mediator and a control. Peruvian soccer continued to be practiced on an amateur level, but the popular spontaneity connected with its early days, particularly in regard to the formation and functioning of clubs, began to decline at a rapid pace.

The full impact of institutionalization would not become evident until Peruvian national teams were formed in the late 1920s to compete in international tournaments. Throughout that decade, however, there were other forces that increasingly militated against spontaneous popular soccer. The most important of these was the progressive use of so-called "tips" to pay players informally. These payments were made possible with the charge for admission to the games. During the 1920s, particularly after the founding of the federation, tips became the norm for nearly all the major teams. The tip was not a fixed salary, but rather a percentage of the gate. The federation received its share, the club took another 20 percent, and the rest was divided equally among all the players. Although, in the eyes of the fans, specific soccer idols had clearly emerged, this fact was not reflected in higher payments to the best players.

Despite the extension of the payment of tips and the growing crowds at the games, until the 1930s there was not a single soccer player who made a living exclusively from his play. The case of the famous right wing of Alianza Lima and the national team, José María Lavalle, is illustrative in this context. A brickmaker by trade, Lavalle got up every morning at 4 A.M. to prepare his bricks, after which, according to his long-time friend and teammate Miguel Rostaing, "he worked all day, and he went to Santa Beatriz in the afternoons to train. And when the tickets were so cheap, how much did they pay him? A pittance. He had nothing."[36]

The tendency toward the integration or co-optation of popular soccer by the dominant elites, either through institutionalization or through tips, did not have the same effect on all clubs. The majority of the best clubs quickly succumbed to the new order. Others never played outside their neighborhoods, competing entirely on the local level. The contradiction between soccer as popular expression and soccer as social control was no more clearly seen than with the premier team of the period, Alianza Lima. At the same time that Alianza continued through the 1920s to be a faithful representative of spontaneous popular soccer, it was also subject to the same pressures toward informal professionalism as the rest of the teams. In fact, because of its superior performance on the field, Alianza was the focus of additional forces promoting its integration into institutionalized soccer. The story of Alianza in these years illustrates the tensions within popular soccer, and its response to institutional pressures at the end of the decade, in moments when Peru was fielding its first national teams in international competition, would mark the end of the formative era in Peruvian soccer.

From its formation in 1901, Alianza was like the other local teams; it had no ambitions outside the boundaries of its own neighborhood, the working class *barrio* of La Victoria. But the very quality of its players, the increasing competitiveness of the sport, and the simple desire to become known soon lured Alianza beyond those local streets and makeshift fields. By the 1920s, it had become Lima's most popular soccer club for various reasons. First, Alianza was truly popular in its origins. Never linked to a factory or any particular firm, its players worked at a variety of jobs, including construction, printing, textiles, and truck driving. Furthermore, the Alianza of the post-World War I years distinguished itself through its unusual ethnic composition; unlike most teams, its players were largely black. Alianza represented a mixture of what was clearly identifiable as lower class, and this was no where more evident than in the color of its black "idols," especially Alejandro "Manguera" Villanueva, José María Lavalle, Miguel "Quemado" Rostaing, and Alberto "Culebra" Montellanos.

The fact that a black team was able to gain prominence as not only the best but also the most popular club had implications that went far beyond the sports sphere. In some ways Alianza's success put a positive value on blackness, on the particular qualities of society's traditionally lowest racial stratum.

"Soccer is the sport of the blacks" became an oft-heard refrain, which not only recognized obvious virtues, but could also be interpreted to imply the incapacity of this group to excel in other activities, such as business or politics. With the success of Alianza, we see the self-affirmation of the individual lower class soccer player being acted out on a larger social canvas. Whatever the interpretation, the dominance of lower class and black soccer players meant that, in at least one area of society, the recreational area, the popular sectors could reign supreme.

But this supremacy too was ambiguous. Alianza's appeal and its successes constituted one of the instances for the exploited to defeat their exploiters, for the poor to defeat the rich, for the blacks to defeat the whites. Soccer was a mirror that reflected larger social conflicts, but it was an imperfect mirror that inverted or distorted them. Democracy reigned on the soccer field, while it was missing from the general society. Hence, the victories of popular soccer remained largely symbolic. After the match ended, life resumed its normal course: the worker returned to the factory, the black or mestizo to his marginal existence.

Although popular dominance through soccer was mainly symbolic, it was not meaningless or illusory. Indeed, the virtual hegemony of Alianza in the 1920s was a primary motive for the creation of a new team in 1927 to mount an upper and middle class challenge to the lower class supremacy of Alianza. The Universitario de Deportes, made up largely of university students and appealing to a "higher category" of spectators, quickly became and remains the major rival of Alianza. The matches between Alianza and Universitario, which on occasion took the form of virtual warfare, became cultural representations of class and ethnic conflict. A popular sports magazine of the period openly described that "class conflict" in the following terms:

> The University team, made up mainly of young men who have always aspired to take first place in Peruvian soccer, is the incarnation of the idea of a renewal of our values in this sport . . . . Alianza Lima, a popular team which has garnered the support and admiration of all good fans, represents the athletic abilities of the more modest class: the people. On one side are the youthful students and on the other the workers.[37]

This same magazine characterized Alianza-Universitario games in terms of racial conflict by referring to the teams as coffee and milk:

> A coffee with milk,
> with Quality milk [read Universitario]
> and coffee highly esteemed
> as is Alianza Lima . . . .
> The match of the little blacks [negritos]
> with the doctors will be a competition between
> milk and coffee in which the best qualities
> of these products will decide the winner.[38]

The players themselves recognized this element of racial antagonism in the Alianza-Universitario games, and it appears to have had an effect on their output. According to ex-Alianza player Miguel Rostaing, "These games turned into fights between blacks and whites. The newspapers built them up as such to attract spectators . . . . Of course, we played with greater intensity against Universitario because there was this rivalry: Alianza blacks, Universitario whites."[39]

These conflicts transcended the playing field to involve the fans who attended the games in support of their particular teams. Universitario attracted ethnically white, upper and middle class fans, while Alianza maintained enormous lower class backing. Miguel Rostaing described the two groups of fans:

> The Alianza fans were from different neighborhoods, of course, the majority from La Victoria, but also from Abajo el Puente, from Malambo [a major black neighborhood]. Alianza was the people, the workers. The Universitario fans were connected to the University. Alianza represented the poor people and Universitario the rich people. That's why they called them black and white.[40]

These fans often engaged in the same racial warfare they saw being played out in front of them. Pedro Frías recalls the virulence of racial insults on the occasion of one Alianza-Universitario match:

> It was a game with Universitario that all of a sudden in less than five or ten minutes they kicked two goals against Valdivieso [the Alianza goalie], and Alianza lost. When the Alianza players were leaving the field, [the Universitario fans] called them "blacks, slaves, cooks from Alianza Lima."[41]

Despite all precautions, it appeared that by the late 1920s, with the creation of Universitario, the elites had unwittingly made soccer more than ever before the focus of the profound tensions within the society of the massifying city. Indeed, in those years two sets of related contradictions were brewing at the core of Peruvian soccer: poor/black versus rich/white; and spontaneous/social expression versus institutionalization/social control. Their resolution would take place in the context of the two international soccer competitions in 1929 and 1930, the South American Cup in Buenos Aires and the World Cup in Montevideo.

The 1929 South American Cup marked the first official Peruvian participation in a major international tournament. The Soccer Federation announced the selection of a national team made up of the best players from the Lima clubs. To ensure successful recruitment and to focus public attention on the national team, the federation canceled regular local play. Ironically, those decisions, which seemed to emerge from a growing recognition of Peru's national identity, indicated an overriding interest in "international culture" on the part of Soccer Federation members and constituted a form of contempt for local culture. Given their continued supremacy on the soccer field, a large proportion of the national team was to be composed of players from Alianza Lima. In the majority of cases, however, these players did not share the priorities of the federation leaders. Alianza's main concern was to maintain close relations with their working-class fans and to compete with their traditional rivals. Furthermore, the tips derived from these games represented a significant form of supplementary income. To spend a full year dedicated entirely to the national team, without being able to fulfill its role as the popular club in local competition, went against the grain and interests of Alianza Lima. Alleging that they "did not want to be held responsible for any 'failure' of the national team," after some indecision the majority of the Alianza players decided not to participate.[42]

Racial discrimination appears to have been another strong motive for the withdrawal of the Aliancistas. It became clear from the first practice sessions that Alianza's players were being segregated from the more "distinguished" players of Universitario, and that they would be relegated to the role of reserves in the actual competition. This determination on the part of the team's management may have emerged from the perception that, were Peru to be represented in Buenos Aires by a team composed largely of blacks, the country might be viewed internationally as a nation of "barbarians." A newspaper story in 1930 openly explained these fears: "How are we going to send a team of blacks to a championship . . . . They will say that we are a country of people from this race!"[43] In the end racial concerns appeared to outweigh all else when it came to Peru's international image, on and off the soccer field.

The withdrawal of the Alianza players from the national team, despite their subordination to the "doctors of soccer," provoked a bitter response from the Soccer Federation. This rebellion of "the blacks from La Victoria" could not be permitted. The federation's incensed directors expelled the club from their ranks, thereby prohibiting it from playing in any official league game or tournament--in other words, from any event in which admission was charged. This "unpatriotic, undisciplined" team found itself abolished, or at least banished, a club with no official status.[44]

The response of Alianza to this sanction was fascinating. The players fell back on the more spontaneous popular soccer of earlier years. Prohibited from using the stadiums, Alianza returned to the open, dirt fields, seeking out teams from Lima's working-class neighborhoods and from the provinces. The reports of their games harken back to an era of sport for pure enjoyment that seemed to have passed away in the surging institutionalization of Lima soccer:

> Alianza Lima's players have become even more popular, if that is possible, as they have partied in Lima and vicinity . . . . We say that they are partying because they have a good time, inside and out. On the outside they make goals against their adversaries like there was no tomorrow, and inside they eat wonderfully with abundant *anticuchos* [barbecues] which they wash down with *chica de jore* [corn beer] or delicious Peruvian cane liquor or pure grape brandy from Ica, depending on what is served . . . . In Pachacamac [a village south of Lima] the thing was fantastic. A band,

lots of applause, and a creole style lunch that made people's mouths water a mile away.[45]

So, despite the absence of the customary percentage of the gate, the Aliancistas certainly did receive concrete material, as well as moral, benefits. If the Soccer Federation would not permit them the "space" to play, they showed themselves capable of creating their own space on their own terms.

In light of the striking success of Alianza's new/old form of competition, the team did not appear to have been terribly disappointed by its expulsion from the Soccer Federation. Rather, the players seemed to be initiating a redirection of Peruvian soccer back toward the seeking of fulfillment *within* the world of Lima's popular masses. Alianza's actions are all the more noteworthy in that they were occurring at the same time that official Peruvian soccer was linking its identity, with a great deal of success, to that of the state in the international arena.

It is evident that the Aliancistas were at least partially conscious of the implications of their actions, as demonstrated by the following dialogue between the captain of the team, Jorge Kochoy Sarmiento, and a sports reporter:

"They say, Señor Kochoy, that the expulsion of Alianza will be lifted.
. . . "

"Alianza doesn't need to have the expulsion lifted. Its players are happy with the attention everybody pays us when we play with the people . . . ."
"Yes, but you don't make enough money to even buy a pair of shoes or a shirt."
"With the federation it's the same thing. We don't make anything and they screw us."
"So Alianza is content with its situation?"
"You can say in the paper that Alianza is content."[46]

Despite Kochoy's statements, the disastrous performance of Peru's National Team in the South American Cup, where they lost all their games, in most cases by wide margins, abruptly changed the panorama. Comparisons between the disgraceful defeats in Buenos Aires and Alianza's successes on the local scene filled Lima's sports pages. Public indignation with the national team was matched by public admiration for the Aliancistas, more than ever recognized as "the idols of the day."[47] But this admiration did not produce the consolidation of Alianza's "people's soccer." Rather it had something of an opposite effect.

In the face of the extensive criticism and painfully conscious that the World Cup was less than a year away, the Soccer Federation approached Alianza with an offer to reinstate the team if they would simply sign a letter of apology. The spokesmen of the federation understood, so they stated, that "after all, these people who lack culture are not fully conscious of what they are doing."[48] Alianza agreed to the federation's terms.

Alianza's readiness to return to the official fold was the product of a complex set of circumstances. The players may have truly missed the relatively steady income derived from their weekly percentage of the admissions; also, they probably were not happy at being the target of criticism from many segments of Lima's society. Perhaps the Aliancistas too were looking forward to proving their athletic quality at the Montevideo World Cup. What is clear is that when Alianza resumed its place as part of official soccer, it had lost none of its touch. In their first game, they beat 3-0 an Argentine team that had soundly drubbed every other local club. At the game and subsequently, the Lima fans reconfirmed en masse their support for the ever popular team:

> The public's reception of Alianza when they ran on the field was without precedent. They were given a thunderous ovation which must be interpreted at the least as the recognition of their controversial quality.[49]

At the same time that Alianza once again became a "legitimate team," a new club president, Juan Bromely, was named, a high-ranking official in Lima's municipal government. It is not clear to what extent the choice of Bromely was a condition of Alianza's rehabilitation, nor was it clear then that he would be successful in "establishing order" over the "undisciplined" Aliancistas. As one magazine of the period speculated:

> There are those who doubt the ability of don Juan Bromely to manage Alianza with success. His personal integrity, his class, together with his lack of knowledge about the world in which soccer is played are considered hindrances for a task in which you need, more than ability in sport, a "native sharpness" [viveza criolla]: he'll have to spend a lot of time burning incense around certain personalities and he'll have to keep up with the thousands of intrigues that occur on a daily basis.[50]

There is no evidence that Bromely actually burned incense, but he had more potent weapons with which to achieve the pacification of his players: hard cash and the offer of relatively well-paid jobs. Proceeding on the paternalistic model that had been introduced years earlier by the factory clubs, Bromely secured city hall jobs for all those players who wanted them, and he made customary personal loans to all who requested them.

Alianza, a team that had never had a president with sufficient material resources to offer such benefits and pressured by official soccerdom, ended up abandoning its own soccer. The last significant bastion and most effective representative of popular soccer finally joined the tide against the sport as autonomous popular culture. Its actions seemed to severely dim the prospect that popular soccer could generate worker solidarity and class consciousness.

While Alianza and similar teams continued to attract mass followings despite their institutionalization and later professionalization, a series of strong forces--from impoverished conditions to an increasingly interventionist state--forced players to set aside, if not abandon, soccer as popular expression.   Soccer became more formally professionalized through the decade of the 1930s and in subsequent years. With the construction of stadiums, larger in size and number, and with the radio and (later) television broadcast of games, soccer gained even greater popularity, if not autonomy, than in its formative years. Disseminated throughout ever larger segments of the Peruvian populace, the sport expanded its capacity to provide living space to the masses, at the same time that it became an increasingly effective mechanism for social control.

Notes

[1]   This paper, originally presented at the Annual Meeting of the American Historical Association, Chicago, December 1984, is the product of joint research with José Deustua Carvallo of the Instituto de Estudios Peruanos (Lima), and Susan C. Stokes of the Department of Political Science, Stanford University.   Data was collected and earlier versions written by the three of us during 1981-1982. Results of that earlier collaboration appeared in *Studies in Latin American Popular Culture* (1984 and 1986), and in my *Lima obrero* (Lima: Editorial de la Universidad de Lima, 1985), vol. 1.

[2]   *El Callao* (3 August 1892); emphasis in the original.

[3]   For a perceptive caricature of the "sport-man" of this period, see the novel written in 1928-1929 by José Diez Canseco, *Duque*, 3rd. ed. (Lima: Ediciones Peisa, 1973).

[4]   *El Comercio* (January - December 1900); *Variedades* (July - November 1911);   and, Jorge Basadre, *Historia de la República* (Lima, 1968-1969), vol. 16, pp. 216-221.

[5]   César Miró, *Los íntimos de La Victoria* (Lima: Editorial El Deporte, 1958), pp. 22-23.

[6]   Interview with Pedro Frías (November 10, 1981).

[7]   Interview with Antonio Maquilón (June 19, 1982).

[8]   Interview with Miguel Rostaing (April 15, 1982).

[9]   Interview with Pedro Frías (November 13, 1981).

[10]   Miguel Rostaing comments (May 6, 1982) that when he played for his first lower division team, Huáscar, between 1914 and 1918, he paid

fifty *centavos* per month to the team. Israel Bravo Ríos, who played for Sporting Tabaco after 1930, recalled (June 20, 1982) that in the 1920s he paid 20 *centavos* per week to play on "minor division" teams.

11 Interview with Antonio Maquilón (June 19, 1982).

12 Interview with Miguel Rostaing (April 29, 1982).

13 Comments made during round table, "Fútbol en el Perú, Historia y Pasión" (Universidad de Lima, August 1982).

14 Interview with Rostaing (June 17, 1982).

15 Interview with Francisco Real (April 28, 1982).

16 Interview with Rostaing (April 29, 1982).

17 Interview with Israel Bravo Ríos (June 3, 1982).

18 Ibid.

19 Interview with Rostaing (May 13, 1982).

20 Interview with Pedro Frías (November 13, 1981).

21 Ibid.

22 Interview with Israel Bravo Ríos (June 3, 1982).

23 Interview with Pedro Méndez (May 24, 1982).

24 Interview with Israel Bravo Ríos (May 3, 1982).

25 Interview with Pedro Méndez (May 24, 1982).

26 Interview with Pedro Frías (November 13, 1981). The cost of a seat in the "Popular" section was equivalent to approximately 10 percent of an average worker's daily wage.

27 Roco Borodi, *Historia de la selección: en campos de antaño* (Lima, 1982), p. 28.

28 *El Sport* (19 April 1930): 5.

29 *El Sport* (26 April 1930): 4.

30 Interview with Antonio Maquilón (July 19, 1982).

[31]   Interview with Pedro Frías (November 13, 1981).

[32]   Interview with Miguel Rostaing (April 22, 1982).

[33]   Interview with Francisco Real (April 28, 1982).

[34]   Soccer was indeed a major factor in the appearance of sports journalism. As the sport grew in popularity, so did the number of sports publications in Lima, rising from two in 1918 to nineteen in 1930. See, República del Perú, *Extracto estadístico del Perú* (Lima: Ministerio de Hacienda, 1943).

[35]   For information on the league and the federation, see Borodi, *Historia de la selección*, pp. 24, 32-33, and *El Intimo* 1:1 (1962): 23-24.

[36]   Interview with Rostaing (May 13, 1982).

[37]   *El Sport* (19 April 1930): 5.

[38]   Ibid.

[39]   Interviews with Rostaing (April 15 and 22, 1982).

[40]   Interview (April 24, 1982).

[41]   Interview with Pedro Frías (April 13, 1982).

[42]   *Toros y Deportes* (21 December 1929): 2. Also, Alianza had been offered a possible tour of the United States, and many players refused to give up such a potential opportunity--which never was realized--to follow the uncertain enterprise of the national team.

[43]   *Toros y Deportes* (22 February 1930): 2.

[44]   Ibid. (7 December 1929): 6.

[45]   Ibid.: 13.

[46]   Ibid. (14 December 1929): 15.

[47]   Ibid. (7 December 1929): 13.

[48]   Ibid. (15 February 1930): 2.

[49]   Ibid.: 15.

[50]   *El Sport* (5 April 1930): 15.

5
Sport in a Fractured Society: Brazil under Military Rule
Janet Lever

Sport belongs in the world of play and leisure, yet business elites, mass media, and government and political leaders recognize its potential for making profits, disseminating propaganda, and eliciting pride. Organized sport prevails virtually everywhere and has developed over the past half century from a relatively minor element of culture into a full-blown social institution.

The careful examination of the role of sport in society remains minimal despite growing recognition that pleasure pursuits provide salient bases for identification in modern life. Not only do people devote more time to playing, watching, and discussing sport than to any other organized activity in public life, but the media, big business, and government manipulate that interest in sport to serve their own interests. Organized sport, as a major social institution, has consequences for any society. Sport can be used and sport can be abused. We need better understanding of the phenomenon to make the distinction.

Sport affects society in many way. This chapter is devoted to an exploration of its most important and universal consequence: *Sport helps complex modern societies cohere.* I will use the case of Brazil to illustrate the point.[1] Creating order amid diversity is a problem that pervades modern thinking; it is not just a problem for developing nations like Brazil. All societies have conflict; cleavages and antagonistic factions are inevitable because of scarcity, injustice, and prejudice. All societies are also integrated to some degree, or they would cease to exist. Despite hostility and divergent interests, individuals, kin groups, towns, cities, and regions somehow get connected into a single national system. Of course the degree of integration in any society varies; a well-integrated society can be defined as one whose members are able to act together to achieve their collectively defined goals.

Sociologists have been justly criticized for their inattention to the central issue: What mechanisms are used to make a society whole?[2] Spectator sport is one mechanism that builds people's consciousness of togetherness. Paradoxically, sport helps bring the whole together by emphasizing the conflict between the parts. Sport is the perfect cultural reflection of our Janus-headed existence; it becomes the arena for displaying allegiance to competing groups while cultivating a shared outlook as the basis for order.

Its unique qualities enable sport to accomplish this antilogical feat. According to Anatol Rapoport, the feature distinguishing games, and especially competitive sports, from other forms of conflict is that the starting point is not disagreement at all, but rather the agreement of opponents to strive for an incompatible goal--only one opponent can win--within the constraints of understood rules and standards of acceptable play.[3] In other words, conflict is not the means to resolve disagreement, but rather the end in itself. Sport is struggle for the sake of struggle, and it is this unique motive that explains the unifying power of its conflict.[4] Sport, then, is the play form of conflict.

We tend to think of conflict as a problem that needs to be solved. But in its play form the benefits of conflict are made more apparent. First, conflict is more exciting than harmony. Second, the staging of conflict demands collaboration. Both sides must agree to the same set of rules, standards of acceptable play, and authorities. Cooperation becomes a product of sport rivalry through the mutual desire to test skills, spirit, and the favors of fate.

If sport simply expressed the paradox inherent in all social interaction, it would serve well as an interpretation of our lives. But its utility extends beyond metaphor. Although sports can display contrived conflicts, such contests are usually dull. Spectator sports engross us most--and make their integrative contribution--wherever they dramatize social divisions that are real and meaningful. The "foundation stone" of nearly every variety of spectator sport, according to sportswriter Michael Roberts, is "the linking of the participant's destiny with the fan's, in terms of a common city, nation, race, religion, or institution of higher learning."[5]

The organization of sport determines which loyalties are tapped. United States sport teams most often represent schools and cities. The territorial monopoly that limits a city to one professional team in a league is unknown outside the United States. Cities elsewhere have more than one team in a sport, and those teams reflect special characteristics of their fan populations.

A look at the soccer rivalries in Rio de Janeiro illustrates the point. There are twelve clubs in the first division in Rio and four of them field world-class teams. Fluminense represents the old rich; Flamengo is the team for the masses of poor and black residents; Vasco da Gama represents the Portuguese immigrants and their Brazilian-born descendants; and Botafogo is identified with the modern middle class. Rio's eight smaller clubs represent the neighborhood districts where they are located. Rio's twelve clubs help break down the urban mass and integrate people into subgroups. Confrontations on the playing fields reflect the real-life antagonisms and jealousies between fan groups. Yet Fluminense, Botafogo, Flamengo, Vasco, and the eight community clubs, united in a metropolitan league, bring their opposing fans together through shared enthusiasm for soccer, the only professionalized team sport.

Sports contests can symbolically represent any groups that claim people's solidarity, but they will arouse the strongest passions where they are linked with the status groups that arouse the most passion. Typically, our strongest sentiments are reserved for our primordial groups, those groups into which we are born, whether they center on language, custom, religion, race, tribe, ethnicity, or locale. Primordial sentiments represent a "consciousness of kind," and that consciousness is pervasive and easily tapped--unlike class consciousness, which usually needs to be cultivated.[6] Soccer in Rio is exciting because it is based on these primordial loyalties.

The resilience of primordial attachments is seen as problematic in new and industrializing nations. Anthropologist Clifford Geertz describes this problem as the clash between primordial and civil sentiments. Primordial sentiments are the basis for the cleavages and prejudices that inhibit unified action. Civil sentiments require subordinating obligations to primordial groups for obligations of citizenship. Being a citizen of a respected nation offers a modern basis for personal identity, yet the more traditional bases for a sense of self typically conflict with the state's need of overarching political unity.[7]

For people in developing nations, political unity is essential to achieving their collective goals of a rising standard of living, more effective political order, greater social justice, and a bigger role in the world system. But, as Geertz observes, primordial sentiments become exaggerated during modernization as status groups fear losing power to a new centralized authority or, worse, being dominated by rival primordial groups. Geertz predicts that a more perfect union between multiple groups will be most successful where the goal is the modernization, not the obliteration, of ethnocentricity.

Instead of viewing them as a hindrance to progress, Geertz advises leaders to harness primordial sentiments to aid national evolution. They are easy to mobilize because they are so apparent and powerful. Seeing them as the roots of personal identification even in modern society, Geertz says they remain essential and deserve to be publicly acknowledged. Geertz's analysis highlights the channeling of ethnic differentiation into "proper" political expression (such as territorial subunits and political parties), but he recognizes that political outlets are not the only way to preserve primordial sentiments while furthering civil unity. He laments that other channels remain obscure.

This essay focuses on the case of soccer in Brazil to demonstrate that large-scale organized sport presents an alternative mechanism for using primordial identities to build political unity and allegiance to the modern civil state. Sport's paradoxical ability to reinforce societal cleavages while transcending them makes soccer, Brazil's most popular sport, the perfect means of achieving a more perfect union among multiple groups. Local soccer teams publicly sanction and express the society's deepest primordial sentiments, tying people together in stable patterns of interaction, while the phenomenal success of the national team heightens the pride of all Brazilians in their citizenship, tying citizens into society conceived in its broadest terms.

Sport gives dramatic expression to the strain between groups, while affirming the solidarity of the whole on multiple levels simultaneously. Brazil is a strategic site for demonstrating this paradox of sport at every level, from interpersonal to international relations. A remarkable record of achievements in soccer boosted Brazilian nationalism, yet also linked Brazilians into a global folk culture of idols and teams: Brazil is the only country to have qualified for all thirteen World Cup championships, has accumulated the highest points total, and was the first to win the cherished Jules Remet trophy three times; three of the world's five all-time highest goal scorers (Friedenreich, Flavio, and Pelé) are Brazilians; and Brazil boasts seven of the world's largest stadiums, Rio's Maracanã (capacity 220,000) being the largest.[8]

National consciousness in developing nations is often retarded by foreign domination of local political, economic, and cultural institutions. Popular culture--be it distinctive art, literature, music, or folklore--can play a crucial role in providing a national self-image that helps integrate diverse (and subordinated) peoples. International recognition for products of a culture foster pride that can be a key instrument for change. Nothing has exceeded soccer in its contribution to cultural nationalism in Brazil.

Insofar as the aim of this analysis is to demonstrate how sport helps complex, modern societies cohere, it is imperative to focus on a site where integration is problematic. Brazil's issues of social order are significant, whether examined at the metropolitan or national level. Therefore, a brief look at the place of soccer in Rio de Janeiro is here followed by closer consideration of soccer's contribution to the development of the nation-state.

Big cities are, almost by definition, full of strangers and in need of integration. But the need is acute in the major cities of the developing nations of Asia, Africa, and Latin America. The sheer number of people and the speed of unplanned urban growth put severe strains on the cities' infrastructures and on the psyches of their residents. In 1940, 69 percent of all Brazilians lived in the countryside and 31 percent in the cities; that ratio has now been reversed.[9] Brazil's two largest metropolises--São Paulo with eight million inhabitants and Rio with five million--are models of mass society concerns and ideal places to explore how organized sport can help hold a complex metropolis together.

Brazilian cities resemble North American "melting pot" cities like Chicago, having drawn in many of the same European nationalities. An estimated 5.5 million immigrants made their new homes in Brazil.[10] Until World War II, newcomers were mostly immigrants who brought their foreign cultures with them. After the war, the majority of newcomers to Brazilian cities arrived from other parts of the country with their regional variations of the "national" culture. Nearly 40 percent of Rio's current population consists of internal migrants.[11] No formal institutions were set up to help these strangers adapt to city life. Many were aided by extended families or acquaintances who had come to the city ahead of them. Others sought help from the church, local charities, or their employers, if they were lucky enough to find work.[12] Soccer clubs have received little attention, but they were also important in helping new arrivals adjust to city life.

Huge and diverse populations make it difficult for urban dwellers to sense they belong to an integrated society. While Rio's multiteam soccer league encourages public expression of divided loyalties, fan club affiliations also affirm a sense of belonging to a common, greater metropolis. Newspapers, radio, and television play a crucial role in circulating shared images and information on local heroes and team standings. Insofar as soccer contests constitute main events in city life, residents who know about them feel like full participants. People need something to talk about, and soccer provides one of those common interests and topics. Unlike most forms of conflict that make interaction difficult or even impossible, the play form of conflict prolongs contact by promoting communication; fans understand that their rivalry is all in fun. Intracity rivalries heighten feelings of involvement, because each fan group, sensing its solidarity against the others, competes to demonstrate the strongest support.

The foundation of sport in Brazil is the private soccer club. Organized as non-profit institutions run by volunteer directors, soccer/sports clubs put their revenues back into the professional and apprentice soccer teams, as well as the numerous other (mostly) amateur sports they support. Soccer clubs in Latin America, unlike most in Europe, are social membership clubs open to neighbors as well as fans who can afford the low initiation and monthly fees. Members are entitled to use the clubs' athletic complex, view the teams' training sessions, and attend social gatherings; special categories of members get to vote in club elections for the directorate. In urban centers with few public facilities, the soccer clubs' promotion of physical recreation and social life is especially important.

Rio's team of the masses, Flamengo, has as its symbol a black vulture. Roughly one-third of Rio's population pledges allegiance to the Flamengo Club; over 65,000 are card-carrying members. As the most famous club in Brazil, Flamengo is often adopted by migrants when they arrive in Rio because they have heard of it back home, thereby further swelling its huge following among the urban poor. Taking the club as their own offers migrants an immediate tie to their new home and plugs them into the local culture.

Flamengo's greatest foe, Fluminense, thought of as the team of the elite, has the second largest following in the city. The team's nickname is "white powder," referring to the powder used to lighten the faces of the aristocracy in an earlier era. Fluminense's pretensions are best reflected in the fact that it is one of the few soccer clubs in the country that restricts its social membership. Applicants who pass the rigorous screening can use the club's massive gymnasium, tennis courts, three swimming pools, steam baths, library, bar, and restaurants.

Vasco da Gama has the third largest following in Rio. The club was well known in Portugal, so many immigrants joined on arrival. This ready-made community eased their entry by providing contacts for those who came alone and a place to socialize for those with extended family and friends already in Rio. The Botafogo Club appeals more to the young, the urbane, the *politicos*, and the nouveau riche of Rio.

Most of Rio's smaller clubs are named after the districts in which they are situated. Like the samba "schools"--clubs that organize the community's parade for the annual, citywide competition during Carnival--soccer clubs form important links that hold the periphery to the central city. In Latin America, the suburbs are for the poor, as they are far from employment sources and adequate public transportation and often lack basic city services like water and electricity. Not only do samba schools and soccer clubs offer the only organized social activities; they are also the only collective representation of community pride.

The central position of the soccer club in Brazilian communities sustains pluralism by giving people of similar backgrounds a place to meet. The clubs, by providing athletic facilities and hosting dances and parties, focus social life for many people in towns and cities. Participating in club events builds a family feeling among fans, and volunteering time to club fund-raising projects brings personal satisfaction and some recognition. Access to team training sessions and victory dances reduces the distance between fans and their idols. And fans retain some control over management through voting and through access to directors and their ledgers. The soccer club was often a community's *first* voluntary organization, and even today soccer clubs offer millions of people their *only* experience with grassroots democracy.

There are even greater obstacles to unity at the national level. Brazil is an enormous country, the fifth largest in the world, with a culturally and racially diverse population.   Poor transportation and communications keep regional differences strong. Sheer distance impedes communication between far-away regions, while Brazil's dense jungles and mountainous terrain impede transportation even between neighboring states.   Foreign investments exacerbate divisions within and between regions by bringing modernity more to some cities than to others, while leaving the hinterland even farther behind.

Geographical integration has been a top priority of the military governments that dominated Brazil after 1964, making this the world's fastest-developing, new industrial country. Federal investments in highways, railroads, and telecommunications have begun to link distant regions, but the task is enormous.   In a nation like Brazil, sport's contribution to social integration is special, because it can *precede* technology's contribution and even promote modernization goals. By 1914 a network of soccer clubs belonging to a nationwide sports federation united Brazil, long before communication and transportation technologies could surmount problems of territorial integration, and long before the federal bureaucracy, established by President Getulio Vargas between 1930 and 1945, could connect the sprawling country administratively. For decades, club directorates, state federations, and the Confederation of Brazilian Sports have brought together men in key socio-political and economic positions who form alliances that complement more formal leadership networks. United by soccer, a diversified group of prominent men can go on to promote other political and economic actions.

Today over 5000 soccer clubs and their leaders connect Brazil's backland towns to the coastal cities and unite its many regions almost effortlessly as they pursue their sporting goals. While some benefits of integration are unintentional, of more interest are those contributions to geographic unification, social welfarism, and cultural nationalism that are owed to intentional manipulation by government authorities. The symbiosis between soccer and government antedates Brazil's military regime. Sport has helped numerous civilian politicians court popularity; in return, these same leaders have often spurred the growth of spectator and participant sports. But here we will concentrate on the success the military regime has had in harnessing the lure of sport to promote its own nationalistic goals.

The symbiosis between sport and politics is perhaps best illustrated by the national sport lottery, created in 1969 by the Department of Finance to raise much needed revenue for official projects. Modeled after European sport lotteries, Brazil's is the most successful of the publicly controlled gambling operations. In 1977 it took in more than $376 million.[13] The government directs soccer's contribution to social welfarism by using the enormous lottery profits to support the aged, handicapped, and orphaned and to fund hygiene programs, in addition to financing the construction of parks, swimming pools, basketball courts, and other athletic facilities. The Ministry of Education and Culture has used these facilities and the lure of sports to attract people in 2128 municipalities to programs that are aimed at eradicating illiteracy along with providing recreation.[14] In a country where 76 percent of the men fail the medical exam for the armed services, the programs' impact on physical fitness alone cannot be ignored.[15]

In addition to producing revenue, the soccer lottery has made an intended contribution to territorial unification, for it was designed to stimulate among Brazilians awareness of their own imposing geography. Strict policy dictates that the thirteen games included in the weekly lottery pool must represent *all* regions of the country, even though the best soccer is played in the southern states. Many people in the northeast cannot name the states or major cities of the south, and vice versa. Brazilian lottery players are supposed to learn about their country while trying to amass their fortune. Seventy million blank lottery fliers are distributed weekly with the names of all the teams and their home states. Those who read newspaper summaries of the teams' recent performances before placing their bets get additional exposure to names and places. The lottery has been so successful that all municipalities with populations greater than 5000 participate in the system; it has made a major contribution to bringing Brazil's disparate regions and peoples together in a single national culture.[16]

The promotion of the sport lottery led to a direct change in the structure of Brazilian soccer that has also enhanced geographic unification. The government urged the Confederation of Brazilian Sports to establish a national championship, so there would be lottery games all year long. In return for extending the soccer season from forty to eighty-five games, the Ministry of Education and Culture offered the Brazilian soccer authorities enough lottery money to subsidize both the costly air transportation needed to conduct a national championship and the exorbitant expenses connected with preparing a World Cup team.

Other soccer-playing nations have long had national championships, but in Brazil, where transportation between distant cities was poor, a national competition had to await air transport that was both available and affordable. In 1970 the tournament included only seven states, but by 1978 the Brazilian soccer authorities had ruled enough clubs eligible so that all states participated. The president of the Brazilian Sports Federation, Admiral Heleno Nunes, also presided over ARENA, the official government political party, in the state of Rio de Janeiro. He stood accused of putting political interests ahead of the good of the game. Critics complained that many of the provincial state leagues had been included for purposes of national integration and political support, even though their low caliber teams offer little skill and spectacle. These critics continue to worry that the year-long schedule and extensive travel are exhausting the nation's best players.

Whatever it costs, the national championship adds to the crisscrossing of multiple loyalties that bring the whole together in spite of the differences between the parts. To show solidarity and civic pride in Rio, fans of rival local teams have called momentary truces. For example, the other three clubs sent their mascots to support Botafogo in the national finals against a São Paulo team. Similarly, regional jealousies are suspended when international contests elicit patriotic support. The threatening attacker from that São Paulo rival, now one of the stars of the Brazilian Selection, is cheered by fans in Rio who hated him during the national championship. Even people who are not ordinarily attentive to soccer at the local level are drawn in when the national team represents them in important elimination rounds for the World Cup. Televised Selection games capture very close to 100 percent of the audience throughout Brazil; compare that with slightly less than 50 percent of the television audience in the United States tuned to the Super Bowl, the country's highest rated sports spectacle! Backwoodsmen and urbanites; northeastern plantation hands and southern factory workers; men, women, and children--all alike know that everybody in one vast land is supporting their team.

The lottery and national championship no doubt furthered the government's goal of a unified Brazil, but nothing did more to arouse nationalistic fervor than the Brazilian Selection's three World Cup wins, culminating in the first-ever tri-championship in 1970. And the military government took steps to share the spoils of victory by linking political with cultural nationalism. Right after the final game, President Médici addressed the nation, saying:

> I feel profound happiness at seeing the joy of our people in this highest form of patriotism. I identify this victory won in the brotherhood of good sportsmanship with the rise of faith in our fight for national development.[17]

Returning from the Mexican World Cup, the team's first stop was Brasilia, where the players received a presidential welcome from the proud Médici. The government declared the day of the team's return a national holiday, so everyone could take to the streets in a mass celebration. In a generous mood, Médici astounded the nation by opening the doors of the presidential palace to the people. Those doors had remained closed following the coup d'état of 1964 and have not been opened again since that jubilant day in June of 1970; political observers called this the "miracle of soccer." At his lunch for the team, Médici bestowed on each player a tax-free U.S. $18,000 bonus. Photographs of the president holding the newly acquired trophy, surrounded by the national heroes, were published in newspapers and magazines throughout Brazil.

After the initial celebration ended, Médici continued to exploit the soccer triumph. Miguel Gustavo's marching tune "Pra Frente Brasil" ("Forward, Brazil"), written to inspire the World Cup team, became the theme song of the regime, played by army bands at all official occasions and aired frequently on radio and television. The regime juxtaposed its nationalistic slogan "ninguem segura mais o Brasil" ("no one will hold Brazil back now") with a picture of Pelé in mid-air after a goal, and plastered the new poster on billboards across the country.[18] The tri-championship was to be merely the first step toward realizing Brazil's manifest destiny. In a survey taken right after the 1970 victory, 90 percent of the lower class respondents identified Brazilian soccer with Brazilian nationalism.[19]

National consciousness is an important element of integration, and soccer has made a significant contribution to national pride in Brazil. But we cannot assume that integration is always a good thing. Social order can promote social welfare, but it can also deprive people of their freedom and keep them in "their place." Whether we think the power of soccer was used or abused to help Brazil's military regime achieve its nationalistic goals is linked to our political judgment about the nature of social order in that country. We can condemn a regime's cruel tactics of social control and restrictions on civil liberties without condemning soccer only if we do not believe that soccer is an opiate that prevents revolution.

In fact, sport is often linked with violence and disorder. If a country is on the brink of civil war, contests that dramatize the intense social conflict might be banned for fear they could serve as the catalyst that sets off the fighting. Sport is no opiate because of its paradox: ritual unification does not displace social schisms. Regionalism and other bases for personal identification are not sacrificed as the price of cohesion. Rather, cleavages and rivalries are reinforced and get public sanction through this channel for expression. Geertz's hope for modernization instead of obliteration of ethnocentricity is realized in the case of Brazilian soccer. The playful competitive framework of sport dramatizes the conflict between multiple groups, while still serving as one of the threads that holds them together.

Even in countries like Brazil, with its terrible scarcities and inequities, people share collective goals. All governments, be they authoritarian or democratic, will try to capitalize on opportunities like major sporting victories to legitimate themselves. Yet few Brazilians are fooled by the government's manipulation of sport for its nationalistic goals; it is not "false consciousness" that makes people support their teams. They want to share both the wealth of a modern nation and the excitement offered by winning soccer teams.

People in developing nations, and not just their governments, want a more influential role in the world system. They have suffered from what Geertz calls a "humiliating sense of exclusion" and see citizenship in a respected nation as their "most broadly negotiable claim to personal significance."[20] Sporting victories can grant the international recognition that helps developing nations shed their inferiority complexes. One special feature of the play form of conflict is that David *can* beat Goliath. Long before economic and military strength can back up political clout, sport offers a nation an opportunity for a high ranking in at least one sphere of the world system.

Does the cohesion produced by sports victories last, or is the euphoria only temporary? The general structure of sporting competition sustains cohesion: the vanquished take comfort in next season's new chance, while victors cannot last on their laurels for long. The specific structure of the World Cup involves participating nations in two years of qualifying rounds before the quadrennial finale; and contributions to cohesion can take a material form that have a permanent impact. The 1970 World Cup provided the occasion to lease space from orbiting communications satellites that established the first telecommunications link between northern and southern Brazil.[21] A similar advance took place in Spain as part of that country's preparation to host the 1982 Cup. The Spanish government approved a $150 million budget for improvements on its state-owned television system. Because of the games, Spain now has permanent production facilities, better reception, and an expanded second channel.[22]

Such material contributions to development are unmistakable, although we must ask whether enormous expenditures for sporting events are warranted in impoverished countries. That is a difficult question to answer, because we cannot easily attach a monetary value to abstractions like national pride and collective identity. Even illiterate peasants in the remote interior, listening to the games on their transistor radios, knew Brazil had earned the respect and admiration of the whole world. The awareness that so many others are sharing the same event makes it an experience above the ordinary, an occasion for togetherness that makes a society greater than the arithmetic sum of its parts.

Notes

1   An earlier draft of this paper was presented at the Fourth Clemson University Conference on Sport and Society (1984); much of the data for the analysis is found in the author's *Soccer Madness* (Chicago: University of Chicago Press, 1983).

2   Edward Shils, *Center and Periphery: Essays in Macro-Sociology* (Chicago: University of Chicago Press, 1975).

3   Anatol Rapoport, *Fights, Games, and Debates* (Ann Arbor: University of Michigan Press, 1960).

4   Georg Simmel, *Conflict and the Web of Group-Affiliation*, trans. Kurt H. Wolff (New York: Free Press, 1955), pp. 34-35.

5   Michael Roberts, "The Vicarious Heroism of the Sports Spectator," *New Republic* (23 November 1974): 17.

6   Immanuel Wallerstein, *The Capitalist World Economy* (Cambridge: Cambridge University Press, 1979), chapter 10.

7   Clifford Geertz, "The Integrative Revolution: Primordial Sentiments and Civil Politics in New States," in *Old Societies and New States: The Quest for Modernity in Asia and Africa*, ed. Clifford Geertz (Glencoe, Illinois: Free Press, 1963), pp. 105-57.

8   Richard Henshaw, *The Encyclopedia of World Soccer* (Washington, DC: New Republic Books, 1979), pp. 90-105.

9   Janice E. Perlman, *The Myth of Marginality: Urban Poverty and Politics in Rio de Janeiro* (Berkeley: University of California Press, 1976).

10   *Encyclopedia Americana* (1978 edition), vol. 4, pp. 454-63.

11   *Encyclopaedia Britannica* (1974 edition), vol. 15.

12   Alejandro Portes and John Walton, *Urban Latin America: The Political Condition Above and Below* (Austin: University of Texas Press, 1976).

[13]   I gratefully acknowledge the receipt of materials from Mr. W. Baumann, secretary general of INTERTOTO, Basel, Switzerland (16 January 1979).

[14]   *Banco Real Economic Letter* (July 1978): 2.

[15]   J. A. Pires Gonçalves, *Subsidios para implantação de uma politica de desportes* (Brasília, 1971).

[16]   Figures provided by Afro Furtado de Carvalho, Superintendent of Lotteries, in personal correspondence (17 March 1978).

[17]   Author's translation of the text of Médici's speech as printed in the *Jornal do Brasil* (21 June 1970): 5.

[18]   Peter Flynn, "Sambas, Soccer, and Nationalism," *New Society* 18:464 (19 August 1971): 327-30.

[19]   Marplan Survey No. 160.

[20]   Geertz, "The Integrative Revolution," p. 108.

[21]   Robert M. Levine, "Sport and Society: The Case of Brazilian *Futebol*," *Luso-Brazilian Review* 17:2 (Winter 1980): 233-52.

[22]   *Variety* (30 July 1980): 54.

6
Sócrates, Corinthians, and Questions of Democracy and Citizenship
Matthew Shirts

Contrary to what the title might suggest to less than fanatical fans of international soccer, the article that follows does not discuss Greece, but Brazil. The Corinthians in question travel rarely (if ever) by boat, and this Sócrates, although given to philosophizing, is a popular soccer hero, better known for his athletic abilities. "Corinthian Democracy," to get to the point, refers to a political movement developed by team administrators and soccer players in an attempt to alter the management/labor relations of a São Paulo club called "Corinthians." The movement came to the public eye in a big way for the first time in 1982 on the eve of elections for club president, in part because of the soccer stars involved and in part because of the similarity between internal club politics and the Brazilian political moment. Two tickets competed for the presidency of the Corinthians, the "third most important position in the country, after the governorship of São Paulo and the presidency of the Republic"[1] : "Order and Truth" and "Corinthian Democracy." The nature of the dispute was clear from the beginning. Corinthian Democracy, already in power at the time of the election, represented the *abertura* ticket, an expression of the political liberalization underway at the level of national politics in Brazil since the late 1970s.[2] Its platform was antiauthoritarian above all else, proposing new forms of team administration based on the participation of players, administrators, and fans in club operations. "Order and Truth," however, proposed quite the opposite: authoritarian and personalistic control of the club in the hands of the "folkloric" soccer *caudillo*, the former club president, Vicente Matheus. The soccer magazine *Placar* summed up the dispute as a battle between "liberalization and heavy handedness, efficiency or paternalism, new times or old methods, Waldemar Pires or Vicente Matheus."[3]

The Corinthians, like athletic teams almost everywhere outside the United States, is a non-profit organization governed, in principle, by club members (title holders), who elect a body of counselors, which in turn selects the administrators of the organization. In practice, however, this form of governance has translated into paternalistic, clientelistic control of Brazilian soccer by entrenched administrators popularly known as *cartolas*, or "top hats." These are typically middle-aged businessmen who obtain positions within the club by demonstrating their dedication to the team, frequently via monetary donations. The top hats' motives, as Janet Lever has explained, are not always entirely altruistic. The importance of soccer in Brazil is such that club administrators are able to use their positions in alliances with representatives of the military, legal, and governmental systems.[4] Laudo Natal, to cite the best known example, moved from the presidency of the São Paulo Futebol Club to the governorship of São Paulo.[5] The attention generated by Corinthian Democracy, moreover, derived in part from the ambitiousness of any attempt to change this well-rooted oligarchical system of control.

The novel character of Corinthian Democracy's platform increased the excitement and urgency of the 1982 elections. The climate, according to *Placar*, was the same as that of "a real election."[6] And if there were any doubts, the importance of the event was confirmed by the campaign expenses of the two tickets--somewhere in the neighborhood of U.S. $500,000.[7] Commercials were placed on television and radio; campaign T-shirts, caps, costumes, and musical groups guaranteed a festive air. Several players made public their support for the Democracy ticket, running for the position of club counselor. They were supporting not only Waldemar Pires for president and the sociologist Adílson Monteiro Alves (one of the theoreticians of the movement) for director of *futebol*, but, most important, a philosophy of management and a new interpretation of soccer's place in Brazilian society. Sócrates, a lanky, bearded medical doctor, captain of Brazil's 1982 World Cup team and the Corinthians' star player, contributed to the urgency of the elections, making his position clear beforehand: he would retire from soccer in the event of an "Order and Truth" victory.

With the hindsight of a Monday morning quarterback, the electoral victory of 1982 appears as but one among many of Corinthian Democracy's accomplishments. Between 1982 and 1984 the movement spilled over the walls of the club and into the national political arena, where it played an interesting role in the political liberalization (*abertura*) underway in Brazil since the late 1970s and, more directly, in the 1984 campaign for free elections. The elegance of the soccer played by Casagrande, Sócrates, Wladimir and company, the 1982 state title, won with "Democracia Corintiana" printed on their uniforms, together with the presence of the team in the increasingly refreshing events of national politics, sent fans into near delirium. The best selling author Marcelo Rubens Paiva, a dedicated fan, went so far as to write that "if ET shows up around here, the Corinthians is the only team he'll invite for a match on his planet."[8]

It had never felt so good to be a *corintiano*. An element of Brazil's rich and mysterious, carnivalesque and spirited urban popular culture, the Corinthians suddenly appeared in the forefront of national politics, along-side unions, opposition parties, and social movements. Drawing cultural identity into the realm of political action and debate, moreover, Corinthian Democracy clarified a theoretical point for social scientists that, in retro-spect, seems rather obvious: Sport is not only a reflection, but just as important, a part of society.

Sport, Brazilian Soccer, and Popular Culture

But what part? Clearly, the nature of the relationship between sport and society depends upon the nature of the society in question. In this sense, two points need be made at the outset. First, soccer, as Anatol Rosenfeld observed in 1956, is not one among many, but rather *the* sport in Brazil.[9] In spite of the growing (and, in most cases, somewhat recent) interest in basketball, surfing, and many other sports, soccer continues to occupy a privileged place in the spectrum of Brazilian athletics.[10] The difference, and this is the second point, is that soccer, unlike all other sports--with the possible exception of *capoeira*[11] --is part of the characteristic and unique popular culture that emerged in Brazilian cities around the turn of the century, while volleyball, surfing, squash, etc., certainly are not. As such, *futebol*, to use the Brazilian term, should be grouped not with other sports, but within a tradition that includes cultural manifestations such as carni-val, Afro-Brazilian religions, popular music, and Catholicism.

Gilberto Freyre, Anatol Rosenfeld, amd the journalist Mário Filho count among the first analysts to approach soccer as a revealing and characteristic element of Brazilian culture.[12] Rosenfeld, for example, citing Shiller, compares *futebol* to the horseraces in London, bullfights in Madrid, and the "gay good life" of the processions of Rome, in an attempt to get at the character of Brazilian society, remarking that "the unrivaled success of soccer in Brazil, with the complete suppression of rugby, played with equal enthusiasm early on, certainly offers food for thought."[13] The renowned sociologist Gilberto Freyre examines the game in light of his understanding of "racial democracy" and national character: "In soccer, as in politics, Brazilian 'mulattoness' is characterized by the pleasure of elasticity, surprise, and rhetoric, bringing to mind capoeira moves, or the steps of a dance."[14]

For my own purposes of analysis, it is not so much national char-acter or "mulattoness" that draw soccers into the realm of carnival, popular religiosity, and music, but rather a common history, a tradition, and most significant, the ability to generate social, national, and individual identities. Without an understanding of this cultural context, part of the relevance of Corinthian Democracy within the history of soccer is lost. In February

1983, for instance, shortly before carnival, Sócrates set forth the objectives of his activities in the Corinthian Democracy movement:

> I'm struggling for freedom, for respect for human beings, for equality, for ample and unrestricted discussions, for a professional democratization of unforeseen limits, and all of this as a soccer player, preserving the ludic, joyous, and pleasurable nature of this activity.[15]

If it did not come from an athlete referring to professional soccer, this combination of "pleasure," "joy," "struggle," "freedom," and "democracy" would quite possibly go unnoticed, say, in the Paris of May 1968. Sócrates's vision of the nature and possibilities of soccer in Brazil, however, are less a result of the influence of the artistic vanguard or intellectual left than of the Corinthian fans and the carnivalesque climate they generate in the stadium. When he started to play for the team, Sócrates "commemorated goals in championship games like you swat a fly." "Today," continues Marcelo Rubens Paiva, writing in 1982, "even when the team is winning 10 to 1 he commemorates a goal like an adolescent beginning his career."[16] The atmosphere generated by the Corinthian following, the second largest in the country after Flamengo in Rio de Janeiro, is, in other words, contagious.

Soccer in Brazil shares the exuberance and certain of the festive forms of carnival and Brazilian popular music's mistrust of labor; all three of these cultural expressions insist on the values of spontaneity, pleasure, and enthusiasm. These common elements stem from a common history, very different from the history of popular culture in most of Spanish America, Europe, and the United States. Writing of popular music, José Miguel Wisnik has set out the specificity of urban popular culture in Brazil compared with European manifestations:

> If in Europe the advance of capital seems to have contributed to the discontinuation of carnivalesque festivals from early on, undermining the common denominator of the public celebration, in Brazil industrialization and modernization (I'm thinking of the first decades of the century) contributed initally towards an amplification of the celebration, of the space of the city, the record industry, giving an electric and urban voice to the carnivalesque substratum active in popular culture, and creating, in this manner, the very phenomenon of Brazilian popular music as a mixture of classes in a dialectic of order and disorder.[17]

In their current forms, carnival, soccer, and popular music developed in Brazil at about the same time as the urban proletariate, a fact that deeply marked their character and content. "The sphere of labor," writes Gilberto Vasconcellos, "projects itself over Brazilian popular music as a powerful *inverted image*; the systematic and radical negation of the values elevated into a positive light by work became the preferred poetic theme of our popular composer in the twenties and thirties--one of the richest and most notable periods in Brazilian popular music."[18] The popular composer inverts this image, according to Vasconcellos, by way of the figure of the *malandro*, a bohemian rascalesque character of Brazilian lore who, with skill and savoir faire, moves between the spheres of "order" and "disorder" in Brazilian society, taking advantage of the breaches and gaps in both.

> Mommy, I don't want
> Mommy, I don't want
> to work from sun up to sun down,
> I want to be a singer on the radio
> a soccer player . . . .[19]

Florestan Fernandes, Fernando Henrique Cardoso, and José de Souza Martins have shown in their studies of slavery and abolition how labor emerged for the newly freed black as the inhuman activity par excellence. In Cardoso's words:

> the free black had to opt between continuing to work under the same conditions as before with the formal status of a citizen, or rebelling against everything that labor--disqualified by slavery--represented, living in idleness and disorder.[20]

Idleness and disorder were not, however, the only reactions of groups excluded by the economic and social order to the new sort of social life emerging in Brazilian cities at the beginning of the century. In music, carnival, religion, and soccer, popular classes, or better, segments of them, brought their energies to bear, altering the trajectory of Brazilian culture.[21] To the dark poverty of lower class life and the (new sorts of) rigors brought on by proletarianization and/or economic marginalization, they opposed the joy and sensuality of dance, the irreverence of carnival and the ambivalent, somtimes tragic life of the *malandro*, master in the art of ducking the severity and inflexibility of labor. Without disregarding differences across regions and genres (important, in the final analysis), it is possible to see the mark of a common aesthetic, in Brazilian popular culture, the mark of a carnivalesque substratum perhaps.

Soccer in Brazil incorporated elements of this aesthetic both in the stands and on the field at about the same time as popular music generated its critique of labor. Football, as it was called at the time, was a pastime limited almost entirely to the sphere of urban elites in the first decades of the century.[22] A refined game, something like tennis, polo, or squash in the country today, it was played at aristocratic clubs where English was spoken on the field and important matches were followed, not with exuberant celebrations in the street, but with fashionable, formal balls animated by waltzes. The popularization of football in Brazil, started around 1900 and officialized with professionalization in 1933, changed the style of play, the character of the fans, altering the overall aesthetic of the game in the process. Soccer, in short, took on an increasingly carnivalesque aspect as fans turned the stadium into a celebratory space.[23]

On the field, the popularization of soccer generated a new sort of player--acrobatic, elastic, full of unexpected moves, elegance, and individual power. It is even possible to say that the message offered up in the lyrics of Vasconcellos's composers, clear at the level of content, is passed along on the feet of Brazilian soccer players. Players such as Leonidas in the thirties and forties, Garrincha in the fifties and sixties, Pelé in the fifties, sixties, and seventies--to cite some of the better known--are the highest expressions of this individualistic, acrobatic, happy style.[24] The anthropologist Roberto Da Matta explains this style in terms of soccer's liberating place within a highly structured, hierarchical social order:

> . . . in the institutionalized and "structured" spheres of Brazilian society, the dominant and explicit mode of relationship is "hierarchization" by means of networks of personal relations. In this plane, everything has its place and individual variations are impossible. In areas such as *soccer, carnival*, and *umbanda*, individual variations are possible and consequently individualism and "hot-dogging" are the dominant ideologies.[25]

The game comes to be interpreted as ludic celebration and irreverence-- Pelé kicking the ball lightly over a defender's head and running past him to receive it himself; or Garrincha, who, ahead 3-0, "dribbled three adversaries, obliged the goalie to make a spectacular leap and fall flat on his face, and then, with an open net for the final shot, he waited for the fullback Robotti to arrive, dribbled him in front of the goal and only then knocked the ball in."[26] As an unsuspect journalist, Alastair Reid, writing of the 1982 World Cup in *The New Yorker* put it: "Brazil's whole play seemed more instinct than design, and it was clear that the Brazilians relished playing the game--an impression that came all too rarely in the Mundial."[27]

Christian Messenger, in his study of sport in American literature, has examined the contradictory nature of sport in North American society: "It liberates in play, but binds its players in strenuous work."[28] "America's puritanical society with its fierce work ethic has nurtured a deep suspicion of play," he writes, going on to point out that this explains, in part at least, the highly disciplined nature of American sports at the level of ideology and practice.[29] In its popular form, Brazilian soccer, in contrast, was born as a liberation from labor and a society hierarchical in nature, a fact which its style reflects. It is interesting to note that the Corinthian Democracy movement picked up on this aspect of the Brazilian soccer tradition and style, emphasizing the ludic quality of the game, as well as the players' right to the control of their own bodies and personal lives. It succeeded in doing away with pre-game "confinement," brought beer into the locker room, and generally made it clear that what the players did on their own time was their own and not the club's business. Rejecting the hypocritical moralism of previous generations of soccer stars, Sócrates and Casagrande, for instance, gave interviews in bars, revealed their taste for a *cervejinha* or two, and explained that they really enjoyed smoking cigarettes and did not plan to quit. What was at stake, broadly speaking, was the athlete's control over his body and, just as important, an interpretation of soccer, not as discipline, but as enjoyment. To use Sócrates's words, Corinthian

Democracy sought to preserve the "ludic, joyous, and pleasurable" nature of the game.

Identity, Soccer, Corinthian Democracy, and Citizenship

The novelty of Corinthian Democracy, of a social movement within a soccer club, raises a series of questions and revives others with respect to the significance and role of the game in Brazil. Among them: Does soccer merely reflect the structures of domination in the country, or can it be seen as a creative intervention in Brazilian society? The two most common interpretations of *futebol* to date--that which sees it as the "opium of the people" and that which highlights its role in national integration--have emphasized soccer's subordination to ideologies and the state. The "opium of the people" thesis interprets the intense popular interest and identification generated by soccer in a negative light as a form of massification which, in keeping the masses' attentions turned from more serious concerns, results in alienation and social manipulation. The national integration thesis exalts popular identification with the game insofar as it strengthens the cultural strings that tie the nation together. In both interpretations soccer emerges as a sort of empty container, filled by the political and ideological structures of the moment.[30]

Corinthian Democracy, on the surface of things at least, would seem to challenge such perspectives insofar as it proposes to unite players, fans, and administrators in an attempt to achieve soccer's autonomy vis-á-vis the authoritarianism of Brazilian society, forging an independent set of values. Or should Corinthian Democracy be considered merely the exception that confirms the rule? Or the reflection in sports of the redemocratization underway in the country since the late 1970s? What sort of autonomy, if any, does Corinthian Democracy, or soccer in general, present with respect to the state and ideologies in Brazil?

The World Cup of 1970 vividly confirmed interpretations that looked upon soccer as a form of social manipulation. The Médici government, the most violent and repressive in the history of the dictatorship installed in 1964, went to great lengths to reap the political benefits of the national team's victory. Médici declared a national holiday in recognition of the victory, received the team in Brasília, was photographed with the Jules Remet trophy, and took it upon himself to reward each player with the equivalent of U.S. $18,500 tax free. In a speech shortly after the World Cup, Medici offered his own interpretation of the relationship between soccer and society in Brazil: "I identify this victory, achieved in the fraternity of sport, with the ascension of faith in our struggle for national development."[31]

The dictatorship felt compelled to do more than merely use soccer for propaganda purposes, however. After 1970 it began to take the game seriously, remaking the national team in its own image. Captain Claudio Coutinho was given the task of "modernizing" the Brazilian style of play and, as Joel Rufino dos Santos points out, his technique and goals betrayed a number of commonalities with the military's efforts to "modernize" the Brazilian economy.[32] In practice this modernization translated into an emphasis on discipline and obedience to the detriment of improvisation, on teamwork in place of individual expression, on physical force instead of art, and on imported technocratic jargon where popular wisdom had previously prevailed. In his article "A implantação de un modelo alienígena exótico e outras questões pertinentes: A Seleção Brasileira de futebol - 1978," the art critic Jacob Klintowitz shows how Coutinho made a point of avoiding players who, for one reason or another, were capable of calling into question this dull and authoritarian style of play, players such as Paulo César Caju, Marinho, Falcao, Serginho, and others who were "dribblers known for a happy style, or expressive."[33] Coutinho, observes Dos Santos, went so far as to define the "dribble, our speciality, 'as a waste of time and proof of our weakness.'"[34]

Given the success of Brazilian soccer in the fifties, sixties, and early seventies, it seems paradoxical that the government felt compelled to undertake such a drastic reformulation. In 1970, after all, Brazil had won its third of the four previous World Cups and was generally considered the country with the best soccer in the world. Pelé in turn was internationally recognized as the best player in the history of the game. One Argentine journalist put the difference between the 1978 team and those of previous decades in racial terms: "Pero, ¿dónde están los negritos? Cuando Brasil venía con unos negros bicudos jugaba bien; ahora vienen unos rubios de pelo largo y no juegan nada."[35]

Understandably, leftist intellectuals reacted strongly to the euphemistic, nationalistic propaganda that surrounded the 1970 World Cup, some even going so far as to root against the Brazilian squad.[36] To my queries about the period, for example, one Brazilian friend replied that "the cheers of the fans drown out the screams of the torture victims." The film P'ra Frente Brasil, which takes Brazil's 1970 World Cup victory march as a title, makes use of the same juxtaposition. If there were any doubts beforehand, it was clear to intellectuals by the end of the Cup that soccer, to use the Althusserian language of the period, served as an ideological state apparatus, the opium of the people, or some combination of the two. From a different political perspective, Janet Lever arrives at a not dissimilar conclusion, arguing that soccer in the Médici period facilitated national integration and buttressed the dictatorships, but that its political significance depends ultimately on one's opinion of the government's objectives.[37]

In light of abertura, the demilitarization of the 1982 World Cup team, and Corinthian Democracy, however, the relationship between politics and soccer--which seemed fairly clear in the 1970s--comes to appear more complex and can be interpreted in a different manner. What is significant in retrospect, in other words, is not so much the identity between the state, its ideologies, and soccer, but precisely the distance between the military regime and the nature of the game in Brazil; the fact that in spite of the success of the country's soccer, the government felt obliged to undertake a complete overhaul of this form of popular expression, attempting to alter what had come to be recognized as the Brazilian style of play, sometimes called "samba soccer" in the international press; from which it can perhaps be concluded that the dictatorship did not feel entirely comfortable with a form of play based on improvisation, individual prowess, irreverence--that is, filled with carnivalesque elements. Ultimately, the military proved incapable of absorbing the game's meaning and attempted, via militarization, to use soccer as a vehicle for another set of messages closer, much closer, to its own set of values and ideology.

Seen as a cultural form that expresses more than either facile nationalism or the gray neutrality of sheer alienation, the problem of popular identification with soccer in Brazil takes on a richer, more complex weave than that offered up in the "national integration" or "opium of the masses" theories, and remains unresolved. The opinion poll cited by Lever to the effect that 90 percent of Brazil's lower classes identified soccer with the nation in 1970, for example, does not answer, but rather raises, a question: With what nation? What is at issue, to put it another way, is not the fact that social and national identifications and identities are generated, in part, by way of *futebol*, but the content of these identities and the nature of soccer's role in their creation.[38]

An analysis that takes as its central element not the proximity but the distance between soccer and the military regime in the decade of the seventies finds support in certain recent treatments of Brazilian culture. Anthropologist Roberto Da Matta traces the importance of popular cultural manifestations in the creation of social and national identities in Brazil:

> If carnival, popular religiosity and soccer are in fact so basic in Brazil, everything would indicate that in contrast to certain European countries and North America, our sources of social identity are not institutions central to the social order, such as laws, the constitution, the university system, the financial order, etc., but rather certain activities which are taken as secondary sources of identity in the center and dominant countries.[39]

This reflects, on the one hand, the strength of popular cultural manifestations in the country, as well as, on the other, the weakness--at the level of social reproduction--of both the Brazilian state and of certain institutions typical of civil societies in Western capitalist countries. Wanderley Guilherme dos Santos, for example, concludes in his study of liberalism and the state in Brazil that:

> Aside from keeping a few radicals under control and aside from the use of police power to break up strikes, the state apparatus (in Brazil) is of little value and has never been seen as a strategic structure for social reproduction.[40]

Richard Morse, drawing on literary examples, registers the bourgeoisie's inability to impose an identity on Brazilian society:

> If today it takes three adjectives to divide the Brazilian bourgeoisie--national, international, bureaucratic--they are still walk-ons without hegemonic penetration. Their presence has not yet disenchanted Mário (de Andrade's) city (São Paulo), much less its salacious rival, Rio. In Mariátegui's terms, if the European bourgeoisie is crepuscular, the creole one is unauthentic.[41]

Finally, Da Matta goes on to point out that the identities created by popular culture on the one hand, and official institutions on the other, do not converge, but rather run parallel to each other:

> In comparison with the United States, we have, then, a relationship which is entirely inverted as well as very interesting from a sociological point of view. In the United States society is reproduced by way of its modern and individualistic civic structure which is identical to the nation and society. In Brazil, however, national identity is multiple. On the one hand it is produced at one social level by the popular institutions mentioned above (carnival, hospitality, umbanda, soccer, etc.). But, on the other hand, it continues to reproduce (although with difficulty), the North American and European models at the level of the "nation" and the "government," where such paradigms are obviously in force.[42]

It is, moreover, precisely this gap, the empty spaces between the multiplicity of identities Da Matta speaks of, that makes Corinthian Democracy so interesting: it draws on the unofficial, supposedly (and in fact) less than serious side of Brazilian culture in order to formulate an explicit critique of one of the country's serious sides--its political structure.

Corinthian Democracy assailed official culture on different flanks. It criticized the paternalism of the Brazilian soccer establishment as well as the authoritarianism of Brazilian society in general. The players established a sort of dialogue with the cheering masses of fans in the stands, entering the field during the deciding game of the 1982 São Paulo state championship with a banner that read: "Win of Lose, but Always with Democracy." Labor relations, club hierarchy, soccer tactics, national politics, and the internal regulations of the team were discussed among the players, as Corinthian Democracy took its place among the social movements that gained strength and form in the 1980s. In this sense, Corinthian Democracy was very much a product of the political liberalization underway in Brazil since the late 1970s. Prior to this time, players who called into question the policies of the soccer establishment or the practices of the military regime, "pre-Socratics,"[43] such as Reinaldo or Afonsinho, were, as Dos Santos shows, marginalized.[44] There was, particularly at the level of the national team, little room for independence or irreverence on or off the field between 1970 and 1978. *Abertura* changed this, permitting freer expression both in terms of political opinions and style of play. Corinthian Democracy took creative advantage of the new possibilities opened up by the political moment, dismantling some of the barriers between leisure and politics, play and seriousness.

Abertura, as Bernardo Kozinski among others has argued, was the product of crisis.[45] The end of the Brazilian "economic miracle," financial scandal, growing foreign debt, and inflation contributed to undermining whatever legitimacy the dictatorship might have had prior to the second half of the 1970s. Brazilian civil society took advantage of this breach in the authoritarianism of previous years, reorganizing itself. The labor movement, professional organizations, ecclesiastical base communities, housing associations, feminist groups, etc., came together and widened cracks that the military government was unable to plug. The crisis of authoritarianism posed a question that has long troubled not only Brazil, but almost all Latin American countries: The legitimacy of political representation. The military governments had attempted to legitimize themselves in power, in large part anyway, on the basis of force. The social movements and opposition parties that challenged the regime in recent years looked, not to force, but to an identity of objectives and goals with the Brazilian people, to representativity, as their major source of political legitimation. They claimed to express (and did to varying and unknown degrees) the needs and desires of *the people*--a central concept in recent years.

Attacking the dictatorship for its lack of representativity, the social movements and opposition parties of the *abertura* period called for increased popular political participation and posed, implicitly and explicitly, a question as yet unresolved: The basis and character of citizenship in the country.[46] "What are we?" asked Celso Furtado in a 1984 article on politics and culture; Afonso Romano de Sant'ana asked the same question with the title of a recent book: "What Country Is This?" (*Que país é esse?*), as did Roberto Da Matta with his "What Makes Brazil, Brazil?" (*O que faz Brasil o Brasil?*).[47] It is probably not by chance that re-examination of the identity and fundamental values of Brazilian society are appearing with increased frequency in recent years. The imminent political reorganization of the country urges a discussion of what it means (or should, or might) to be a Brazilian citizen.

Implicitly, Corinthian Democracy answered the "What Country Is This?" question as follows: One of soccer fans and players. Which is not to say that soccer (or carnival, or samba, etc.) is all that Brazilians know how to do, but rather that they take the game seriously as a source of identity and form of expression. With this response, Corinthian Democracy added its contribution to the political debate of the moment, broadening the concept of Brazilian citizenship to the point where it could incorporate social and national identities generated by popular cultural expressions, in this case soccer. In a sense, this was nothing new. Soccer has long served as one of the many forms of "unofficial" citizenship in a country that has had difficulty realizing official forms. For decades Brazilians--or at least segments of Brazilian society--have recognized themselves as such based on a common identification with soccer and the way it is played in the country. The specific contribution of Corinthian

Democracy on this score was to legitimate what had been unofficial, taking advantage of the carnivalesque climate of the free elections to do so.

Corinthian Democracy reached its apotheosis at the April 1984 free election rally in São Paulo, a few days before the Congressional vote on the constitutional amendment re-establishing free elections was scheduled to take place. Sócrates, moved by the event, and speaking before some 1,500,000 people, pledged that were the amendment to pass he would refuse a million-dollar offer to play in Italy and stay in Brazil to participate in the reconstruction of democracy. It was a polemical gesture, criticized by many as demagogic, but absolutely consistent with Corinthian Democracy. As a representative who gave voice to at least certain popular aspirations, he felt obligated (excited might be a better word) to stay in the country and help finish what he had helped start. Those who considered the vow demagogic betrayed, in the final analysis, discomfort with a player who drew on the identification and legitimacy generated by soccer to make a political statement.

The free elections amendment did not pass. Sócrates went to play for Fiorentina in Florence, where he spent part of his time auditing political science classes. Apparently he had difficulty adapting to the Italian style of play and made the following assessment of Italian soccer: "The players are excellent professionals, but their game lacks joy."[48] Casagrande, another symbol of Corinthian Democracy, was lent to the São Paulo Futebol Club. He watched the Corinthians lose the 1984 São Paulo state championship to Santos in the final; the television cameras picked him out in the stands, crying amidst the crowd.

Corinthian Democracy faded into the background together with the free elections campaign in Brazil. Its future as a movement is unknown.[49] It made its mark, leaving behind a sense that soccer in Brazil would never be quite the same. Corinthian Democracy added a new dimension to the sociability that revolves around *futebol* in São Paulo and in Brazil. In the press, on the radio, on television before and after games, and in bars--principally in bars--throughout the city, fans, journalists, and announcers discussed whether or not soccer belonged in politics. Following the lead of the Corinthians, teams throughout the country developed movements supporting the free elections campaign.[50] Intellectuals who had been skeptical of the nature of the game's influence in society found themselves obliged to look at it in a slightly different light.

Soccer in Brazil would never be quite the same after Corinthian Democracy . . . or would it? Those who continued to see soccer as little more than the opium of the masses tended to consider Dr. Sócrates almost entirely responsible for a movement that represented "the exception that proved the rule." In the wake of Corinthian Democracy, however, it became more difficult to ignore the force of soccer--and of popular cultural manifestations in general--in Brazilian society. *Futebol* invaded politics, traditionally the terrain of elites in the country. In doing so, it revealed (paradoxically) an autonomy vis-á-vis political structures that has been overlooked, in large part, by intellectuals concerned with the relationship of popular culture and power, popular culture and ideology. This autonomy, moreover, obliges a recasting of the notion that soccer integrates the nation: if it does so in fact, it is in a manner not necessarily in tune with the integration carried out by dominant political and economic structures.

The history of soccer in Brazil is such that it ended up as more than a sport. Closer to carnival, it has generated an identity that has served as a sort of unofficial citizenship in the country. A form of cultural expression, *futebol* interprets the world around it, but the aesthetic dimension of the game as it is played in Brazil has been all but ignored by analysts of sport and society. The result is a sociological analysis of a cultural manifestation that ignores content and form, and consequently collapses culture into politics and economics. Corinthian Democracy was able to draw on the tradition of the game and on the identity generated by soccer in Brazil to effect its political critique precisely because it did not make this same mistake . . . and because Sócrates, Casagrande, Wladimir & Co. played great soccer.

Notes

1   According to Wadih Helu, a former president of the club, cited in "A vitória da Democracia," *Placar* (11 March 1982): 15.

2   Robert M. Levine, "Brazil: The Dimensions of Democracy," *Current History* (February 1982): 60-63, 86-87.

3   "A vitória da Democracia," p. 14.

4   Janet Lever, *A loucura do futebol* (Rio de Janeiro, 1983), pp. 85-86.

5   Lever provides further examples in Ibid., p. 90.

6   "A vitória da Democracia," pp. 14-15.

7   Ibid., p. 14.

8   "Corinthians, ou o sonho que não acabou," *Placar* (11 March 1982): 37.

9   "O futebol no Brasil," *Argumento* 4: 61-86.

10   The magazine *Placar*, formerly dedicated almost exclusively to soccer, has recently changed its format to become, in its own words, "the magazine of all sports in Brazil."

11   *Capoeira* is a dance/fight practiced originally by slaves in Brazil. It is performed as a show, used as a form of self-defense, and is currently practiced in competition. The question is to what extent or in what sense it can (or should) be considered a sport.

12   Mário Filho, *O negro no futebol brasileiro*, 2nd ed. (Rio de Janeiro, 1962); Rosenfeld, "O futebol no Brasil"; Gilberto Freyre, *Sociologia* (Rio de Janeiro, 1945); and Freyre's preface to the Filho volume.

13   "O futebol no Brasil," p. 61.

14   Freyre, *Sociologia*, cited in Rosenfeld, "O futebol no Brasil," p. 82.

15   *Folha de São Paulo* (13 February 1983): 23.

16   Paiva, "Corinthians, ou o sonho que não acabou," p. 37.

17   Cited in Gilberto Vasconcellos and Matinas Suzuki, Jr., "A maladragem e a formação da música popular brasileira," in *Historia geral da civilização brasileira, III: O Brasil republicano, Vol. 4, Economia e cultura (1930-1964)*, ed. Boris Fausto (São Paulo, 1984), p. 508.

18   Ibid., p. 505.

19   Ibid., p. 510.

20   Ibid., p. 513. See also Florestan Fernandes, *A integração do negro na sociedade de classes*, 2nd ed. (São Paulo, 1977), and José de Souza Martins, *O cativeiro da terra* (São Paulo, 1980).

21   On carnival see José Carlos Sebe, *Carnaval, carnavais* (São Paulo, in press). On Umbanda in this period, see Renato Ortiz, *A norte branca do feiticeiro negro* (Petrópolis, 1981). On soccer see Filho, *O negro no futebol brasileiro*, and Joel Rufino dos Santos, *História política do futebol brasileiro* (São Paulo, 1982).

22   Filho, *O negro no futebol brasileiro*; see also Robert M. Levine, "Esporte e sociedade: o caso do futebol brasileiro," in *Futebol e cultura: coletanea*, eds. José Sebastião Witter and José Carlos Sebe (São Paulo, 1982).

23   See Rosenfeld, "O futebol no Brasil."

24   For Leonidas, see Rosenfeld, "O futebol no Brasil"; for Garrincha, see Telmo Zanini, *Mané Garrincha: o anjo torto* (São Paulo, 1984). There is good material on Pelé's style of play in Armando Nogueira, *Bola na rede*, 2nd ed. (Rio de Janeiro, 1974).

25   Roberto Da Matta, "Futebol: opio do povo vs. drama social," *Novos Estudos Cebrap*, 1:4 (1982): 60.

26   Zanini, *Mané Garrincha*, p. 27.

27   Alastair Reid, "The Sporting Scene," *The New Yorker* (1 November 1982): 118.

28   *Sport and the Spirit of Play in American Fiction: Hawthorne to Faulkner* (New York, 1981), p. 2.

29   Ibid.

30   The "opium of the people" thesis is difficult to find in the Brazilian literature on soccer. It is sufficiently commonplace, however, to draw responses from Da Matta in "Futebol"; Paiva in "Corinthians"; and Juca Kfouri in *A emoção Corinthians* (São Paulo, 1983). Roberto Ramos, *Futebol: ideologia do poder* (Petrópolis, 1984) takes to extremes the "soccer as a state ideological apparatus" argument. The best formulation of the national integration thesis is found in Lever, *A loucura do futebol*.

31   Lever, *A loucura do futebol*, p. 92.

32   Rufino Dos Santos, "Na CBD até o papagaio bate continencia," *Encontros com a Civilização Brasileira* 5 (December 1978): 121.

33   In *Encontros com a Civilização Brasileira* 5 (December 1978): 115-16.

34   Dos Santos, "Na CBD," p. 121. On the militarization of soccer in Brazil in the 1970s, see also Isney Savoy and Júlio Cezar Garcia, "No país do futebol," *Retrato do Brasil* 19 (1984): 217-22.

35   Cited in Rufino Dos Santos, "Na CBD," p. 122.

36   This was a fairly common attitude among certain sectors of the left in this period. Fernando Gabeira, *O que é isso, companheiro* (Rio de Janeiro, 1980) offers some interesting insights into the left and Brazilian soccer in the late 1960s.

37   Lever, *O loucura do futebol*, pp. 194-98.

38   Ibid., p. 197.

39   "Futebol," p. 60.

40   *Ordem burguesa e liberalismo político* (São Paulo, 1978), p. 115.

41   Richard Morse, "Brazilianists, God Bless'em! What in the World Is to Be Done?" *Stanford/Berkeley Occasional Papers in Latin American Studies* 5 (Winter 1983): 7. For a more developed treatment of the same point see Morse's *El espejo de Próspero* (Mexico City, 1983).

42   Da Matta, "Futebol," p. 60.

43   Thanks to Milton Lahuerta for this term.

44   Dos Santos, "Na CBD"; Levine, "Esporte e sociedade," p. 37. See the interview with Sócrates and Afonsinho in the Bar do Bexiga, reported in Chico Malfitani, "Sócrates e Afonsinho, douteres em liberdade," *Folha de São Paulo* (10 June 1984).

45   Bernardo Kozinski, *Abertura, história de uma crise* (São Paulo, 1982).

46   On social movements and citizenship, see Eunice Ribeiro Durham, "Movimentos sociais, a construção da cidadania," *Novos Estudos Cebrap* 10 (October 1984): 24-31.

47   Betty Milan cites these titles as a case of "symptomatic repetition" that reveals the intelligentsia's inability to resolve the question of identity; *Isso é o país* (São Paulo, 1984).

48   "Fiorentina não libera Sócrates," *Folha de São Paulo* (31 January 1985): 38.

49   After three games without a victory, an article appeared in the local press calling for the "de-bureaucratization" of Corinthian Democracy; Matinas Suzuki, Jr., "Adílson deve pensar em abrir uma 'Burocracia Corintiana,'" *Folha de São Paulo* (4 March 1985): 20.

50   Carlos Maranhão, "O futebol entrou na festa," *Placar* (3 February 1984): 24-27.

7
Sport in Revolutionary Societies: Cuba and Nicaragua
Eric A. Wagner

Cuba and Nicaragua have long Spanish colonial traditions, nearly a century of substantial political and economic influence and intervention by the United States, and a socialist way of life brought about by revolutionary means. Both also have a passion for the same national sport--baseball. These two societies are dissimilar, however, in the recency of their revolutions and in the scope of popular involvement in their insurrections. Cuba now has a revolutionary experience that spans a quarter of a century, and a clearly elaborated social structure. Nicaragua has an experience of only a few years with its revolution, and it is not yet clear how society will ultimately be organized. Cuba's "new" government came to power after a relatively short insurrection in which only a small fraction of the population was involved, while the Sandinistas assumed control after a long, bloody insurrection that effectively mobilized most Nicaraguans. Comparing sport in these two countries requires an awareness of both these similarities and differences.

My purpose in this chapter is to describe and analyze the social aspects of sport in Cuba and Nicaragua. I hope to explore the evolution of sport in these societies, participation in sport, and the way in which sport is organized and controlled. I will attempt to show how sport contributes to social divisiveness and/or integration, the effects of foreign penetration on sport, the political uses of sport, and class, sex, age, and urban/rural divisions evident in sport in these countries. Because it is the dominant sport in each country, baseball will be the focus of much of my attention.

Revolution is a key variable in this analysis, because it alters the nature of a society fundamentally. Two aspects of revolution are important for our purposes: the insurrectionary phase in which some members of a society overthrow the established order, and the revolutionary phase in which basic social institutions are changed. The latter involves a reallocation of resources toward the mass of people who have previously been exploited.

In Cuba, the direct roots of revolution were relatively short, essentially extending from 1953 to 1959. Indirect roots go back much further, to the Cuban colonial experience with Spain, slavery, and dependence on a sugar cane economy. Independence came late to Cuba, in 1898, almost a century after most of the rest of Latin America. But independence was more in name than in fact, as Cuba simply exchanged dependence on Spain for dependence on the United States. Strong bonds with the United States led eventually to a very stratified class structure. By 1933, "about sixty percent of the Cuban people were living at a submarginal level."[1] Governments came and went, heavily influenced by the economic and political interests of the United States. Politics was a pastime of the upper classes, and political changes generally did not concern the masses. Thus when Fidel Castro and his supporters began their opposition to the Batista regime in 1953, most Cubans took little notice. For the next five years, Fidel and his small band of followers, generally numbering fewer than one thousand, waged intermittent guerrilla warfare against the Batista government in Havana. This warfare was primarily rural. By the time Batista fled into exile the last night of 1958, allowing Castro to assume power, most Cubans had not been involved in the insurrection.

In Nicaragua, most people were involved. Such involvement had deep roots in Nicaragua's history. During the centuries when Nicaragua was a colony of Spain, land and wealth were concentrated in the hands of a small minority. With independence in 1838, little changed, except that now the minority had control of the government. Over the next seventy years, Liberal and Conservative factions squabbled over political control, and the possibility of a canal through Nicaragua led to heightened interest in this country by the United States. Throughout this period, and especially in 1881, rural poor opposed the increasing takeover of their lands by the rich. For most of the time from 1912 to 1933, Nicaragua was occupied by U.S. troops in an attempt to bring about pro-U.S. stability. Many nationalistic rural poor opposed this occupation by a foreign force, and engaged in guerrilla warfare, which from 1927 to 1933 was headed by Augusto César Sandino. In 1933, the United Stated withdrew its troops, having trained a National Guard to maintain law and order. The head of the National Guard, Anastasio Somoza García, soon seized control of the government and established a family dictatorship, which lasted until 1979. Sandino was murdered in 1934, but his ideals of rural guerrilla warfare and devotion to the peasants lived on.

For the next forty years, peasant unrest smoldered and occasionally flared into activity. As the atrocities and brutality of the Somoza regime grew, so did the opposition. By 1975 peasants had been joined by many of the urban poor in their opposition to the Somozas, and by the late 1970s even many among the middle and upper classes had joined the insurrection. By 1978, it is fair to say that the vast majority of the Nicaraguan people were in revolt against the Somoza government. Faced with overwhelming opposition, Somoza fled the country in July 1979, and the Sandinistas took control.

Fidel Castro took over a Cuba in which there was only slight damage to the physical infrastructure of the society, while the Sandinistas took over a country in which a substantial portion of the infrastructure had been destroyed. In Nicaragua, nearly everyone was mobilized and active during the final months of the insurrection. In Cuba, only a small minority was deeply involved in the insurrection against Batista, and most of these activists operated in the rural areas. With the structure of society essentially intact, Castro had time to consider changes in the organization of sport, and it was several years before sport received substantial attention from his government. The National Institute of Sport, Physical Education, and Recreation (INDER) was founded in late February 1961, more than two years after Fidel Castro seized power.

Nicaragua was another matter. Most of the sport installations in the country were damaged. The country emerged from the insurrection without trainers, without fields, without sports equipment. Yet when I was in Nicaragua in August and September 1980, the Nicaraguan Institute of Sports was functioning, and neighborhood-level sports committees had been established in a number of cities. Much of the local organizing for sport had taken place spontaneously, without direction from above.

What effect does a revolutionary framework have on sport? Sport is a deeply entrenched social institution, and revolution is not likely to change fundamental interests in sport. People who have been involved in sport continue to be involved. However, the nature and level of this involvement is likely to be affected by the revolutionary experience, and in a revolutionary society there may be more opportunity to rise and diversify. The revolutionary experiences of Cuba and Nicaragua were different, and this has affected involvement in sport. Most Cuban people, without active insurrectionary participation, waited for sport to be brought to them by the government. When it did come, sport could be structured in ways that supported wide social and political goals of the government. This structure, fashioned from the top, led to more elite, more political sport, designed to enhance Cuba's international image. In Nicaragua, the masses, especially poor people, were central to the insurrection and had been actively involved; and "to a greater degree than in Cuba, the widespread insurrection in Nicaragua blurred the urban-rural dichotomy almost entirely."[2] With success, the Nicaraguan people did not wait for the government to organize society. Instead they began setting up their own grassroots organizations, in areas such as education, public sanitation, police protection, and especially recreation and sport. Local sports organizations, and local competitions, were formed before there was any coherent national structure within which they could operate. This, I would contend, is likely to lead to a sports structure that is more attuned to needs from below than to decisions from the top. If this proves prophetic, then Nicaraguan sport is more likely to lead to mass involvement, and less likely to lead to elite, political sport used to enhance Nicaragua's international image.

Other aspects of sport also may stem from the revolutionary experience. In Nicaragua, women were heavily involved in insurrectionary activities and quickly served notice that they intended to be a part of all phases of the "new" Nicaraguan society.[3] Would this extend to sport, an institution in which they had had only limited participation? Cuban women have expanded their role in socialist Cuba, but their participation in sport still lags substantially behind that of men.[4] Is sport a key factor in providing social cohesion, as Janet Lever puts it, a basic element in helping "complex modern societies cohere"?[5] In revolutionary societies, where many of the basic structures of society have been swept asunder by the chaos of insurrection and revolutionary change, one certainly could agree that the conservative nature of the stable values and interests of sport would have a cohesive effect. Certainly in Cuba that proved to be the case, providing that country with a focus and a success around which Cubans could rally. But what was the price of this cohesion? Was it a façade to mask serious economic and social problems, or did it enhance meaning and give worth to peoples' lives? In Nicaragua, baseball has been maintained and supported, as Edgard Tijerino Mantilla puts it, at the insistence of the people.[6] Is this to provide a familiar structure, an opiate as some would call it, to help maintain order and support during the difficult years of building a revolution? Clearly, sport can have cohesive qualities. But it can also be devisive, to the extent that it distracts the attention of the people from pressing social problems or authoritarian political control. To amplify these questions, we need to examine the development and organization of sport in Cuba and Nicaragua.

Development of Sport

The roots of sport go back to antiquity. Long before Europeans set foot in the New World, there were various forms of games, often linked to religious celebrations. Throughout Mesoamerica, ball-game ceremonies were held. Versions of the games varied, depending on time and location. "In one version, players, always members of the priestly or military elite, may have passed a rubber ball through a narrow stone hoop set in a ball-court wall."[7] Over time, these games became more secular and were played for recreation and entertainment. While we know little of the rules of such games, the archaeological remains of a large number of ball courts make it clear that the games were widespread. Other sport activities, such as games of chance using dice, and running events also took place. How widespread these events were in pre-Columbian Nicaragua we do not know; little is known of daily life in that country prior to the coming of the Europeans.

Daily life in precolonial Cuba is likewise mostly unknown. There were, however, several ancient games, though we know little about the extent to which they were played or their rules and organization. One of these was a game utilizing a stick, a ball, and bases of stone, perhaps a precursor of modern baseball. The other game was similar to soccer, with two groups of players sending a ball back and forth by kicking it or hitting it with various parts of the body.[8] These games mostly died out before or during the early colonial period, as the colonial literature about Cuba makes virtually no reference to them. It is likely, as happened with the Puritans in North America, that the early colonial emphasis on bringing Christianity to the New World led to an elimination of those aspects of the culture that might have been viewed as part of native religions. Most of these games/sports did originate as part of religious observances, and the Spaniards may therefore have frowned upon them.

During the centuries of colonialism in Cuba and Nicaragua there was little attention to sport, and almost no mention of it in the literature. Several reasons for this seem probable. First, the native inhabitants of these areas, numbering in the hundreds of thousands at the time of the arrival of the Spanish, and perhaps a million in Nicaragua, were quickly decimated through disease and slavery, and many of their customs and pastimes died with them.[9] Second, endless labor for their masters left the common people with no time or energy for pastimes such as sports. It seems likely that native sports simply died out.

In the middle of the nineteenth century, modern sports began to be disseminated, primarily from England, to the rest of the world. The whole nature of sport appears to have changed, from the connection of primitive sport and religion, and sport and a warrior ethos, and the later connection of sport and preparation for combat in feudal Europe, to a sport based on the modern British ideas of sportsmanship, of fairness, and of sport as a recreational pastime. Cuba and Nicaragua were very much a part of this global process of the dissemination of modern sport. However, they differed in several important respects from the rest of Latin America. For most of the world, and for Latin America, sport was brought by the British through their colonial and neo-colonial contacts. Generally, this was not a conscious process, but occurred by chance; often it was by British sailors. Having learned the rapidly expanding game of soccer in England, they sometimes played it in the port cities they visited. Latin American workers in the dock areas joined in and learned the game. With incipient urbanization and increasing leisure, the situation was ripe for a new pastime, and soccer spread rapidly in ports such as Rio de Janeiro, Santos (São Paulo), Montevideo, Buenos Aires, Valparaíso (Santiago), and Callao/Lima. In all of these places, England had substantial commercial interests, and contacts were frequent.

In Cuba and Nicaragua, contacts were not so much with the British as with North Americans. It was North America that had used Nicaragua as a place to cross the Central American isthmus in the years following the California gold rush, and it was an American adventurer--William Walker--who briefly took over Nicaragua in 1855. American interest in that country continued and grew, as did American interest in Cuba, where United States investments were increasing. In the 1860s in Cuba, and sometime prior to the 1890s in Nicaragua, baseball was introduced and took hold. Modern sport, once firmly set in the society, became a major institution that is hard to modify. Thus Cuba and Nicaragua, unlike much of the rest of Latin America, had planted in their soils the seeds of baseball from the United States, rather than the seeds of soccer from England. The seeds would soon be nourished and grow rapidly.

Cuba and Nicaragua also differ from most of the rest of Latin America in another respect. Soccer, brought to port cities that were growing rapidly, became primarily an urban game, and only later spread into the countryside. Steve Stein shows that the growth of soccer and urbanization were closely linked in Peru,[10] and Janet Lever argues that soccer clubs in Brazil were "important in helping newcomers adjust to city life."[11] Soccer became an entertainment for the masses, and these masses were located in urban areas. Baseball is a more pastoral, rural game, played in the countryside more than in the city. In Nicaragua and Cuba, the countryside provides baseball's most passionate adherents. One might well argue that baseball took hold so easily in Nicaragua and Cuba precisely because these were rural societies that were not beginning the urbanization process taking hold in Argentina, Brazil, Uruguay, Chile, and Peru, the countries of Latin America where soccer was spreading most rapidly. It is true that Havana in the late nineteenth century was a growing city, but baseball began not in Havana but in Matanzas, a provincial town about fifty miles east of Havana. To this day, baseball as a counter to the "big city" is one of the joys of the rural provinces.

Luis Hernández argues that baseball first came to Cuba in 1864, when a Cuban by the name of Nemesio Guillot, who had been studying in the United States, brought a bat and ball with him when he returned from his studies.[12] When a ship from the United States docked in Matanzas in 1866, the crew invited the Cuban cargo handlers to play baseball with them.[13] The game spread quickly, and organized play began. Teams and leagues were set up, and the first Cuban baseball championship was held in 1878.[14] Passion for baseball swept the country, and it became a major part of Cuban society. Significantly, it was a game of the common people, and they cling to it even now.

Although baseball dominated sports for the masses in the pre-revolutionary period in Cuba, there were other sports activities. Cuba was one of the early participants in the modern Olympics, first fielding a team in 1900, when a Cuban won a gold medal in fencing. This was followed by additional individual and team medals in fencing at the 1904 Olympic Games. While Cubans participated in several other Olympics prior to the triumph of Fidel Castro in 1959 and had an excellent sprinter at the 1948 Games in London, they won no more medals. In addition to its Olympic participation, "Cuba was one of the three founder members of the inaugural Central American and Caribbean Games."[15] Cuba also has a substantial history of activity in chess, starting at least as early as the 1850s. (In Latin America, chess is often regarded as a sport, and it will be so treated in this chapter.) There were a number of notable Cuban chess players, and one Cuban--José Raul Capablanca--is regarded by many chess experts as "the greatest player of all time."[16] Today, a Capablanca memorial tournament is held annually in Cuba, and chess almost always has several pages of the Cuban sports weekly *Semanario Deportivo LPV* (*Sports Weekly LPV*, with LPV [*listos para vencer*] meaning "willing to win" or "ready to win") devoted to it. Boxing was also popular among the lower classes, who saw professional boxing as a possible road to riches. Except for boxing and baseball, amateur sports in Cuba were pretty much dominated by the more well off members of society. This would change when Fidel Castro seized power.

In Nicaragua, literature on the development of sport prior to the Sandinista revolution in 1979 is virtually non-existent. Baseball, we know, began prior to 1890, because by the 1890s baseball leagues were well organized in Nicaragua, and results were reported regularly in the newspapers.[17] By the middle of the twentieth century, baseball was played everywhere in Nicaragua, even among the Miskito Indians of the Atlantic coast.[18] Boxing was also popular among the people, as was soccer, though neither of these sports approached the popularity of baseball. Volleyball, swimming, basketball, table tennis, track, chess, and softball were also played by some Nicaraguans. However, nothing rivaled interest in baseball; Nicaraguans were (and are) crazy about baseball. On Sundays, thousands of Nicaraguans headed to the baseball fields. Everyone loved it, but especially the rural poor. "Among the poorest of the rural agricultural workers, in little towns like San Juan Oriente near Masaya, baseball was a matter of enormous interest."[19] For the rich, there was golf in Managua, but the course was changed to other uses when the Sandinistas came to power.

The Organization of Sport

The coming to power of revolutionary governments in Cuba and Nicaragua brought about a new structure for sport. In Cuba, there was a two-year transitional phase from 1959 to 1961, when sport was managed by a general sports directorate. This gave way in 1961 to the National Institute of Sports, Physical Education, and Recreation (INDER), which became the top sports organization in Cuba, and continues as such to this day. Its headquarters are in Ciudad Deportiva (Sport City), a suburban part of metropolitan Havana. Clustered in Sport City are a large number of facilities for the athletes of the Havana area, as well as most of the high level sports research institutes in Cuba. The National Training Center is here, various sports schools, and the National Institute for Sports Medicine. According to the law by which INDER was established, its functions are "to develop a valid system of national physical education and sport, to prepare regulations and rules for developing Cuba's sport under specific recognition of recreation, school sports at all levels, athletics, teaching and research in sport and sportive competition on all levels, as well as to secure a qualitative organization of all projects."[20] Over the past twenty or more years, INDER has made major strides in carrying out these goals. Both scholastic and military physical education was promoted intensively, and tests of physical ability have become a standard part of Cuban school and military life. Professional sport was abolished in 1962, with the argument "that professionalism is a typical phenomenon of capitalism, since it is an exploitation of individuals and, therefore, does not have a place in a socialistic state."[21] INDER also worked hard to promote a sporting goods industry, since sports equipment was cut off by the United States economic blockade of Cuba, and abolished entrance fees at sporting events in 1967.[22] Today, Cubans are able to enjoy sports events free of charge, and this has certainly not hurt the popularity of organized baseball in Cuba.

Providing sport for all Cubans was one of INDER's chief goals. Since this goal required large numbers of teachers and trainers, Cuba at first had to rely on experts sent from the Soviet Union, the German Democratic Republic, and Czechoslovakia, and on sending Cubans to these countries to study. In 1964, a College of Physical Education opened in Cuba, which has now graduated about 10,000 sports teachers and trainers. Research is quite active, and Cuban scholars often prepare papers for international audiences. More than a dozen Cubans were scheduled to present papers at the Olympic Scientific Congress in Eugene, Oregon, in July 1984, but did not attend because of complications surrounding the Soviet-bloc boycott of the 1984 Olympics in Los Angeles. In schools, sport is emphasized, and time, adequate facilities, and trained teachers are all provided. Students in schools, at universities (for the first three years), and those in the armed forces must participate in sport or physical education. I observed one large primary school in Santiago de Cuba, where each day forty-five minutes were devoted to sport and physical education. During this time six physical education teachers and one gymnastics instructor taught the fundamentals of twenty-six different sports.[23] In addition to providing national-level facilities and training, there are branches of INDER in each of the fourteen provinces and on the Isle of Youth. Each of these provinces also has children's schools which specialize in sport and physical education. At the provincial and local level, INDER helps organize and coordinate, with the cooperation of labor unions and other organizations, local voluntary sports councils. They organize sports and physical recreation in factories, schools, local neighborhoods, universities, and military units.[24] What is interesting about the high level of organized sports activity in Cuba is that "sport has been incorporated into other social institutions; . . . factories and worker groups, schools and universities, the armed forces, and rural groups all are active in organizing sports activities."[25]

Nicaragua has not yet progressed to the level of having sport activities substantially integrated into other social institutions. Some of these, of course, do occur, but the organization of sport in Nicaragua, like its revolution, is much more recent, and has not yet been clearly and comprehensively articulated into the social structure. The new structure for sports is in clear contrast to the level of organization that existed prior to the revolution. Then, a General Directorate of Physical Education and Sport came under the Ministry of Education and was not given much emphasis. Sports federations and the Nicaraguan Olympic Committee were mostly under the effective control of high ranking military officers. With the assumption of control by the Sandinistas, sport was placed under the Ministry of Culture, headed by a Catholic priest. The Ministry directs sport through an Advisory Committee, which has responsibility for both the Nicaraguan Olympic Committee and the Institute of Sports. This Advisory Committee includes representatives from the Institute of Sports, the Olympic Committee, and others. The Olympic Committee, formed in January 1980, is headed by Moisés Hassan, who served on the governmental Junta. Among the other members of the Olympic Committee are four vice presidents (the coordinator of the basketball federation, a member of the track federation, a director of the baseball federation who also happens to be the Minister of Defense, and a member of the cycling federation who also serves as the Vice Minister of Planning), a treasurer (who is a planning adviser in the Ministry of Education), the Director of the Institute of Sports, and a number of other members. With so many key officials involved, it is clear that sport is strongly supported by the government. Under the Olympic Committee (but functioning relatively autonomously) are the national federations for sixteen different sports: baseball, soccer, basketball, boxing, track and field, cycling, judo, billiards, weightlifting, swimming, tennis, motorcycling, softball, table tennis, volleyball, and chess.[26]

The Institute of Sports, directed by former *La Prensa* sports editor Edgard Tijerino Mantilla, was founded in September 1979, fewer than two months after the Sandinistas seized power. Thus Nicaragua acted more quickly than Cuba in establishing a permanent structure for sport. The Institute of Sports is divided into four main operating units-- administration, sports activities, physical education and recreation, and voluntary sports committees (CVDs). The sports activities unit maintains close liaison and coordination with the sixteen Nicaraguan sports federations, while the physical education and recreation unit fosters games and recreation for youth in neighborhood settings. The unit dealing with voluntary sports committees, the CVDs, is perhaps the most interesting. The CVDs mostly appeared spontaneously, as outgrowths of the defense committees that had been established by local groups during the insurrectionary phase of the revolution. Hundreds of the CVDs had been established in the first year of Sandinista Nicaragua. They were actively pursuing mass involvement of the people in sports, sports facilities (particularly baseball fields), and organizing leagues and tournaments.[27] Much of this activity occurred before the Institute of Sports became organized and active, leading to much decision-making and organization at the grassroots level, and acquiescence at departmental and national levels, rather than the more common procedure of organization from the top down. Whether this high level of local organization and control can continue remains to be seen; however, the keen interest of many high government leaders in sport makes continuing local control somewhat unlikely. Also of interest in this structure is the lack of close organizational coordination between sport and education. Nicaragua's sport structure is to a substantial degree modeled on that of Cuba, where such coordination is quite evident.

Below the national-level Institute of Sports are departmental sports councils, one in each of Nicaragua's sixteen departments. The two primary functions of these councils are to coordinate the various sports activities in the departments with local sections of each of the national sport federations, and to oversee and coordinate the activities of the voluntary sports committees, the CVDs. Each of these local CVDs has local volunteers who take responsibility for an individual sport. Thus the staffing of Nicaragua's burgeoning sport activities is mostly handled by volunteers at the local level, and many of the ideas, plans, and competitions originate there. In addition to organizing formal sports activities, it is at the local level that most of the work for children's recreation takes place. "These activities were organized under the 'Plan de la Calle' [Plan of the Street], and obviously modeled after the Cuban plan of the same name."[28] Included in this plan for childhood recreation are a number of games designed to teach children the physical movements prerequisite for effective sports activity in later years, and to form "from the earliest ages good social habits and the love of sport."[29] "Specific objectives were: (1) to make possible through different games the participation of masses of youth in recreational activities that would satisfy the needs of their age; (2) to facilitate a program of extracurricular activities as a continuity to physical education programs; (3) to develop through games and sports socially acceptable habits, such as respect for established laws, discipline, self-control, collectivism, and a sense of responsibility; (4) to use dynamic elements in a child's free time to help contribute to physical, social, and intellectual development; and, (5) to give an opportunity to children to help contribute to socio-political and ideological development."[30] In fact, much of the structure of sport in Nicaragua at both the local and national levels was modeled after that of Cuba. This is not surprising, since the key technical adviser in sport to the Nicaraguan government was Raul Noda, a Cuban who headed the Havana sports committee.

Sports Today

Contemporary Cuban sport appears to have two main emphases. First, there is a strong push to get young children in both the local neighborhoods and the schools involved in physical education and sport activities. Through the process of mass socialization into sport at an age when lifelong habits are being formed, it is hoped that adult Cubans will continue their involvement in physical recreation. To encourage and support these habits, organizations such as factories, labor unions, the armed forces, local neighborhoods, and even service organizations such as hospitals encourage active sport participation. Second, Cuba sees sport as a way to gain international recognition and prestige, to show the world that the "Cuban social system" is successful. Therefore, great emphasis is placed on elite sports, on winning tournaments, and on making strong showings in international competitions. International success in sports is also a major means by which the Cuban government hopes to gain continued support from the people, by constantly reminding them of the endless successes of their system of sport. When reading through hundreds of issues of the weekly sports magazine *Semanario Deportivo LPV*, which is published by the government, I was struck by the great emphasis on tournaments, both national and international, and the incessant reporting of the constantly improving record of Cuban sports, and the success of the Cuban system. This emphasis has been quite consistent from the late 1960s to the most recent issue (October 1984) I have seen. Even the initials LPV in the title of this magazine echo the theme. As noted, LPV stands for *"listos para vencer,"* generally translated as "willing to win" or "ready to win."

In many respects, the first goal feeds into the second. By introducing all young Cuban children to sport, and by making specialized sport schools and training available to those whose tests show strong athletic potential, Cuba is building the base that will enable it to select only the best for international competition. However, the great emphasis placed on international success may not be fully matched by a commitment to life-long sport participation. There is a great deal of rhetoric about adult sport participation in Cuba, but I was often struck by the number of adult Cubans who complained to me that if one weren't good in sports, the authorities didn't seem especially interested in providing facilities and opportunities to play. Elite athletes and national teams always had priority in facilities, equipment, and support.

Data on sports participation in Cuba tends to confirm these observations. In interviews with 105 people in Cuba in 1981, I found that 77 percent of those under age twenty participated actively in sport (active being defined as participating on the average at least once a week). For those between twenty and forty, participation ranged from 40 to 60 percent, which is reasonably high. Beyond age forty, participation was low, less than 20 percent. Such data is difficult to assess, for two reasons. First, the sample is small and not completely representative (males, urbanites, and older people tend to be slightly overrepresented). Second, those over age forty went to school before Cuba's socialist exposure to sport activities. Pickering shows that in 1975, 2,136,466 people participated in school sports, and 1,367,964 people participated in sports in general (presumably non-school sports).[31] Out of a population of between eight and nine million people at that time, his figures are roughly comparable to mine in terms of sport participation. Looking at participation by sex, I found that 70 percent of males and 32 percent of females are actively involved in sport. While my sample is not large enough for statistical analysis of female participation by age, my observations in Cuba make it clear that active sport participation by women beyond the school years was quite low. Sport participation by residence and social class in Cuba conforms to patterns that have been widely reported in the literature.[32] Urban residents participate more frequently (57 percent) than do rural residents (50 percent), and upper/middle class respondents participate much more often (73 percent) than do working/lower class respondents (48 percent).[33]

Which sports are most popular today in Cuba? Of the 105 Cubans whom I interviewed, forty-six did not participate in sports. Of those fifty-nine who did, twenty (nearly one-third) participated in baseball; sixteen participated in volleyball, thirteen in swimming, and eleven each in soccer and basketball. Twelve other sports were listed by three or fewer respondents. (The totals add to more than fifty-nine, because many respondents participated in two or three sports.) What is interesting about this data, and I think is typical of contemporary Cuba, is the wide diversity of sports activities. Cuba, through the two main sports magazines published by INDER, *Semanario Deportivo LPV* (*Sports Weekley LPV*), and the monthly *El Deporte--Derecho del Pueblo* (*Sport--Right of the People*), puts great emphasis on a wide variety of sports, and tries to get Cubans to participate in as many different sports as possible. Only with wide participation across the whole spectrum of sports will Cuba have the depth from which to draw elite athletes who can represent the country in international competition. One must not overemphasize elite sport, though, because it is rather clear that Cuba does value participation in sport for its own sake. That participation is valued is documented by the emphasis Cuba places on recreational sports such as camping, roller hockey, archery, fishing, orienteering, and games, which draw millions of participants.[34] Often, people will give responses such as fishing or orienteering when asked about their sports, and these recreational activities are sometimes included in the sport magazines.

In order to show the diversity of sport and recreation in Cuba, to ascertain whether there has been any significant change in emphasis on certain sports over time, and to examine whether the Cuban government, through INDER's publication of a weekly sports magazine, is trying to downplay the "Yankee" sport of baseball,[35] a content analysis of *Semanario Deportivo LPV* was undertaken. One hundred and twenty-seven issues from the 1969-1972 period,[36] and fifty issues from 1982-1983[37] were reviewed. It is important that a full year, or several years, are utilized for each time period, because various sports have their seasons, and coverage will vary accordingly. Each page of each magazine was assigned to a specific sport if one sport filled the majority of the page. If two or more sports were depicted or discussed, the page was assigned to a mixed sports category. If the page discussed sports in general terms, portrayed national or international games, or showed general sports facilities, it was assigned to a miscellaneous category. Pages that were clearly about sports in schools were assigned to a school sports category. A large number of pages, nearly one-third of the 1982-1983 issues, ended up in the miscellaneous category. Primarily, this reflects the great emphasis that is placed on major competitions, including extensive coverage of the locale, the officials involved, the background and history of the events and other pageantry surrounding these activities; nearly one hundred pages in several special issues in 1982 were devoted to the Central American and Caribbean Games held in Cuba that year.

TABLE 1

CONTENT ANALYSIS OF *SEMANARIO DEPORTIVO LPV*

SPORTS AND OTHER ACTIVITIES	127 Issues 1969-1972			50 Issues 1982-1983		
Specific Sports	Number of Times on Front or Back Cover	Total Pages	Average Pages Per Issue	Number of Times on Front or Back Cover	Total Pages	Average Pages Per Issue
Baseball	52	843	6.64	5	159	3.18
Chess	7	301	2.37	0	115	2.30
Track and Field	16	300	2.36	13	74	1.48
Soccer	13	286	2.25	2	61	1.22
Gymnastics	18	172	1.35	4	50	1.00
Bicycling	8	152	1.20	4	39	.78
Volleyball	9	146	1.15	2	33	.66
Basketball	13	129	1.02	5	49	.98
Swimming/Diving	7	122	.96	9	47	.94
Boxing	6	108	.85	7	85	1.70
Sailing, Fishing	10	95	.75	1	22	.44
Fencing	10	94	.74	6	20	.40
Rowing	5	87	.69	1	27	.54
Weightlifting	2	76	.60	4	31	.62
Motorcycling	7	62	.49	1	15	.30
Wrestling	4	57	.45	4	31	.62
Rifle, Shooting	4	56	.44	2	17	.34
Tennis	3	55	.43	1	11	.22
Judo	2	49	.39	4	19	.38
Water Polo	4	40	.31	2	11	.22
Table Tennis	0	40	.31	2	11	.22
Non-Specific Sport-Related Activities						
Miscellaneous	27	426	3.35	17	476	9.52
Mixed Sports	9	357	2.81	3	193	3.86
School Sports	18	268	2.11	1	38	.76
TOTALS	254	4321	34.02	100	1634	32.68

Source: Content analysis by the author.

Even a cursory examination of Table 1 leaves little doubt that baseball is still the dominant sport in Cuba. While its dominance, at least in
the pages of *Semanario Deportivo LPV*, is not quite so pronounced in
1982-1983 as it was in 1969-1972, no sport appeared to be challenging it.
Many people will probably be surprised to see that chess has steadily remained in second place and seems to have improved its position over the

past decade. While their relative positions changed slightly, the next eight most covered sports (track and field, soccer, gymnastics, bicycling, volleyball, basketball, swimming/diving, and boxing) were the same in 1982-1983 as they were in 1969-1972. Among them only boxing seemed to have received a substantial increase in attention. This is probably due to the great international success Cuban boxers have achieved during the past ten or fifteen years. What is probably most striking about this sports coverage is the consistency from one period to the next: there has been no significant change in emphasis on particular sports during the decade of the 1970s. There is no evidence that the "Yankee" sport of baseball is being downplayed in favor of a sport such as soccer.

One of the most interesting questions about sport in Cuba centers around the extent to which a socialist system has been able to reduce sexual and racial differences. Unfortunately, such an issue is almost impossible to document empirically, given the difficulty of doing social research in Cuba. However, there is some evidence that Cuba is still a society where substantial sexual differences exist. While it is probably true that elite female athletes are treated in much the same way as elite male athletes and afforded similar opportunities, data cited earlier in this chapter on sport participation indicates that males are more than twice as likely to participate as females, and the gap is probably much greater among adults. That traditional male *machismo* has not been eradicated from the world of sport, even in government publications, was vividly shown in the May 22, 1984, issue of *Semanario Deportivo LPV*. On page thirteen, a group of young women are shown lounging around a pool in bikinis, with the focus on one young woman leaning back and partially exposing her breasts. The caption reads *"Caballeros, i que calor!"* (Men, how hot!) Racism, if it exists, is not nearly so apparent. In fact, the impression one gets in looking at the many pictures in *Semanario Deportivo LPV* is that both dark and light people seem to be pretty well distributed among the various sports. Nonetheless, some traditional distinctions are still in evidence. Boxing, traditionally a lower class sport, tends to have a fairly large percentage of darker participants, while sailing, traditionally an upper class sport, still seems to be dominated by lighter skinned people. These traditional distinctions, though, are generally overwhelmed by the rather egalitarian impressions one gains of the color of sport participants in the pages of *Semanario Deportivo LPV*.

Cuba has been very successful in international sport in recent years. Several Cuban athletes--notably boxer Teófilo Stevenson and sprinter Alberto Juantorena--have justifiably won world-wide acclaim. I would contend that, while it has been argued that Cuba has only become a sports power in the last decade or two, "having been before a completely unimportant sport nation,"[38] a solid basis for international sports success had been laid earlier, and that the Cuban love of sport was ready and waiting for further development when Fidel Castro came to power. In 1900, Cuba was one of the first twenty nations to compete in the Modern Olympics and was almost alone among Third World nations in winning Olympic medals in the early years of the century. True, it was not until 1964 that

Cuba recaptured the success of 1900 and 1904 by winning a silver medal. But the Olympics are not the only international sports forum, and Cuba has found success in other settings. The first Central American and Caribbean championships were held in 1926, and Cubans competed and won medals. Cuba hosted those games in 1930 and again did well. In 1951, the Pan-American Games began and over the years Cuba has steadily improved its level of success.

Cuba's most notable pre-revolutionary sport success came in its national sport, baseball. Cubans have played in all the major amateur baseball competitions open to them--the Central American Games, the Pan-American Games, and the World Series. In the Central American Games, they won first place in 1926, and much of the time since then. They won first place in the Pan-American Games in their inaugural in 1951, and won first place in the World Series in Cuba's first appearance in 1939. In these three major international baseball competitions, "during the years 1926-74 Cuba's record of 23 first places is more than the 15 first places gained by all the other countries combined."[39] In baseball, Cuba was clearly a major power long before the coming of Fidel Castro.

With the ascent of socialism in 1959, Cuba began its quest for success in virtually all areas of sport. (Winter sports were excluded, given Cuba's semi-tropical climate.) While success was slow at first, by the middle of the 1960s Cuba was doing well in international sport. In the Central American Games, they went from 52 medals in 1962, to 363 medals in 1970; since 1966 they have dominated. In the Pan-American Games, they went from 20 medals in 1959 to 275 medals in 1975. Since 1971, they have been second only to the United States in their success (and in per capita terms, have won far more medals). In the Summer Olympics, they won one medal in 1964, ten medals in 1968, twenty-two medals in 1972 (including three gold medals, their first since 1904), thirteen medals in 1976 (six gold), and twenty medals in 1980 (eight gold).[40] They did not compete in the 1984 Summer Olympics, joining the Soviet-bloc boycott of these games. By any account, Cuba in the 1980s is a powerful nation in sport, dominating regional competitions and competing strongly at the world level. On a per capita basis, only the German Democratic Republic is stronger in the Olympics, and Cuba is the strongest sport power among Third World nations.

Compared with Cuba, Nicaragua is a very weak sport nation. Only in baseball did Nicaragua compete in a number of international competitions, meeting with limited success. One of the high points was in 1972, when they hosted the World Series in Managua. They finished second, but did manage to beat the champion Cuban team in a classic game, described by Edgard Tijerino Mantilla in *El Mundial Nica* (*The Nicaraguan World Series*).[41] Nicaraguans were delirious with joy and excitement over the game, for they had beaten the acknowledged best in the world. (Unfortunately, they had not been able to beat several other teams, and finished second overall.) Nicaragua has also participated in the Olympics, without much success. In 1976 in Montreal, they sent a small team. One of their swimmers, Enrique Portocarrero (who is a Somoza relative, but a

sports official in Sandinista Nicaragua), told me that they "weren't competitive."[42] Still recovering from the revolutionary insurrection in 1979,
they did not send a team to compete in Moscow in 1980. In 1984, they
did send a delegation to the Los Angeles Summer Olympics, though they
won no medals.

Within Nicaragua, sport is a major pastime of the people. Participation levels are relatively high for an underdeveloped country. In ana-
lyzing data taken from 2337 applications for employment with the
Nicaraguan electric company, I found that 64 percent of these people listed
themselves as active participants in one or more sports.[43] The surprise in
looking at participation by age was that levels of participation remained
quite high all the way up to athletes aged fifty. Unlike Cuba, participation
did not drop dramatically when athletes reached age forty. My informal
observations confirmed this. Men of virtually all ages and some women
played baseball. My data shows that from the young teenage years to
twenty, 75 percent of the people participated in sport; for the ages twenty
to twenty-four, 66 percent participated; 60 percent of those twenty-five to
thirty-nine participated in sport, while 52 percent of those forty to forty-
nine did so. Above the age of fifty, 31 percent participated, which is quite
high for that age group. One must be cautious in using such data; as
discussed in the notes, the data base is comprised mostly of males. In
terms of differential participation by sex, 75 percent of males participated
in sport, while only 34 percent of females did so. More rural (72 percent)
people participated than urban (64 percent), and more middle/upper class
people (76 percent) participated than did working/lower class people (62
percent).[44] It is normal for participation levels to increase as one looks at
higher social class levels. However, urban people (presumably with more
leisure time) generally participate at higher levels than do rural people.
That this does not hold in Nicaragua is probably attributable to three
factors. First, baseball is the dominant Nicaraguan sport, and it is
quintessentially a rural pastime.[45] Second, some of the urban respondents
from Managua lived in neighborhoods where the density of settlement may
have made it difficult to find adequate space for baseball. Third, the real
poverty and struggle for existence of many of the urban poor probably did
not leave them with the leisure time that is normally associated with urban
life.

What sports are played most by the Nicaraguan people? Even more
than in Cuba, baseball is the number one sport, and it dominates the
Nicaraguan sports scene. Soccer is second, though it is followed closely
by volleyball, swimming, basketball, table tennis, track, and chess. A
breakdown of the sports participated in by the 2337 Nicaraguans for whom
I have data is presented in Table 2. The reader should be aware that this
data is from employment applications submitted from 1978-1980. Thus
they portray a picture of Nicaragua during the time of change from
Somoza family to Sandinista control.

Since the early 1980s, the emphasis of sport in Sandinista Nicaragua
has been on fostering widespread popular involvement. Throughout the
country, posters depict the basics of sport skills; posters on baseball show

TABLE 2

SPORT PARTICIPATION IN NICARAGUA

Sport in Which Participate	Number of Respondents	Percent of Respondents
None	837	35.8
Baseball	688	29.4
Soccer	196	8.4
Volleyball	179	7.7
Swimming	167	7.1
Basketball	155	6.6
Table Tennis	125	5.3
Track, Running	88	3.8
Chess	86	3.7
Softball	58	2.5
Boxing	58	2.5
Kickball	37	1.6
Sports (in general)	26	1.1
Karate, Judo	23	1.0
Physical Exercise	21	0.9
Tennis	21	0.9
Billiards	20	0.9
Weightlifting	17	0.7
Fishing	17	0.7
Cycling	11	0.5
Gymnastics	10	0.4
Walking	9	0.4
Motorcycling	4	0.2
Yoga	4	0.2
Handball	3	0.1
Bowling	3	0.1
Checkers	2	0.1
Hunting	1	0.1
Equitation	1	0.1
	2867	122.8

(Because of multiple responses, the number of respondents does not add to 2,337, nor do the percentages to 100.)

Source: Wagner, "Sport and Revolution in Nicaragua," p. 293.

the proper way to pitch, bat, catch, and field a baseball, while posters on soccer show skills needed to participate in that sport. In bold lettering on all of the posters are *"Por la Masificación del Deporte"* (For the Massification of Sport). Like Cuba, Nicaragua wants to encourage all of its people to be sport participants, because they believe that an active physical life will lead to better health. The Nicaraguan Junta decreed in the *Statute on the Rights of Nicaraguans* that "Nicaraguans have the right to enjoy the highest level of physical and mental health. The state has an obligation to adopt measures to achieve . . . intensive and systematic development of sports."[46]

Since the assumption of power by the Sandinistas, baseball has continued as the most prominent national sport. There is no attempt to replace it with soccer, or to downplay it. As Tijerino notes, the people demand baseball; it is a sport in which everyone participates--it is important because it has been massified spontaneously.[47] It is the people's sport. Today in Nicaragua there are about eight national baseball teams, and over a thousand organized community and youth league teams.[48] Nearly every small town in Nicaragua has at least one baseball team, and people are beginning to pay more attention to their own local sports activities and organizations. The emphasis is on these local teams, rather than on national and international baseball teams--though the Nicaraguan newspapers and people still follow the major leagues in the United States.

Reasons for Sport

Why is there such obvious emphasis on sport in Cuba and Nicaragua? First, there is widespread support in many countries, socialist and non-socialist alike, for the political uses of sport. Domestically, arguments have been made that sport contributes to the cohesion and integration of the society. Internationally, sport can be used to "prove" that a given social system works and to gain international prestige. Second, arguments have been made that sport helps promote better health, fitness, and preparation for life. Fitter people are more productive people. And, particularly germane to Nicaragua and Cuba, a physically fit population is an important part of preparation for defense from outside aggression. Third, sport can be used to teach socialist values. Fourth, in both Cuba and Nicaragua there has been strong leadership support for and interest in sport.

Reflecting these ideas are the four basic themes of Nicaraguan sports ideology elaborated by Edgard Tijerino. The Sandinistas want to use sport to help integrate the society; there is a desire for widespread participation, or massification of sport, which involves broad access to sport; they want to create local involvement in building the organization of sport; and there is a desire to instill a collective mentality through working together on sport teams.[49] All of these themes are, to a certain extent, reflected in baseball. Through the organization of baseball teams, leagues, and tournaments, people are being brought together and are working together; thus collective effort is certainly helping to integrate the society. Many people are participating, and are doing so in nearly every locality in the country. The masses are involved, and their involvement is growing each year.

In Cuba, too, the masses are involved in sport, and especially in baseball. Baseball was, from the beginning, rooted in the popular classes and has remained a passion of the common people to this day. First, it was originally played by cargo handlers, and it was they who introduced it to their countrymen. Unlike most modern sports, which were first played by the privileged classes and then diffused to the masses, baseball in Cuba started and remained among the poor. Second, it started in Matanzas, rather than in Havana, the cultural center of the country. Thus much of the history of Cuban baseball is the history of outlying parts of the country challenging the center in Havana, and the outlying areas sometimes won. Not often could the center be so successfully challenged. Third, the sport of baseball was rooted in the masses, and so is the revolutionary government. The popular classes brought their sport with them when they gained power. The Revolution, badly needing popular support in the first difficult years when it was revolutionizing the political and economic institutions of the country, was only too glad to support and enhance a sport to which the masses were so passionately attached. Fourth, Cuba's long history of success in international baseball competitions, begun more than thirty years before the Revolution, gave the new government a ready-made instrument for gaining national prestige and international support. They were quick to seize upon this means to credibility, and to expand it to other sports. Their success, recognized by leaders of the Revolution, has been supported and enhanced to bring prestige and recognition to the Cuban way of life. Just as the German Democratic Republic (East Germany) used its success in sport to gain international political recognition as an independent nation, so Cuba has used success in sport and baseball to gain prestige abroad, particularly among Third World peoples. Sport became, and continues to be, an important facet of Cuban foreign policy.

Sport in Cuba and in Nicaragua has the support of the top leadership. Fidel Castro has long been viewed as that country's number one baseball and sports fan, and he has had life-long involvement in sport. In Nicaragua, many in the top leadership roles in the country are active in sport. Junta member Moisés Hassan heads the Olympic Committee, the Minister of Defense is a baseball fanatic, and the Vice Minister of Planning is a bicyclist. Practically all of the widespread Sandinista leadership plays one sport or another. All of these leaders feel sport is an integral part of society, and believe it is a key part of the cohesive interests that help to bond a society together, to integrate the many diverse constituencies and regions.

To a substantial degree, the rhetoric of Castro and the reality of baseball coincide. Among Castro's sport themes are: (1) people learn collective work in sport; (2) sport should be open to all, young and old, men and women; (3) sport should both promote health and welfare and produce champions; and, (4) sport should develop recreation for everyone, instead of being the privilege of an elite. As our review of sport, and especially baseball, has shown, these themes are reflected in sport activities. The emphasis on learning collective work through sport is being carried out by the extensive sport and recreation programs supported by Cubans and especially by the Cuban workers confederations. Sport is open to all, with data clearly showing steadily increasing sport participation. However, certain groups, in particular women and older people, are only very slowly beginning to participate. The social structure of a Latin American country, where *machismo* and sport are often connected, is not rapidly or easily going to allow the full participation of women. Sport for the privileged few has ended--though it is certainly clear that the best players have far more opportunities and support than those engaged in sport merely for recreation. Sport, and in particular baseball, continues to produce champions; sport is probably promoting better health, and health has improved noticeably in post-revolutionary Cuba, though there is no data to show any causal connection between health and sport. In Cuba, sport activities and ideological rhetoric are closely tied.

Nicaraguan Tijerino argued that in the early stages of building a new Nicaragua, sport must play a fundamental role in reactivating the society, because sport serves to harmonize the great number of personalities, temperaments, and characters which unite on the sports field. All must have a chance to become involved in sport, and it is sport that will help integrate the society.

In both Cuba and Nicaragua, sport continues to reflect the society. The ideologies of these countries are not only reflected in the institution of sport, but sport itself has helped shape ideology. No leaders in Cuba or Nicaragua have advocated abandoning their people's passionate interest in sport, and especially in baseball, which not only continues to reflect the society, but serves as a stabilizing force tying people to their social traditions. Rather, they have built upon this strong tie to tradition, and have channeled this interest in directions that are supportive of their revolutionary goals.

Notes

1   Douglas S. Butterworth, *The People of Buena Ventura: Relocation of Slum Dwellers in Postrevolutionary Cuba* (Urbana: University of Illinois Press, 1980), p. 4.

2   Max Azicri, "A Cuban Perspective on the Nicaraguan Revolution," in *Nicaragua in Revolution*, ed., Thomas W. Walker (New York: Praeger Publishers, 1982), p. 364.

3   Susan E. Ramírez-Horton, "The Role of Women in the Nicaraguan Revolution," in *Nicaragua in Revolution*, ed. Thomas W. Walker (New York: Praeger Publishers, 1982), pp. 147-59, includes a discussion of women's involvement in Nicaraguan society.

4   Eric A. Wagner, "Sport Participation in Latin America," *International Review of Sport Sociology* 17:2 (1982): 29-39.

5   Janet Lever, *Soccer Madness* (Chicago: The University of Chicago Press, 1983), p. 3.

6   Edgard Tijerino Mantilla, interview in Managua, Nicaragua, September 1980.

7   S. Jeffrey K. Wilkerson, "Man's Eighty Centuries in Veracruz," *National Geographic* 158:2 (August 1980): 222.

8   Celso Enríquez, *Sports in Pre-Hispanic America* (México, D.F.: Litográfica Machado, S.A., 1968).

9   Thomas W. Walker, *Nicaragua in Revolution*, p. 11.

10   See the essay by Steve Stein in this collection.

11   Janet Lever, *Soccer Madness,* p. 70.

12   Luis Hernández, "Un siglo de béisbol en Cuba," *Semanario Deportivo LPV* (2 December 1969): 8-9.

13   Enrique Capetillo, "103 años de béisbol," *Semanario Deportivo LPV* (30 November 1971): 14-17.

14   Eric A Wagner, "Baseball in Cuba," *Journal of Popular Culture* 18:1 (1984): 113-20.

15   R. J. Pickering, "Cuba," in *Sport Under Communism*, ed., James Riordan (Montreal: McGill-Queen's University Press, 1978), p. 149.

16   José Casimiro Ortal and Edward J. Tassinari, "Chess, Propaganda and the Cuban Media" (Paper presented at the Conference on Latin American Culture, Las Cruces, New Mexico, March 1981), p. 4.

17   Personal communication from historian Charles L. Stansifer, 20 March 1981.

18   Mary W. Helms, *Asano: Adaptations to Culture Contact in a Miskito Community* (Gainesville: University of Florida Press, 1971), pp. 84, 223.

19   Wagner, "Sport and Revolution in Nicaragua," in *Nicaragua in Revolution*, ed., Thomas W. Walker (New York: Praeger Publishers, 1982), p. 292.

20   Manfred Komorowski, "Cuba's Way to a Country with Strong In-
     fluence in Sport Politics--The Development of Sport in Cuba Since
     1959," *International Journal of Physical Education* 14 (1977): 28.

21   Ibid.

22   Ibid.

23   Eric A. Wagner, "Sport After Revolution: A Comparative Study of
     Cuba and Nicaragua," *Studies in Latin American Popular Culture,* 1
     (1982): 68.

24   Pickering, "Cuba," pp. 141-74.

25   Wagner, "Sport After Revolution: A Comparative Study of Cuba and
     Nicaragua," p. 68.

26   Wagner, "Sport and Revolution in Nicaragua."

27   Ibid.

28   Ibid., p. 298.

29   Ministerio de Cultura--Instituto Nicaragüense de Deportes, *Plan de
     la Calle* (Managua, 10 January 1980); Ministerio de Cultura--Instituto
     Nicaragüense de Deportes, *Tercer Folleto de Recreación. Plan de la
     Calle* (Managua, July 1980).

30   Wagner, "Sport and Revolution in Nicaragua," p. 298, and Ministerio
     de Cultura, *Plan de la Calle* (10 January 1980).

31   Pickering, "Cuba," p. 151.

32   Wagner, "Sport Participation in Latin America."

33   Wagner, "Sport After Revolution: A Comparative Study of Cuba and
     Nicaragua," p. 71.

34   Pickering, "Cuba," p. 161.

35   It has occasionally been contended that baseball is no longer Cuba's
     most popular sport, having been overtaken by soccer and perhaps
     boxing, and that the government has opposed baseball since the rev-
     olution. My data and my observations provide no evidence for such
     a contention, and the government sport magazines certainly do not
     downplay baseball, as any content analysis would make clear. It is
     true that Cuba is placing emphasis on a wider variety of sports, and
     that baseball is not seen as the only sport, but to argue that "the tra-

ditional love for baseball in Cuba recently has subsided in favor of soccer and boxing as that country's first and second most popular sports, in part due to an official campaign against baseball since the 1959 revolution" is simply not supported by the evidence.   The quoted remarks are from *Update*, Newsletter of the Outreach Services of the African, Asian, Latin American and Russian Studies Centers, University of Illinois at Urbana-Champaign (December 1983): 3.

[36]   Coverage extends from August of 1969 to May of 1972. With the exception of a few missing issues, coverage from November of 1969 to May of 1972 is complete. Grateful thanks are extended to the librarians in the Latin American Collection of the University of Florida Library for their help in locating these magazines and facilitating their use by a visitor.

[37]   Coverage extends from July 6, 1982, to July 5, 1983, with two issues missing. These copies are from the author's collection.

[38]   Komorowski, "Cuba's Way to a Country with Strong Influence in Sport Politics--The Development of Sport in Cuba Since 1959," p. 26.

[39]   Wagner, "Baseball in Cuba," p. 117.

[40]   Pickering, "Cuba," p. 150, includes a listing of the numbers of gold, silver, and bronze medals won by Cuba in these three main competitions from 1959 to 1976. *Spiele der XXII. Olympiade Moskau 1980* (Berlin: Sportverlag, 1981), p. 451, lists the medals won by Cuba in the 1980 Moscow Olympics. Ten of Cuba's medals, and six of the gold medals, were in boxing.

[41]   Edgard Tijerino Mantilla, *El Mundial Nica* (Managua: Imprenta Copiaco, 1973).

[42]   Enrique Portocarrero, interview in Managua, Nicaragua, September 1980.

[43]   Caution must be exercised in interpreting this data. Most (92 percent) lived in the Managua metropolitan area, were working or lower class (86 percent, compared to 14 percent middle/upper class), were male (74 percent), and were in young working ages;   16 percent were nineteen or under, 41 percent were twenty to twenty-four, 22 percent were twenty-five to twenty-nine, 15 percent were in their thirties, and only 6 percent were forty or older.   Thanks are expressed to Ricardo Chavarria for making these employment applications available to me.

[44]   Wagner, "Sport Participation in Latin America," pp. 34-35.

45   D. Stanley Eitzen, "The Structure of Sport and Society" in *Sport in Contemporary Society*, ed., D. Stanley Eitzen, (New York: St. Martin's Press, 1984), pp. 51-57, discusses the rural nature of baseball.

46   Pedro Camejo and Fred Murphy, *The Nicaraguan Revolution* (New York: Pathfinder Press, 1979), p. 52.

47   Tijerino, interview in Managua, Nicaragua, September 1980.

48   David Russell, "Baseball, Hollywood, and Nicaragua," *Monthly Review* 34:10 (March 1983): 23.

49   Tijerino, interview in Managua, Nicaragua, September 1980.

8
Sport as Dramaturgy for Society: A Concluding Chapter
Robert M. Levine

In the recent past, more than a few observers dissatisfied with conventional explanations of Latin American society have turned to the study of sports, a subject easily approached and richly symbolic on a number of levels. The reasons for this new interest are many. Sports transcend social and economic class. Sports information pervades modern life, from rabid and intricate sports journalism to sophisticated analogies by social scientists. Sportive rituals are exotic. Sport contests reflect passionate rivalries, escapism, and changing social values. Theories about sports flow easily, a fact rooted in the myriad ways in which sports touch everyday life; this summary chapter will consider several of them and weigh them against examples drawn from Latin American experiences.

Critics approach sports from a variety of angles. Social anthropologists use sports to measure social aggression, to examine collective behavior, and to trace patterns of body contact and incursions into territoriality.[1] Political scientists and historians study foreign penetration, nationalism, and the political uses of sport. Language specialists list ways that sports have affected vocabulary; urbanologists use sports to look at cities, psychological space, and mass social interaction. Philosophers have called athletes "proxy warriors" in larger ideological conflicts.[2] Others search for evidence of racial conflict (or harmony). Some praise sports for its integrative role. Still others decry its hypnotic powers to manipulate the underclass and to impose cynical social control.

Latin American sports conjure up even more colorful and often disturbing images. North Americans, who continue to be puzzled by soccer, despite the heavy-handed marketing blitzes of the mid-1970s, think of moated stadiums and rioting crowds when they hear about that sport in Latin America. Political scientists study the 1970 "Soccer War" between El Salvador and Honduras, begun when disputed calls during World Cup regional elimination matches between the two hostile neighbors spilled over into a formal break in diplomatic relations. Itamaratí, the Brazilian Foreign Ministry, used the diversion generated by the opening of the 1978 World Cup in Buenos Aires to call off, without warning, the tripartite talks scheduled with Argentina and Paraguay over regional hydroelectric cooperation. Commentators noted that the Argentines were particularly vulnerable at that moment because "all of their resources" were concentrated on the football extravaganza.[3] Some have observed the extreme lengths to which sports and ideology have become intertwined, not only in societies such as Castro's Cuba and Sandinista Nicaragua, as Eric A. Wagner has shown, but in virtually every country in the hemisphere at one time or another.

Assessing sport in Latin America is difficult because the region lacks homogeneity. One can argue without much hope of meaningful resolution about the boundaries of "Latin America" itself, about whether the French-, Dutch-, and English-speaking Caribbean, for example, deserves inclusion. Puerto Rico poses another dilemma: Should a United States territory be termed part of Latin America? Two spectator sports dominate the island societies of the Caribbean--cricket and baseball. The first stands quintessentially rooted in the lands of the British Empire/Commonwealth; the second was implanted mostly during times of United States intervention, as in Puerto Rico, Cuba, and Nicaragua, and in places dominated by an American presence, as in the Dominican Republic, Venezuela, Panama, and Mexico's Yucatán. An ironic extension of this circumstance exists in São Paulo, Brazil, where Nippo-Brazilians, residents of the largest overseas community of Japanese in the world, play baseball, introduced earlier to the Far East by Americans and carried to Brazil by Japanese who migrated to South America.

There is also the question of sports practiced exclusively among moneyed segments of the upper classes. These include polo-playing and equestrian Argentines and Uruguayans; Brazilian and Chilean yachtsmen; Formula One racing drivers, often also from Argentina and Brazil; world-class tennis players out of the private clubs of rich and poor countries alike. Yet even if trained as scholarship athletes at Stanford or the University of Southern California or if taking permanent residence in the south of France while pursuing the globe-trotting circuit of professional tennis, should not an Andrés Gimeno or María Bueno be considered Latin American and representative of Latin American society?

At the other end of the scale are the surviving aboriginal contests: team log-racing among the Shavante Indians of Central Brazil, for example. Are these events part of "Latin American" sports? The questions need not be analyzed to death, but it serves to point out the difficulty of generalizing either for the geographic region or the society of Latin America as a whole. Once in a while, moreover, something occurs that contradicts stereotypes. Early in 1985, for example, a wealthy engineer and entrepreneur left in his will a fortune of $360 million in stocks, paintings, real estate, and cash to the Bangú club of Rio de Janeiro, originally a factory team and over the years identified with working-class fans from the remote neighborhoods of the city's Zona Norte. Was this an ironic act of symbolic defiance from a man who by convention should have changed his allegiance to Fluminense, the team of the elite? Or was it an isolated act of stubbornness attributable to the perversity of fandom and the survival of team loyalty despite upward social mobility?

"Latin America" is defined in this chapter to include the Spanish-speaking countries of the Western hemisphere, as well as Brazil. The time frame, as throughout this book, covers the period from the late nineteenth century to the present, a century roughly characterized by urbanization, the rise of mass culture, and efforts to use forms of popular culture to achieve social or political integration or to attain nationalistic ends. The chapter focuses on those spectator sports appealing to large segments of the population. For the most part, this translates into soccer, probably the only institution in Latin America besides the Roman Catholic Church to touch the lives of rich and poor, the educated elite, and the hereditarily illiterate underclass. Yet, as Gilbert M. Joseph demonstrates, regional distinctiveness in Mexico, coupled with the arrival of workers and technicians from outside--Cuban merchant seamen and cargo handlers, as well as North American mining engineers and railroad employees--planted the seeds of *béisbolmanía*. By the turn of the century baseball had become the major sport of the small, emerging middle classes, and, in the aftermath of the Mexican Revolution, officials of Yucatán's Socialist Party promoted baseball among the rural Mayan population and laid the groundwork for the sport's institutional growth.

Various hypotheses have emerged out of the heated debates over the role and meaning of sports in Latin American life. The list does not pretend to be a complete inventory of theories about sport, nor does it touch on all social groups or geographic regions. It focuses on areas of convergence, where elite culture and popular culture interact. Its bias is historical, and it seeks to extract from sportive activity, especially as it impacts on the general population, ways of viewing the social dimensions of culture and public behavior. Robert Darton warns us that this kind of non-systematic analysis should not lead us to imply that "anything goes in cultural history because anything can pass as anthropology."[4] Rather, the theories about sports that have emerged from under the social scientists' microscopes are all the more provocative because they attempt to say so much about the larger world.

1. *Sports express human needs, and, as such, have become for many Latin Americans a pervasive way of life.* Sociologists distinguish among "play," "games," and "sport" as components of the sportive world. "Play" is voluntary, given to spontaneity and fantasy, and involves few formal rules; it is viewed by participants and observers both as being momentary, removed from the "serious" side of life and work. "Games" are competitive; they involve skills and follow standardized rules, but they are con-

sidered to be equally dependent upon luck.   Winning or losing is transitory, and there is little or no continuity between one game and another.[5]

"Sport" represents a kind of Darwinian evolution in the direction of serious competition, the highest levels of training and skill, and is valued for its own sake as well as for the meaning and emotions it imparts to spectators as well as the participants themselves. For the athletes, sport may provide access to higher income and social status than they usually can hope to attain. Sport brings recognition and, for some, fame and fortune, if only brief-lived. More than most other forms of social activity, sport offers opportunities for the most talented persons to break through obstacles placed against upward social mobility, especially those based on educational attainment, race, or ethnic status.

Warnings that sports were harmful to the less privileged rang out as soon as sports began to take hold in urban life. Thorstein Veblen, who reviled them as a wasteful form of unproductive leisure, warned that addiction to sports not only gripped the productive sectors of the population, but was shared with "the lower-class delinquents, and with such atavistic elements throughout the body of the community as are endowed with a dominant predacious trend." Veblen thought that "individuals among the industrial classes" could not fully comprehend the refined appeal of the sporting life. Their interest in sports, he wrote in 1899, amounted to more of a diversion in the nature of a reminiscence than a true "organic" commitment, and therefore it was not yet too late to save the unwashed masses from the "barbarian traits" that emerged when watching sporting contests.

Veblen's fear of barbarism notwithstanding, the shaping of modern urban life narrowed the gap between the workplace and the playground. Around the turn of the twentieth century, factories in working-class industrial neighborhoods of major Latin American cities began to sponsor employee soccer teams, usually coached by the English managers and engineers who had helped introduce the sport to the New World in previous decades. Some of the earliest "crack" athletes, the superstars of the pre-media age, emerged out of these working-class environments. They raised the level of play, paving the way for both the advent of professionalization and the acceptance of lower class soccer players of immigrant and even non-white origins.

Abetted by the rise of tabloid journalism, the radio, and the social acceptance of public enthusiasm along class and, to some degree, racial lines for individual teams, sports for many Latin American urban residents by the late 1920s did in fact become a pervasive way of life. Sports, we are told, help complex modern societies to cohere. Given the fears among Latin American elites that urban life would violently disrupt social stability, that socialism and other nostrums would infiltrate the shabby working-class neighborhoods and exacerbate class antagonisms, spectator sports, mainly soccer, seemed to provide a legitimate and relatively healthful outlet for resolution of frustrations rooted in conflicting interests. Whether the dynamics were understood in the crudest sense or not, sports offered a safety valve, filling up the non-working hours of workingmen, permitting them to blow off emotional steam and, at the same time, cultivating a shared outlook as the basis for social order.

The differences between sports in Latin America and sports elsewhere come to mind here. Perhaps the most interesting difference is that, in Latin America, sports have retained their singularly vicarious flavor. Latin Americans love their sports heroes, but do not as a whole emulate them as human beings. Another way of saying this is that the sociology of Latin American sports emphasizes the symbolic victories and setbacks of the teams, not of individual performances. The North American obsession with sports statistics, especially measurable record achievements, is for the most part foreign to the Latin American sportive tradition.

European expressionists in the 1920s and 1930s and their modern-day successors weaned on sports journalism and television, in later decades focused on sport's power to serve as a tangible index of intensifying human performance. But Latin American sports fever historically centered on the symbolic personalities of teams *and their supporters*. Thus Matthew Shirts finds "Corinthian Democracy" in the broadest context of the world of Brazilian soccer to be more significant than the won-and-lost record of the Corinthians Football Club.

Herein lies another distinction between sports organization in Latin America and its counterpart in the United States. Professional sports teams in Latin America are owned and managed by their collective membership. In the United States, proud of its tradition of democracy, most professional sports teams are headed by corporate syndicates, individual entrepreneurs, or family dynasties. Commercialism talks: teams have become willing to abandon hallowed generations of fan loyalty for the lure of higher profits in other locations. The cynical kidnapping of the Dodgers and Giants by their owners to California, the cowardly departure of the Baltimore Colts to Indianapolis in hired moving vans at midnight, and the tantrums of the Steinbrenners, Irsays, and Toses would stun and disorient Latin American sports enthusiasts.

Even if we know that the motives of the Latin American *cartolas* are also less than perfectly altruistic, as Shirts and Lever reveal, the basic link between teams and their supporters--usually a complex affair attributable less to geography than to social standing, group perceptions, and unwritten nuances of status and symbolism--remains inviolate. Individual players are permitted to be sold for club profit; but teams live and die in situ, even as neighborhoods change or fashions ebb, rather than to desert their origins for greener corporate pastures. Teams in Latin America cannot be permitted the luxury of such capricious behavior. After all, as Lever has demonstrated, sport's paradoxical ability to reinforce social cleavages while transcending them makes the public's passion for sports the ideal vehicle for social integration.

2. *The emergence of large-scale spectator sports coincided with booming and accelerating urban growth. In turn, officials used this popularity to manipulate public behavior.* The thesis that sports as a substitute for conflict divert attention from more unsavory pressures from within society is relatively mild. More forceful is the assertion that sports reflect

outright manipulation. Social order can promote social welfare, we are reminded, but it can also deprive people of their freedom. Detractors use harsh words to condemn sports as an opiate, a circus by which the dominant class fools the masses into sublimating the misery of their lives in the fleeting success of a team victory. This view accepts sport as neutral and morally innocent, yet easily differentiated into divergent ideological messages.[6] But, as we have seen, regimes of all types have used sports events to divert attention or to focus local pride: Examples range from the Argentine dictatorship's use of the 1978 World Cup to the Sandinistas' decree that managers use pitchers less in order to save their arms from damage. There is little evidence that the role of sports in self-styled revolutionary societies is much different from that elsewhere. Further, where politicians have attempted to create interest artificially--as in the case of Cuba's attempt to promote soccer in order to capitalize (no pun) on its Third World appeal--their efforts have invariably failed.

The social control argument is elusive. Even if it is demonstrated statistically that social cohesion results from dramatic sports victories or that defeat on the playing field yields lower productivity, higher absenteeism, and documented cases of depression and suicide, there is still little evidence that the euphoria (or disappointment) rubs off on other areas of consciousness and remains for any measurable period of time. Sports victories and failures carry intense psychological impact, but they evaporate quickly, melting into the air even if stretched out by clever journalists and propagandists.

Cases where devotion to individual teams or star athletes is so great as to permeate daily behavior are rare, and usually anecdotal. Corinthians fans relish their reputation as "sufferers" and "fanatics," and Shirts argues convincingly that followers of São Paulo's "people's team" share a fellowship of collective potential that extends beyond soccer into politics and social behavior. It was no coincidence, *corintiano* historian Juca Kfouri noted, that the first banner in favor of political amnesty in Brazil was unfurled in the midst of a Corinthian *torcida*.[7] But the degree to which such emotions penetrate the social fabric and move sports fans to action remains to be demonstrated. Fandom creates intense emotions but stops short of imposing social control, except in individual cases that represent the unusual, not the rule.

The dark side of the social control argument would be more convincing if there were not evidence that the spectators themselves understand that sports represent a world of fleeting emotions and momentary fantasy. What strengthens the feeling of release is the act of spectator participation itself--the thrill of crowd emotion, the cheering, the classless cameraderie, the pain of defeat. But when the game ends, class distinctions reassert themselves, and life goes on. And for every opportunity for vicarious self-esteem and pride in a victorious team or sporting phenomenon, there are far more occasions of mediocre play, or lost chances, or average performance not nearly of the sort to mobilize mass emotion or influence social and political behavior.

The evolution of Yucatecan "street ball" into commercialized baseball illustrates the milder side of the manipulation theorem. The sport,
Joseph notes, fits nicely into the local oligarchy's sense of *noblesse oblige*
and its vision of a dynamic and prosperous society founded on the virtues
of physical competition and vigor. Economic fluctuations slowed efforts
to harness the spontaneity of street baseball, but urban growth brought the
sport to the city's periphery and beyond to the small towns in the Yucatán
linked to Mérida by rail. A strong impulse to harness baseball's popularity
to ideological ends accompanied the efforts by revolutionary-era officials
to extend government to the people and therefore achieve a form of co-
opted legitimacy. Baseball's popularity would likely have grown in any
case in the Yucatán, especially with the introduction of Cuban and North
American "ringers" and barnstorming Negro League teams. Even the
Revolution took five years before reaching the isolated peninsula. But
economic prosperity and regional order gave birth to. a golden age of
baseball, reinforced by the government's 1916 decree abolishing debt
peonage and forced labor. The steps by the socialist Partido Socialista del
Sureste (PSS) under Carrillo Puerto to mobilize the rural population
through recognition of the faith of the folk culture of Yucatán's *campesinos*
and emphasis on athletic competition certainly represent political manipulation, but in a manner most observers would find benign. So what if
Yucatán's Liga Central schedules games to coincide with announcements
of government land distributions or cultural events of local resistance
leagues?

3. *The ritualistic expressionism of sports, inherently theatrical, offers
a window for analysis of individual and group behavior.* Examples abound:
the *limeño* "sportmen," from wealthy and prominent families, characterized
by their carefree demeanor and skill with imported gentlemen's games--
soccer, polo, yachting, fencing, and cricket. What better sociological laboratory for study than a closely played soccer match between the "whites"
of Unión Cricket and the fishermen and stevedores of Atlético Chalaco,
or the whites of Universitario and the blacks of Alianza?

Consider Pedro Frías's description of the behavior of lower class fans
from Callao who arrived by train and walked to the stadium, taunted by
the cries of "dynamite Callao!" Yet such incendiary language and behavior
was mostly theatrics. Democracy may have reigned on the field while it
was absent from general society, but the struggle represented by the
matches, so classically symbolic, for the most part *remained* symbolic.
Sports passions over specific contests rarely, we repeat, last more than a
few days.

4. *Sports bring psychological liberation to the underprivileged, creating new forms of "living space" for men and women hemmed in by oppressive
urban confinement within societies characterized as underdeveloped, or
"fractured."* This interpretation, a variant of the first two hypotheses, is
illustrated by some of the ways in which sports contests have brought
(limited) relief to fans. We have the example of members of a rural
Yucatecan team whitewashing walls for a week, their eyes streaming and
red from the astringent lime, to raise money to pay the first-class train fares

and lodging demanded by the visiting middle class team from Mérida. The Mexican bicycling craze triggered a passion for healthful exercise, although it was limited to the prosperous classes. Baseball's popularity extended to the Miskito Indians of the Nicaraguan coast and to the poorest of agricultural workers in the circum-Caribbean. Soccer provided a temporary antidote to the dark lives of urban industrial workers, to the unemployed, and to the miserable. Modern sports have brought to the Latin American mass population a sense of self within society, in Althusser's language, interpolating concrete individuals as concrete subjects. And if civil sentiments and the state's need for overarching political unity require the subordination of obligation to local groups, then there is not much of a difference between co-optation of working-class teams for political purposes in societies that are politically heterogeneous and in self-styled revolutionary ones. Social control, then, is no monopoly of one kind of government or political system. Blanco and Colorado soccer teams in Uruguay functioned as a basic element in maintaining the two party system for decades.

The study of any social phenomenon in isolation opens only a partial window to understanding society at large. In fact, for every question it seems to answer it raises more that defy interpretation. Even within the world of Latin American sports, great internal differences and variations limit possibilities for overarching explanations. The experience of one country or region may not be the same as that of another.

For one thing, it is misleading to compare local ("primordial" to the sociologist) with national circumstances. Looking at national phenomena--the traumatic effects of victories and defeats of national teams in international competition; the linkages between sports and political life and government-initiated manipulation--tends to place the observer within a framework that is broad and to some degree too theoretical. One weakness of this approach is that it does not permit in-depth analysis of important questions. For example, to what degree does the kind of cohesion achieved by sports rub off on other areas of consciousness? To what extent do the passions generated by sports influence day-to-day behavior over the long haul? Do the democratizing effects of sports--forging ties of cameraderie across social or class lines or between age groups--influence interpersonal relations once the fever pitch of the contest evaporates? Do sports in fact internalize the "real-life antagonisms and jealousies" between neighborhood, racial, and ethnic groups? What of the impact of sports in the majority of settings in Latin America, where national teams play mediocre or average soccer, baseball, or basketball, so that they never finish high enough in the rankings to raise the population to fever pitch on the occasion of a victory bringing national jubilation or a crushing loss evoking national disgrace?

In this regard, case studies at the less glamorous local level can shed light on the impact of sports on the day-to-day texture of the lives of ordinary people. We need more analysis of the career trajectories of professional athletes in Latin America, not only the Pelés and the Julio Molinas and the Miguel Rostaings, but also the journeymen, those who rose through the ragged networks of neighborhood and semi-professional teams, perhaps to brief success at the regional level. For these young men, and even those fortunate enough to rise to national prominence, a wealth of detail lies ready for the systematic researcher to examine such issues as race, personal growth, social mobility, and, most poignant, the fate of athletes felled by injury or simply past their prime.

One suspects that the few athletes from lower class origins (the vast majority of professional athletes in Latin America as in most parts of the world) who did manage to capitalize on their fame during their careers sufficiently to remain economically (or socially) prominent after their playing days ended were rare exceptions. Did most fall to the levels from whence they came? Or did they achieve a kind of permanent hero status that brought advantages to them even after they faded back into "civilian" life? Does sports prominence bring with it unwelcome vulnerability? We have the case of a radio sportscaster, Demetrio Martínez, tortured and shot to death by Sendero Luminoso terrorists outside of Lima in mid-1985,[8] presumably because his name was so well known in the region.

A problem with any new discipline or scholarly theme is that initial studies are often based on broad observation and conjecture, not on extensive field or archival research. This is not a criticism of the essays in this volume; they represent careful thought and execution. But the next generation of analysts of Latin American sport must dig deeper into untouched archives and other sources.[9] Most of the sports federations in every major Latin American city and country hold extensive records, some including every professional contract signed by every athlete on every team since its inauguration. Surely these archives can be mined for data in search of answers to the questions posed above. The daily and weekly sports press--popular, combatant, and tremendously influential among large sectors of the population--waits careful reading and analysis by scholars. Thousands of sports figures--coaches, trainers, journalists, referees, radio and television commentators, as well as the athletes--wait to be interviewed. Films using sports as their central themes, novels and biographies about sports figures, merchandising schemes linking sports figures with sales campaigns, the growth of mass advertising, and consumerism all remain virtually unexamined.

Further research is necessary before we can accept fully the kind of overarching hypotheses that preliminary studies lay out. Have sports in revolutionary societies really subdued traditional divisions over ethnic, racial, and economic distinctions? To what extent has the mass merchandising of sports and the packaging of sports personalities by the media truly stripped the vicarious enjoyment of sports of its spontaneity and intensity? Do sports, as Roland Barthes has suggested, represent wholly a "spectacle of excess"?[10] Are athletes really the unwitting victims of "sports socialization"? Is sport really the "play form of conflict"? And if sports yield social cohesion, what is the price of that cohesion? Is sport merely "capitalism in shorts"? Richard D. Mandell has charged that sports events are not very substantial events, that athletes are almost instrinsically boring.[11] Are sports really banal? If so, why then their tremendous power, their ability to integrate ritual, religion, images of warfare, and visions of human transcendence into the lives of millions?

Notes

1   William Arens, "Games Societies Play," *New Scientist* (June 1978): 857.

2   *Latin American Political Report*, 20:22 (9 June 1978): 169.

3   John Hoberman, *Sport and Political Ideology* (Austin: University of Texas Press, 1984), p. 6.

4   Robert Darton, *The Great Cat Massacres and Other Episodes in French Cultural History* (New York: Basic Books, 1984), p. 6.

5   See, for example, Richard D. Mandell, *Sport: A Cultural History* (New York: Columbia University Press, 1984).

6   Hoberman, *Sport and Political Ideology*, pp. 12, 161.

7   Matthew Shirts, in *South Eastern Latin Americanist* 28:4 (March 1985): 47.

8   *Miami Herald* (1 May 1985): 42A.

9   Nicolas Mullins, *Theories and Theory Groups in Contemporary American Sociology*, cited by Eric A. Wagner, "Sports," in *Handbook of Latin American Popular Culture*, eds. Harold E. Hinds, Jr., and Charles M. Tatum (Westport: Greenwood Press, 1985), p. 135.

10   Roland Barthes, *Mythologies*, trans. Annette Lavers (New York: Hill and Wang, 1972), p. 15.

11   Mandell, *Sport: A Cultural History*.

Bibliography

Alencar, Edigar de, *Flamengo: Força e alegria do povo*. Rio de Janeiro: Conquista, 1970.

Angel Jaramillo, Hugo, "Los ídolos del deporte en la sociedad capitalista," *Desarrollo Indoamericano* 12:37 (April 1977), 27-31.

_____. "El profesionalismo deportivo y la juventud," *Desarrollo Indoamericano* 6:20 (June 1973), 53-61.

Arbena, Joseph L., "Sport and Sport Themes in Latin American Literature: A Sampler," forthcoming in *Arete: The Journal of Sport Literature* 5:1 (Fall 1987).

_____. "Winners Without Losers: Perspectives on Latin American Sport," forthcoming in *Studies in Latin American Popular Culture* 7 (1988).

Baker, William J., *Sports in the Western World*. Totowa, NJ: Rowman and Littlefield, 1982.

_____, and Mangan, James A., eds., *Sport in Africa: Essays in Social History*. New York: Africana Publishing Company, 1987.

Bale, John, "International Sports History as Innovation Diffusion," *Canadian Journal of History of Sport* 15:1 (May 1984), 38-63.

Beezley, William H., "The Porfirian Persuasion: Sport and Recreation in Mexico's Society of the 1890's," *Proceedings of the Rocky Mountain Council on Latin American Studies* (1983), 136-45.

_____. "The Rise of Baseball in Mexico and the First Valenzuela," *Studies in Latin American Popular Culture* 4 (1985), 3-13.

Bonilla Aragón, Alfonso, et. al., *Cali Panamericana* 2 vols. Cali: Carvajal & Cía., 1971.

Borodi, Roco, *Historia de la selección: en campos de antaño*. Lima, 1982.

Brohm, Jean-Marie, *Sport--A Prison of Measured Time*. Translated by Ian Fraser. London: Ink Links, 1978.

Cadavel, Alejandro, *El deporte visto por los universitarios*. México, D.F.: Universidad Nacional Autónoma de México, [1979].

Cagigal, José María, *Deporte y agresión*. Barcelona: Editorial Planeta, 1976.

Calabrano, D. Alonso, "La cultura, el deporte y la juventud chilena," *Cuadernos Americanos* 200:3 (1975), 55-68.

Cantelon, Hart, and Gruneau, Richard, eds., *Sport, Culture and the Modern State*. Toronto: University of Toronto Press, 1982.

"La corrupción del deporte," *Criterio* 50:1773 (October 13, 1977), 539-41.

Chandler, Joan M., "Towards the Teaching of Sport History," *Teaching History* 7:1 (Spring 1982), 34-40.

Chauvel, Louis, *Racing Club Haitien; ou, 40 Ans au Service du Sport National*. Port-au-Prince: Imprimerie des Antilles, 1964.

Clignet, R., and M. Stark, "Modernization and the Game of Soccer in Cameroun," *International Review of Sport Sociology* 9:3-4 (1974), 81-98.

Club Colonia Rowing, *Libro de oro*. Colonia, Uruguay: El Ideal, 1973.

Corten, André, and Tahon, Marie-Blanche, "Sport et societé dans une cité pétroliére mexicaine: Biographie d'une équipe de jeunes," *Canadian Journal of Latin American and Caribbean Studies/Revue canadienne des études latino-américaines et caraibes* 9:18 (1984), 57-73.

Cospín, Miguel Angel, *Nuestro fútbol en su época de oro (anecdotario)*. Guatemala: El Imparcial, 1965.

Da Matta, Roberto, "Futebol: ópio do povo x drama de justica social," *Novos Estudos Cebrap* 1:4 (November 1982), 54-60.

_____. "Esporte na sociedade: um ensaio sobre o futebol brasileiro," in *Universo do futebol: esporte e sociedade brasileira*, Roberto Da Matta, et. al., pp. 19-42. Rio de Janeiro: Edições Pinakotheke, 1982.

_____. "Soccer and Brazilian Nationalism." Unpublished paper presented at the Conference on Sport, Culture, and Society, Stanford University, 17-19 April 1986.

Deustua Carvallo, José, Stein, Steve, and Stokes, Susan C., "Soccer and Social Change in Early Twentieth Century Peru," *Studies in Latin American Popular Culture* 3 (1984), 17-27.

Domínguez Dibb., Humberto, *El fútbol paraguayo*. Asunción: Talleres Gráficos Cromos S.R.L., 1977.

Dos Santos, Joel Rufino, *História politica do futebol brasileiro*. São Paulo: Editora Brasilense, 1981.

Enríquez, Celso, *Sports in Pre-Hispanic America*. México, D.F.: Litográfica Machado, 1968.

Escobar M., Gabriel, "The Role of Sports in the Penetration of Urban Culture to the Rural Areas of Peru," *Kroeber Anthropological Society Papers* 40 (1969), 72-81.

Evanson, Philip, "Understanding the People: *Futebol*, Film, Theater and Politics in Present-Day Brazil," *The South Atlantic Quarterly* 81:4 (Autumn 1982), 399-412.

Filho, Mário, *O negro no futebol brasileiro*. 2nd ed.; Rio de Janeiro, 1962.

Flynn, Peter, "Sambas, Soccer and Nationalism," *New Society* 18:464 (19 August 1971), 327-30.

Galeano, Eduardo, ed., *Su majestad el fútbol*. Montevideo: Arca Editorial, 1968.

Gelber, Stephen, "Working at Playing: The Culture of the Workplace and the Rise of Baseball," *Journal of Social History* 16:4 (Summer 1983), 3-22.

Goldemberg, Isaac, *Play by Play*. Translated by Hardie St. Martin. New York: Persea Books, 1985. Originally published in 1984 as *Tiempo al tiempo*.

González, Renato, *El boxeo en Chile*. Vol. 48. *Nosotros los Chilenos*. Santiago: Editora Nacional Quimantú, 1973.

Gruneau, Richard, *Class, Sports, and Social Development.* Amherst: University of Massachusetts Press, 1983.

Guerrero, Carlos, *Grandes del deporte.* No. 15. *Nosotros los Chilenos.* Santiago: Editora Nacional Gabriela Mistral, 1975.

Guttmann, Allen, *From Ritual to Record: The Nature of Modern Sports.* New York: Columbia University Press, 1978.

_____. *Sports Spectators.* New York: Columbia University Press, 1986.

Hardy, Stephen, "Entrepreneurs, Organizations, and the Sport Marketplace: Subjects in Search of Historians," *Journal of Sport History* 13:1 (Spring 1986), 14-33.

Henshaw, Richard, *The Encyclopedia of World Soccer.* Washington, DC: New Republic Books, 1979.

Hoberman, John M., *Sport and Political Ideology.* Austin: University of Texas Press, 1984.

James, C.L.R., *Beyond a Boundary.* New York: Pantheon Books, 1983. (Originally published by Stanley Paul & Co., in 1963.)

Kelly, Isabel, "Notes on a West Coast Survival of the Ancient Mexican Ball Game," *Notes on Middle American Archaeology and Ethnology* no. 26 (1943), 163-75.

Klintowitz, Jacob, "A implantação de um modelo alienígena exótico e outras questões pertinentes: A seleção brasileira de futebol--1978," *Encontros com a Civilização Brasileira* 5 (November 1978), 113-18.

Komorowski, Manfred, "Cuba's Way to a Country with Strong Influence in Sport Politics: The Development of Sport in Cuba since 1959," *International Journal of Physical Education* 14 (1977), 26-32.

Kottack, Conrad Phillip, "Swimming in Cross-Cultural Currents," *Natural History* 94:5 (May 1985), 2-11.

Krotee, March L., "The Rise and Demise of Sport: A Reflection of Uruguayan Society," *The Annals of the American Academy of Political and Social Science* vol. 445 (September 1979), 141-54.

LaFrance, David G., "A Mexican Popular Image of the United States Through the Baseball Hero, Fernando Valenzuela," *Studies in Latin American Popular Culture* 4 (1985), 14-23.

Lara C., Joaquín, *Historia del béisbol en Yucatán (1890-1906)*. Mérida: Editorial "Zamma," 1953.

León Echaiz, René, *Diversiones y juegos típicos chilenos*. Santiago: Editora Nacional Gabriela Mistral, 1974.

Lever, Janet, "Soccer As a Brazilian Way of Life." In *Games, Sport and Power*, edited by Gregory P. Stone, pp. 138-59. New Brunswick: Transaction Books, 1972.

_____. *Soccer Madness*. Chicago: University of Chicago Press, 1983.

Levine, Robert M., "The Burden of Success: *Futebol* and Brazilian Society Through the 1970s," *Journal of Popular Culture* 14:3 (Winter 1980), 453-64.

_____. "Sport and Society: The Case of Brazilian *Futebol*," *Luso-Brazilian Review* 17:2 (Winter 1980), 233-52.

Llanes, Ricardo M., *Canchas de pelotas y reñideros de antaño*. Buenos Aires: Municipalidad de la Ciudad de Buenos Aires, 1981.

Loy, John W., Jr., "The Nature of Sport: A Definitional Effort." In *Sport in the Sociocultural Process*, edited by Marie Hart and Susan Birrell, pp. 21-37. 3rd ed.; Dubuque: Wm C. Brown Company, 1981.

_____. "A Paradigm of Technological Change in the Sports Situation," *International Review of Sport Sociology* 1 (1966), 177-93.

Lyra Filho, João, *Introdução a sociologia dos desportos*. Rio de Janeiro: Bloch Editores, 1973.

Mandell, Richard D., *Sport: A Cultural History*. New York: Columbia University Press, 1984.

Martín Baró, Ignacio, "Munich 72: El ocaso de una mitología," *ECA; Estudios Centro Americanos* 27:288-289 (October - November 1972), 697-701.

Meihy, José Carlos Sebe Bom, and José Sebastião Witter, eds., *Futebol e cultura: coletanea de estudos*. São Paulo: IMESP/DAESP, 1982.

Mera Carrasco, Julio, *De Tokio a México: Los juegos olímpicos*. México, D.F.: Ediciones Deportemas, 1968.

_____. *Fútbol (La Copa del Mundo en sus manos)*. México, D.F.: Editores Mexicanos Unidos, 1970.

Millones, Luis, "Deporte y alienación en el Perú: El fútbol en los barrios limeños," *Estudios Andinos* 1:2 (1970), 87-95.

Miró, César, *Los íntimos de La Victoria*. Lima: Editorial El Deporte, 1958.

Morales, Franklin, *Fútbol: mito y realidad*. No. 22. *Nuestra Tierra*. Montevideo: Editorial "Nuestra Tierra," 1969.

Morales Roca, Diego, *¿Existe el fútbol boliviano? (Problemas del fútbol nacional)*. La Paz: Ediciones Galaxia, 1977.

Morgan, William J., "'Radical' Social Theory of Sport: A Critique and a Conceptual Emendation," *Sociology of Sport Journal* 2:1 (March 1985), 56-71.

Mutis, Alvaro, "La vergüenza del deporte," *Eco* 35:215 (September 1979), 557-59.

Obregón, Osvaldo, "El 'clásico universitario' chileno: un caso singular de teatro de masas," *Revista Canadiense de Estudios Hispánicos* 7:1 (Fall 1982), 67-80.

Ossandón, Carlos A., "Las dos caras del fútbol," *Araucaria de Chile* 20 (1982), 192-94.

[Paniagua S., Benjamín, et. al.], *Guatemala*. Guatemala: Tipografía Nacional, 1950.

Pedroza, Milton, "Presencia del fútbol en la literatura brasileña," *Revista de Cultura Brasileña* 46 (June 1978), 53-88.

Peláez G., Gabriel, and Martín Castro M., *Historia del deporte en Bolivia (y los datos principales del deporte mundial)*. Sucre: Universidad de San Francisco Xavier de Chuquisaca, 1962.

Pereira Salas, Eugenio, *Juegos y alegrías coloniales en Chile*. Santiago: Editora Zig-Zag, 1947.

Pickering, R. J., "Cuba." In *Sport Under Communism*, edited by James Riordan, pp. 141-74. Montreal: McGill-Queen's University Press, 1978.

Ponce, Francisco, "Ocio y deporte," *Revista Mexicana de Ciencias Políticas y Sociales* 25:95-96 (January - June 1979), 79-90.

Rachum, Ilan, "Futebol: The Growth of a Brazilian National Institution," *New Scholar* 7:1/2 (1978), 183-200.

Ramos Mirena, Alí Rafael, *Todos fueron héroes.* [Caracas]:   Ministerio de Información y Turismo, 1982.

Reid, Alastair, "The Sporting Scene: Shades of Tlachtli," *The New Yorker* 46:22 (18 July 1970), 60-71.

Remley, Mary L., "Sport History: A Brief Overview," *OAH Newsletter* 11:3 (August 1983), 15-16.

Reyes Matta, Fernando, "The Olympic Games in the Latin American Press," pp. 194-217 in *Global Ritual: Olympic Media Coverage and International Understanding,* ed. Michael Real.   San Diego: [p.p.], 1986.

Rigauer, Bero, *Sport and Work.*   Translated by Allen Guttmann.   New York: Columbia University Press, 1981.

Rosenfeld, Anatol, "O futebol no Brasil," *Argumento 4* (1956), 61-86.

Ruocco, Angel V., "La trastienda del fútbol."   In *El fútbol (antología),* José Luis Buzzetti, et. al., pp. 73-80.   Montevideo: Centro Editor de América Latina, 1969.

Russell, David, "Baseball, Hollywood, and Nicaragua," *Monthly Review* 34:10 (March 1983), 22-29.

Samper Pizano, Daniel, *Así ganamos . . . (Como fue campeón Santa Fe en 1975).*   Bogotá: Carlos Valencia Editores, 1975.

Sanoja, Eduardo, *Juego de garrote larense.   El método venezolano de defensa personal.*   Caracas: Federación Nacional de la Cultura Popular, 1984.

Scheffler, Lilian, et. al., *El juego de pelota prehispánico y sus supervivencias actuales.*   Tlahuapan, Puebla, México: Premiá Editora, 1985.

Sebreli, Juan José, *Fútbol y masas.*   Buenos Aires: Editorial Galerna, 1981.

Slatta, Richard W., "The Demise of the Gaucho and the Rise of Equestrian Sport in Argentina," *Journal of Sport History* 13:2 (Summar 1986), 97-110.

Snyder, Elden E., and Barbara A. Brown, "Sport and Social Change," *Sociology of Sport Journal* 4:2 (June 1987), 140-43.

Speroni, José, "Firpo-Dempsey: el combate del siglo," *Todo Es Historia* 1:6 (October 1967), 26-32.

Stein, Steve, "Miguel Rostaing: Dodging Blows On and Off the Soccer Field." In *The Human Tradition in Latin America: The Twentieth Century*, edited by William H. Beezley and Judith Ewell, pp. 15-25. Wilmington, DE: Scholarly Resources Inc., 1987.

Suárez Orozco, Marcelo Mario, "A Study of Argentine Soccer: The Dynamics of Its Fans and Their Folklore," *Journal of Psychoanalytic Anthropology* 5:1 (Winter 1982), 7-28.

Taboada, Miguel A., "Con el fútbol espectáculo comenzó la bancarrota que hoy ahoga a los clubes," *La Razón* (15 October 1984), 17.

Terrazas, Silvestre, *El ciclismo: manual de velocipedia*. Chihuahua, México: Tip. de Silvestre Terrazas, 1896.

Velázquez Rojas, Manuel, *Alex Olmedo: el cacique del deporte blanco*. Lima: Editora Contemporanea, 1959.

Vidales, Ernesto, *Nos dejó el tren . . . .* Vol. I. Biblioteca el Teatro del Libro. Bogotá: Editorial Kelly, 1961.

Wagner, Eric A., "Cuban Sports Magazines," *Sociology and Social Research* 72:1 (October 1987), 25-29.

_____. "Sport After Revolution: A Comparative Study of Cuba and Nicaragua," *Studies in Latin American Popular Culture* 1 (1982), 65-73.

_____. "Sport and Revolution in Nicaragua." In *Nicaragua in Revolution*, edited by Thomas W. Walker, pp 291-302. New York: Praeger Publishers, 1982.

_____. "Sport Participation in Latin America," *International Review of Sport Sociology* 17:2 (1982), 29-39.

_____. "Sports." In *Handbook of Latin American Popular Culture*, edited by Harold E. Hinds, Jr., and Charles M. Tatum, pp. 135-50. Westport: Greenwood Press, 1985.

Whitson, David, "Sport and Hegemony: On the Construction of the Dominant Culture," *Sociology of Sport Journal* 1:1 (1984), 64-78.

Whorton, Brad, and Wagner, Eric A., "Nicaraguan Sport Ideology," *Journal of Sport and Social Issues* 9:2 (Summer/Fall 1985), 26-33.

Zurcher, Louis A., and Meadow, Arnold, "On Bullfights and Baseball: An Example of Interaction of Social Institutions," *The International Journal of Comparative Sociology* 8:1 (March 1967), 99-117.

Index

About the Contributors

JOSEPH L. ARBENA received his doctorate in history from the University of Virginia and has been on the faculty of Clemson University since 1965. His research interests include twentieth-century Colombia, political development, music, and sports. He is preparing an annotated bibliography of sport in Latin America to be published by Greenwood Press.

WILLIAM H. BEEZLEY holds his doctorate in history from the University of Nebraska and has numerous publications on the political, social, and cultural history of Mexico since the late nineteenth century. His most recent book, *Judas at the Jockey Club and Other Episodes of Porfirian Mexico* (1987), was a History Book Club selection. He is presently on the faculty of North Carolina State University. He also coaches youth soccer and referees at the collegiate level.

GILBERT M. JOSEPH, a historian and baseball fan, has focused his research principally on the Yucatán region of Mexico. His publications include *Revolution from Without: Yucatán, Mexico, and the United States, 1800-1924* (1982). He currently teaches at the University of North Carolina at Chapel Hill.

STEVE STEIN earned his doctorate from Stanford University and has published extensively on social change in Lima in the early twentieth century. He is the author of *Populism in Peru: The Emergence of the Masses and the Politics of Social Control* (1980). At the University of Miami (Florida) he teaches history and directs programs in international education and study abroad.

JANET LEVER, a sociologist, has taught at Yale, where she also did graduate study, Northwestern, the University of California at San Diego, and the University of California at Los Angeles. Her *Soccer Madness* (1983) was a pioneering study of sport in a Latin American country. She is currently employed by the Rand Corporation.

MATTHEW SHIRTS, a doctoral candidate in history at Stanford University, is a Program Associate at the Program in Latin American Studies of the Woodrow Wilson Center for Scholars. During an extended residence in Brazil, he published several articles on soccer in the local social and political context.

ERIC A. WAGNER, a sociologist on the faculty of Ohio University, is a leading North American student of sport in Cuba, Nicaragua, and other Latin American areas. His 1985 bibliographical essay was the first comprehensive attempt to evaluate the state of sports studies in and about the Latin American region.

ROBERT M. LEVINE has written extensively on Brazilian history, politics, and culture. His publications include monographs, reference works, and numerous articles, several on the meaning of soccer in Brazil. He received his doctorate from Princeton University and taught at the State University of New York at Stony Brook before becoming chairman of the Department of History at the University of Miami (Florida).